Bracero 2.0

Mexican Workers in North American Agriculture

PHILIP MARTIN

OXFORD

UNIVERSITY PRESS

OXFORD
UNIVERSITY PRESS

Oxford University Press is a department of the University of Oxford. It furthers
the University's objective of excellence in research, scholarship, and education
by publishing worldwide. Oxford is a registered trade mark of Oxford University
Press in the UK and certain other countries.

Published in the United States of America by Oxford University Press
198 Madison Avenue, New York, NY 10016, United States of America.

© Oxford University Press 2024

Library of Congress Cataloging-in-Publication Data
Names: Martin, Philip L., 1949– author.
Title: Bracero 2.0 : Mexican workers in North American agriculture / Philip Martin.
Description: New York, NY : Oxford University Press, [2024] |
Includes bibliographical references and index.
Identifiers: LCCN 2023033284 | ISBN 9780197699973 (hardback) |
ISBN 9780197699997 (epub) | ISBN 9780197699980
Subjects: LCSH: Agricultural laborers—Mexico. | Agricultural laborers, Foreign—United States. |
Agricultural laborers, Foreign—Canada. | Foreign workers, Mexican—Government
policy—United States. | Foreign workers, Mexican—Government policy—Canada. |
Seasonal labor—Government policy—North America. | Agriculture—Economic
aspects—North America.
Classification: LCC HD1531.M6 M377 2024 | DDC 331.7/630972—dc23/eng/20230719
LC record available at https://lccn.loc.gov/2023033284

DOI: 10.1093/oso/9780197699973.001.0001

Printed by Integrated Books International, United States of America

Contents

Contents

Preface

Five million Mexican-born farm workers are employed on North American farms sometime during a typical year, including 50,000 in Canada, 3 million in Mexico, and 2 million in the United States. Almost all of these workers were raised in poverty in rural Mexico.

Mexican farm workers employed on American and Canadian farms earn at least ten times more than they would earn in Mexico, whether they are employed as guest workers, legal immigrants or naturalized citizens, or unauthorized workers. Mexican farm workers are also employed in Mexico on farms in the northern and central states that export fruits and vegetables to the United States; this group of workers includes internal migrants from Mexico's poorer southern states.

This book explores the impacts of Mexican migrant workers in Canada, Mexico, and the United States, the alternatives to farm workers in particular commodities, and policies to improve protections for farm workers. Mexican braceros, or guest workers, were a significant share of the US farm workforce in the 1950s, an experience often viewed as a time of failure to protect Mexican and US farm workers. *Bracero 2.0* explores the similarities and differences between the braceros of the past and the migrant farm workers in Canada, Mexico, and the United States today.

Mexican migrants dominate the seasonal farm workforces of Canada, Mexico, and the United States because most local workers in the areas that produce fresh fruits and vegetables are seeking better nonfarm jobs. This book explains who these migrant workers are, their recruitment and employment experiences, and the implications of relying on Mexican-born farm workers.

The three chapters of Part I explore the structure of agriculture and the importance of hired workers in Canada, Mexico, and the United States. Each chapter reviews the evolution of the demand for hired workers in Canadian, Mexican, and US agriculture and the characteristics and earnings of farm workers, emphasizing that the fruit and vegetable subsector of agriculture accounts for less than 20 percent of farm sales in each country but employs more than half of each country's hired farm workers.

Part II turns to migrant workers in the farm labor market. The Seasonal Agricultural Worker Program admits mostly young Mexican men to fill seasonal farm jobs in Ontario, Quebec, and British Columbia, the three provinces that produce most of Canada's fresh fruits and vegetables. In Mexican states such as Baja California, Sonora, Sinaloa, Jalisco, and Michoacán, local workers are joined by internal migrants from southern Mexican states on farms that often partner with US growers and marketers to produce fresh fruits and vegetables for Americans and Canadians.

Mexican-born workers are 70 percent of US crop workers, over half of the workers employed by US dairies and livestock operations, and a significant share of the workers employed in farm-related industries such as food processing and meatpacking. The final chapter of Part II explores the major alternatives to US farm workers, including mechanization, guest workers, and imports.

Part III highlights the interactions between labor-saving technologies and mechanical aids, migrants, and trade policies that determine whether a particular commodity mechanizes and stays in the United States, employs guest workers to maintain US production, or shrinks in the face of rising imports. The race between machines, migrants, and imports yields different answers in different commodities. Blueberries and raisins are likely to mechanize quickly because machines are available and rising imports force US growers to reduce their production costs, while apples, lettuce, and strawberries face less import competition and are likely to use H-2A guest workers as a bridge to full mechanization. US production of melons and tomatoes is likely to shrink in the face of rising imports from lower-wage countries.

The final chapter of Part III lays out policies to improve protections for farm workers, highlighting the potential of the food safety model to improve compliance with labor laws. The revolution in food safety over the past quarter century relies on government regulation, buyer standards and their associated audits and certifications, and civil litigation to ensure that farmers anticipate food safety hazards, monitor water and pesticides to detect and correct problems, and undergo regular audits to ensure that their fruits and vegetables are safe. A similar system could improve compliance with labor laws.

The economies of Canada, Mexico, and the United States have been integrating under the North American Free Trade Agreement (NAFTA) since 1994 and revisions to NAFTA incorporated into the US-Mexico-Canada Agreement (USMCA) since 2020, as symbolized by the evolution of two major sectors, autos and agriculture. Each industry employs about 5 million workers in North America, but autos and agriculture offer different types of jobs to different workers. The auto sector offers year-round jobs to local secondary school graduates in each country, while agriculture offers seasonal jobs to Mexican workers with primary school educations. Almost all autoworkers live near their workplaces, while some farm workers migrate from homes to farms that may be far away or in another country.

The USMCA, which went into effect on July 1, 2020, has 24 revised and 10 new chapters, including a new chapter 23 that requires Mexico to reform its labor laws. Article 23.9 acknowledges that migrant workers are vulnerable and commits the three governments to "ensure that migrant workers are protected under its [each country's] labor laws." As competition between farmers in Canada, Mexico, and the United States intensifies, more attention is being paid to migrant workers, as when complaints of forced and child labor blocked exports of some Mexican tomatoes to the United States in 2022.

This book is unique in several ways. Part I's assessments of the evolution and current parameters of farm labor systems in Canada, Mexico, and the United States help readers to appreciate the past and present roles of migrant workers in each country. Part II's analysis of statistical and survey data paint a reliable portrait of the 5 million people who work for wages on North American farms. Part III takes a realistic look at the alternatives to hand labor in major fruits and vegetables, and the potential of the food safety model to improve labor law compliance.

This book reflects decades of research on agricultural production, farm labor, and labor migration. I am grateful for the insights of many colleagues, as well as to the farm employers, workers, and others who shared their data and perspectives. The research program on which this book is based has been supported by, inter alia, the Colcom, Farm, Giannini, Rosenberg, and Walmart Foundations. None of these supporters reviewed the manuscript, and I am solely responsible for the analysis and conclusions as well as any errors or omissions.

Prologue: Mexicans in the Fields

Juan Martinez picks fresh blueberries. With seven years of schooling and five years of experience, 25-year-old Juan can pick 50 to 75 pounds an hour, depending on yields. In southern Jalisco, Juan earns three times Mexico's minimum wage of 173 pesos ($9) a day in 2022.

Fresh blueberries are an agricultural success story. Consumption of fresh blueberries is rising due to their health benefits, convenient packaging, and year-round availability. Mexico was a latecomer to blueberry production, and benefitted from the development of varieties that thrive in warmer climates. Most Mexican blueberries are produced under plastic-covered hoop structures that protect the berries from birds and weather and reduce weed and pest pressures.

Blueberries are harvested almost year-round in North America, so Juan could follow the sun and harvest blueberries all year. But Juan picks blueberries in Jalisco only from January through April, and then returns to his small farm in Chiapas. As Juan departs for southern Mexico, other Mexican workers are packing their bags to travel to Canada and the United States as legal guest workers, where they will be paid a piece rate wage of $0.50 a pound to pick blueberries and earn $15 to $25 an hour.

Most fresh blueberries are picked into gallon-sized buckets, dumped into field bins that hold 20 to 30 pounds of berries, and transported to packing sheds to be sorted and packed for consumers. The picking and packing process is similar in all three countries, and so are the workers involved, mostly people born in rural Mexico. Canada and the United States import blueberries picked by Mexican workers during the winter months, and Mexico imports blueberries from Canada and the United States that are picked by Mexican-born workers during the summer months.

Jose Rosales is employed in Ford's auto assembly factory in Aguascalientes, a state with eight car plants that assemble over 1.5 million vehicles a year. Jose graduated from secondary school and earns $3 an hour, allowing him to buy a small house near the plant. Mexico produces 4 million cars and light trucks a year and exports 80 percent of them to Canada and the United States.[1]

Unlike agriculture, the auto industry has Mexican workers in Mexican plants, Canadian workers in Canadian plants, and American workers in US plants.

Agriculture is the only North American industry that relies on rural Mexicans in all three countries. This book explores the implications of the growing presence of Mexican-born workers for farm employers and farm workers, consumers, and the economies of Canada, Mexico, and the United States. Mexico's poverty is concentrated in rural areas, and labor-intensive farms in all three countries rely on local and migrant workers from rural Mexico to fill seasonal farm jobs.

This integration of North American commodity and labor markets amid a rising demand for fresh fruits and vegetables raises many questions. Will the further expansion of labor-intensive agriculture encourage farm employers to look further afield for migrant workers, to Central America and beyond, or will farmers mechanize harvesting and other farm tasks that now depend on hand labor? Will more commodities be imported from outside North America, so that low-wage farm labor is embodied in blueberries from Peru or garlic from China?

The farm labor market in North America is at a crossroads. Canada's relatively small fruit and vegetable sector relies on legal guest workers from Mexico and the Caribbean who move under the terms of bilateral agreements negotiated between the labor ministries of Canada and sending countries. Mexico's farms that export fresh fruits and vegetables employ local and migrant workers, often in controlled environment agriculture (CEA) farming structures that lengthen seasonal jobs and make farm work akin to factory work, with controlled entrances and exits to workplaces. US fruit and vegetable production is concentrated on large farms in states such as California and Washington with high state minimum wages and extensive regulation of farm labor markets, encouraging farmers to weigh the choice between machines and migrant guest workers to get crops harvested. Produce buyers seek reliable supplies of low-cost and high-quality fresh produce, which explains the rising share of fresh fruits and vegetables that are imported to Canada and the United States.

This book explains the processes, people, and policies behind the farm labor market in North America, including rising consumer demand for fresh produce year-round. After examining the farm labor history of each country, we explain farm employment patterns and farm worker characteristics before sketching the trajectories of machines, migrants, and imports in particular US fruits and vegetables.

There is an important difference between seasonal farm labor in North America and that in Europe. Polish and Romanian farm workers fill seasonal farm jobs at home *or* abroad in higher-wage Germany and the United Kingdom because northern European countries produce the same commodities in the same areas at the same time. Farms in Italy and Spain producing fresh produce for northern European countries are more analogous to the north-south orientation of North American agriculture. Southern European farmers rely on diverse African and Eastern European migrant workforces, just as Canadian and US farmers rely on Mexican farm workers.

Farmers invest significant capital in orchards and vineyards that can produce fresh fruit for several decades. As fruit and vegetable agriculture globalizes, what is the responsibility of farmers and investors to consider the availability of labor before planting orchards and vineyards in remote areas and assuming that seasonal farm workers will be available? Should governments validate investments in remote apple orchards by admitting guest workers, or should investors consider the availability of labor before they develop orchards in remote areas? Investors make assumptions about how labor costs will evolve over time. What do governments owe investors if labor regulations change and invalidate their labor cost assumptions?

The goal of this book is to help readers to think about the implications of having Mexican workers dominate the seasonal farm workforces of Canada, Mexico, and the United States. There are three major options to ensure a supply of fresh produce: machines that replace workers, guest workers and mechanical aids that raise hand worker productivity, and imports of labor-intensive commodities.

The fight in the fields between machines, migrants, and imports varies by commodity. The harvest of commodities such as raisin grapes could be mechanized quickly if growers invested to re-trellis vineyards and bought machines that are already used to harvest wine grapes. However, most raisin growers are in their late 60s with 20- to 40-acre vineyards, raisin consumption is falling and imports are rising, and many raisin growers plan to sell their land to developers or convert vineyards to almonds rather than invest to mechanize raisin grape production.

Commodities that defy easy mechanization include lettuce, strawberries, and table grapes. Reliance on migrant guest workers and mechanical aids is increasing in these commodities, as with conveyor belts that travel in front of workers who harvest lettuce or strawberries and robots that convey lugs of harvested table grapes from pickers to packers. There is little imported lettuce, but imports of fresh strawberries and table grapes from lower-wage countries are rising.

Apples represent an in-between case. The United States is a net exporter of fresh apples, and proprietary varieties such as Cosmic Crisp are popular with consumers. Newly planted apple orchards have dwarf trees with shallow roots and limbs trained to grow on trellis wires to support trees that grow to 10 to 12 feet. Apples are easier to spot on the trellised limbs, and workers on hydraulic platforms can pick much faster than workers who use ladders to climb into taller trees and pick apples into bags that weigh 50 to 60 pounds when full. Migrants and mechanical aids are likely to be a bridge to full mechanization in apples.

US production of asparagus, apricots, cantaloupes, and mature green tomatoes is shrinking in the face of rising imports and technical and economic challenges that make it difficult to develop machines to harvest these small-acreage commodities. The small market for plants and machines for these crops limits the biological and engineering investments available for mechanization, so imports are likely to increase. For example, if the prototype machine developed to harvest California cantaloupes was perfected, fewer than 50 would be needed to harvest the state's cantaloupes, so even a very high profit margin offers little incentive to machine developers. California produces 60 percent of US cantaloupes.

PART I

AGRICULTURE IN NORTH AMERICA

The three chapters of Part I explain the evolution and current status of hired farm labor in Canada, Mexico, and the United States. Each country's history is different, but the share of employment in agriculture fell sharply in all three countries during the 20th century, especially after World War II.

Many of Canada's immigrants in the late 19th century were eastern Europeans, many of whom became farmers in Canada's western prairies after the completion of Canada's transcontinental railroad in 1885. Eastern European immigrants to the United States in the late 1800s and early 1900s, by contrast, mostly filled factory jobs in eastern and midwestern cities because Black sharecroppers were seasonal farm workers in the South and Chinese, Japanese, and other Asians labored on farms in the West. Canada's climate and geography favored family-sized grain and livestock operations, while the Mediterranean climate of the western United States allowed large dryland wheat farms to be converted into fruit farms that relied on migrant farm workers.

The Spanish and later Mexican governments made large land grants to elites at a time of relatively little immigration, leading to the creation of feudal estates that housed and employed peasants. Efforts to transform these haciendas into family-sized farms failed in the 1850s and again after the Mexican Revolution of 1910–17. Instead, the Mexican government created communal ejidos on land taken from large landowners, creating small farmers who could not sell the land or borrow money against its value. The result was limited investment, widespread rural poverty, and migration to Mexican cities and the United States.

Agriculture is an 80-20 sector in the three North American countries. Small farms are 80 percent of all farms, but they account for only 20 percent of farm output and employ few farm workers. By contrast, the largest

20 percent of farms account for over 80 percent of the production of most farm commodities, and these large farms rely on hired workers from rural Mexico to do most of their hand work.

Canada and the United States began to recruit guest workers from the Caribbean and Mexico at different times, Canada in the 1960s and the United States during World War I, but reliance on guest workers increased in both countries in the 21st century. Mexico has a guest worker program that admits Guatemalans to fill seasonal farm jobs in Chiapas, but far more internal migrants move from poorer southern Mexican states to modern farms in northern and western Mexico.

Many farm labor systems rely on guest workers, but few can match the North American farming system's reliance on rural Mexicans. Southern European countries such as Italy and Spain rely on Africans who remain in the country year-round and eastern Europeans who shuttle in and out of the country seasonally. Plantations in Malaysia rely on Bangladeshi and Indonesian migrants who work and live on palm oil and rubber estates for two or three years. Thai guest workers are employed in Israeli CEA agriculture with multiyear contracts. In some farm labor systems, there is two-step migration, as when Poles migrate to Germany or the United Kingdom to fill seasonal farm jobs, and Ukrainians arrive in Poland to fill seasonal farm jobs.

1

Canada

Agriculture and Labor

Canada is a net exporter of agricultural commodities whose farms rely on 60,000 Mexican-born workers to fill seasonal farm jobs. There are several guest worker programs, including the largest, the Seasonal Agricultural Workers Program (SAWP), which the International Labor Organization (ILO) has deemed a model for bilateral cooperation to manage labor organization. Most farm employers are satisfied with the SAWP, but some NGOs and unions attack the SAWP for exploiting vulnerable workers who are tied to their farm employers by contracts and must leave Canada if they lose their jobs.[1]

Agricultural Evolution

Canada, the sea-to-sea-to-sea country that stretches from the Atlantic to the Pacific and north to the Arctic Ocean, is second only to Russia in total area, with 39 million people spread over 3.5 million square miles. California, by contrast, has 40 million people spread over 156,000 square miles; that is, California has more residents with less than 5 percent of Canada's area.

Canadian residents are concentrated in three ways: most live within an hour of the US border, most are in the three provinces of Ontario, Quebec, and British Columbia, and a third live in three cities, metro Toronto (6.2 million residents), Montreal (4.6 million), and Vancouver (2.6 million). Half of Canadians live between Windsor, Ontario, and Quebec City, the 700-mile-long Via Rail corridor along the Great Lakes and St. Lawrence River.

Canada was colonized by Europeans who did not necessarily want to be there, including Frenchmen who could escape prison sentences by emigrating to Canada and 60,000 British loyalists who moved north after American independence in 1783. The British North American Act of July 1, 1867, united the four colonies of Ontario, Quebec, New Brunswick, and

Bracero 2.0. Philip Martin, Oxford University Press. © Oxford University Press 2024.
DOI: 10.1093/oso/9780197699973.003.0001

Nova Scotia into the Dominion of Canada. Conservative prime minister John A. Macdonald (1867–73 and 1878–91) supported the building of the transcontinental Canadian Pacific Railway to unite Canada's provinces and encouraged immigration to settle the western prairies in the 1880s and 1890s.

The Dominion Lands Act of 1872, Canada's version of the US Homestead Act of 1862, offers farmland in Canada's prairie provinces in 160-acre increments at no charge or for $2.50 an acre (Falconer 2020b, 4).[2] Canada sought immigrant farmers in eastern Europe, and immigration surged to a peak of 400,000 in 1913, unleashing a wheat boom that led to the creation of Alberta and Saskatchewan as provinces.

Canada had 682,000 farms with an average 160 acres in 1911. There was rural-urban migration during the 1920s that was reversed in the 1930s during the Depression, so the agricultural workforce peaked at 1.5 million in 1939. World War II drained farmers and farm workers from agriculture, and many of those returning from military service moved to urban areas, so the total workforce in agriculture fell to 809,000 in 1956, when a seventh of Canadians were employed in agriculture (Haythorne 1960).

Canada opened its doors to Asian immigrants in 1962 and introduced a point system in 1967 that prioritizes the entry of young and educated immigrants who speak English or French, adding points for foreigners with more education and Canadian job offers and work experience. Most of the 400,000 immigrants a year are from the Philippines, India, or China, have college educations, and settle in metro Toronto, Vancouver, and Montreal. Many of the immigrants are already in Canada and adjust their status from student or temporary worker to immigrant.

Temporary foreign workers are a growing share of the workforce in Canadian agriculture. The Canadian Agricultural Human Resource Council (CAHRC) regularly issues reports that highlight farm labor shortages, resulting in the CAHRC receiving government funds to implement the International Phase of the Quality AgriWorkforce Management Program to help farmers to adopt best practices to recruit and retain workers. The Agri-Food Immigration Pilot allows employers of greenhouse, livestock, and meat- and food-processing workers to sponsor up to 2,750 foreign workers to fill year-round farm and farm-related jobs for immigrant visas (OECD 2020, 155–56; Falconer 2020b, 18).[3]

The COVID-19 pandemic did not change the dependence of Canadian farmers on guest workers. Federal and provincial governments created electronic platforms to match jobless Canadian workers with farm jobs and offered incentives to jobless workers to fill farm jobs, but the government also made exceptions to otherwise closed borders for guest workers and subsidized mandatory quarantine periods for newly arrived guest workers. After a brief halt to Mexican guest worker arrivals in May and June 2020 in the wake of several Mexican worker deaths from COVID, labor migration resumed and Mexican and Caribbean guest workers dominated the seasonal hired farm workforce, as had been the case before the pandemic.

Farm Structure and Labor

Canada is a net exporter of farm commodities and the world's leading exporter of canola and maple syrup. Canada exported farm commodities and food worth C$66 billion in 2018, dominated by grains and oil seeds. The most valuable farm exports were canola seeds, oil, and cake, worth C$10 billion, and spring and durum wheat, worth C$5 billion. Canada's farm exports to the United States were worth C$30 billion in 2017, followed by C$7 billion in farm exports to China and C$4 billion to Japan. Canada also imports farm commodities and food worth about C$40 billion, with 60 percent of that from the United States.

Canada had 193,000 farms in 2016, and 15,000 of those (8 percent of all farms) had annual sales of at least C$1 million, collectively accounting for over 60 percent of total farm receipts (Agriculture and Agri-Food Canada 2017). Most farms were small, with annual farm sales of less than C$100,000, and they collectively accounted for less than 5 percent of the value of Canada's farm output in 2016.

Most Canadian farms in 2016 produced wheat (52,000 farms), barley (25,000), and oats (24,000). There were 3,200 farms with tree fruits,[4] 9,300 with berries and grapes, and 10,000 with vegetables.[5] Canola was the largest-acreage crop, 21 million acres planted on a fifth of Canada's cropland, followed by 15 million acres of spring wheat and about 7 million acres each of barley, durum wheat, and soybeans.

Primary agriculture, the production of food and fiber on farms, generated C$60 billion in cash farm receipts in 2016 (Agriculture and Agri-Food Canada 2017, 68). Grains and oil seeds accounted for 37 percent of cash receipts, red meats 22 percent, and fruits and vegetables 11 percent.[6] Farm operating expenses were C$44 billion in 2016, including C$5.4 billion for cash wages and the value of farm-provided housing to hired workers. The average family income on unincorporated farms was C$117,000 in 2016, a sixth higher than the C$100,000 average of all Canadian families with two or more persons (Agriculture and Agri-Food Canada 2017, 67). The average net worth of Canadian farmers was C$2.8 million in 2015.

Fruits and vegetables (worth C$4.5 billion in 2014) employ most of Canada's farm workers, and their production is concentrated in three provinces. Ontario had horticultural sales of C$878 million in 2015, led by greenhouse tomatoes; Quebec had horticultural sales of C$490 million, led by field vegetables; and British Columbia had horticultural sales of C$478 million, led by fruits such as blueberries.

There were 252,000 people employed in Canadian agriculture in 2021, including 130,500 farm operators and their family members and 122,000 hired workers, making hired workers half of average employment in agriculture. Livestock and poultry farms paid about 40 percent of farm wages, greenhouses and nurseries paid a quarter, and fruits and vegetables paid a sixth; that is, fruits, greenhouses, and vegetables accounted for 40 percent of wages paid.

Canada's farm workforce includes more farm operators and unpaid family members (130,500 in 2021) than hired workers (120,000). The number of operators and their family members fell by almost half since 2000, while the number of hired workers was stable. However, Figure 1.1 shows that among

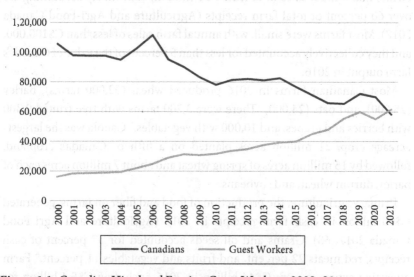

Figure 1.1 Canadian Hired and Foreign Guest Workers, 2000–21
Source: Statistics Canada

Canada's hired farm workers, the number of Canadians fell by almost half since 2000, while the number of foreign guest workers almost tripled, so foreign guest workers now outnumber Canadian farm workers.

Most employment standards laws and data on hired farm workers are province-specific. Ontario had 12,300 farms that hired labor in 2016, and they reported a total of 2.2 million weeks of hired labor in 2011, equivalent to 42,600 full-time jobs. Two-thirds of these weeks of hired farm work involved year-round workers.[7] Ontario's leading commodities by farm sales in 2016 were dairy products, worth C$2 billion, and vegetables and soybeans, worth C$1.6 billion each.

Guest Workers: SAWP

The share of Canada's seasonal farm work that is done by foreign guest workers is rising. Falconer (2020a, 10) reported that 56,000 temporary foreign workers (TFWs) were 21 percent of the total farm workforce in Canadian agriculture in 2019, including farmers, unpaid family workers, and hired workers, and TFWs were 46 percent of all hired farm workers. Most TFWs are employed less than a full year, so their share of the year-round-equivalent farm workforce is lower.

The Seasonal Agricultural Workers Program has been admitting Caribbean (mostly Jamaican) workers since 1966 and Mexican workers since 1974. The SAWP doubled in size between 2000 and 2015 (Figure 1.2).[8] Procedures to recruit workers and to protect them while they are employed in Canada are spelled out in government-to-government memorandums of understanding (MOUs)[9] and employer-worker contracts.

The SAWP, according to the Canadian government, "matches workers from Mexico and the Caribbean countries with Canadian farmers who need temporary support during planting and harvesting seasons, when qualified Canadians or permanent residents are not available." There are about three Mexican workers admitted for each worker from Jamaica, the second-largest sending country. Two-thirds of SAWP workers are in Ontario, almost 20 percent in British Columbia, and 10 percent in Quebec. Between 1974 and 2017, some 351,869 Mexican workers were employed in Canadian agriculture, including many who returned year after year.

The SAWP admissions process begins with Canadian farmers who try to recruit Canadian workers by offering the higher of the minimum or prevailing

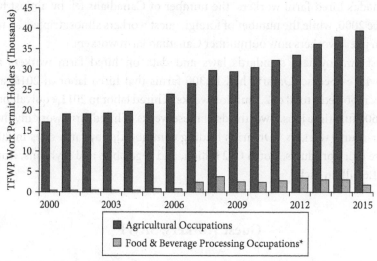

Source: Immigration, Refugees and Citizenship Canada and AAFC calculations.
* Includes tobacco processing.

Figure 1.2 Temporary Foreign Workers in Canadian Agriculture, 2000–15
Source: Agriculture Canada 2017, 48

wage in the area and for the commodity. Canadian minimum wages vary by province and were C$14 in Ontario, C$13.85 in British Columbia, and C$12.50 in Quebec in 2019. If efforts to recruit Canadian workers fail and the government determines that the presence of SAWP workers will not depress the wages of similar Canadian farm workers, farmers are certified by Service Canada to recruit SAWP workers by promising them at least 240 hours of farm work over at least six weeks in Canada.[10]

SAWP workers may stay in Canada up to eight months between January 1 and December 15 each year, and they stay an average 22 weeks or 5.5 months, often working 60 to 70 hours a week. About 2,000 Canadian farms hire SAWP workers, including greenhouses that produce tomatoes around Leamington, Ontario, the self-described tomato greenhouse capital of Canada. Tomato production peaks between April and November, when long hours of daylight contribute to average yields of over 500 metric tons per hectare.

Canadian farmers specify by name over three-fourths of the SAWP workers they want to hire. Mexico's Department of Labor maintains a list of workers who would like to be selected to work in Canada, and employers can select from this work-ready pool if they do not name their preferred workers.

Many Canadian farmers ask current workers to refer friends and relatives, so networks of current workers rather than sending-country worker-ready pools are the primary means of recruiting additional workers. Canadian farmers rely on nonprofit organizations created by farmers to transport SAWP workers to Canada: Foreign Agricultural Resource Management Service (FARMS) in Ontario and FERME in Quebec.

Mexican workers are prohibited from paying recruitment fees to get jobs in Canada, but some do. On June 23, 2008, Canadian Border Services Agency (CBSA) inspectors asked 80 Mexicans arriving with SAWP permits whether they had paid recruitment fees in Mexico. When the workers responded yes, they were not admitted to British Columbia to work. CBSA says that workers who pay recruitment fees are denied entry into Canada because they may not leave at the end of their work contracts.[11]

Both employers and workers sign contracts that spell out wages and working conditions and deductions. Most farmers advance the cost of airfare and visas but deduct some travel and other costs from workers' wages.[12] Employers must offer free housing to SAWP workers on their farms or in nearby commercial establishments; the housing is inspected by Canadian authorities before workers arrive. Farmers must provide transportation between worker housing and workplaces at no charge.

Employers must enroll SAWP workers in provincial or private health insurance programs, and SAWP workers are eligible for health services upon arrival. SAWP workers and their employers pay premiums for the unemployment insurance program, even though SAWP workers are generally not eligible for unemployment benefits because they cannot remain unemployed in Canada looking for jobs after their contracts end.

Farmers evaluate each SAWP worker at the end of the season. SAWP workers are required to present their employer's evaluation to a government agency at home in order to be selected for the next season. Farmers and farm organizations can "blacklist" particular workers and not hire them in the future, and government agencies in sending countries can blacklist particular Canadian famers and not approve sending workers to them. However, Canadian farmers who are blacklisted by the Mexican government can turn to the Caribbean for workers and vice versa.

FARMS, FERME, and other farmers' organizations that bring SAWP workers to Canada and transport them to farms are also involved in reviewing the operation of the Seasonal Agricultural Workers Program in periodic meetings with the Canadian, Mexican, and Caribbean governments. There is no formal role for workers' organizations in these review-of-SAWP- operations meetings, and sending-country governments represent the interests of their workers.

Caribbean government liaison officers interact with workers from their countries while they are in Canada,[13] and the Mexican government has consular officers who interact with Mexican SAWP workers. Some SAWP workers complain that these liaison officers are more interested in maximizing the number of Canadian farm jobs available than in dealing with the grievances of particular workers.[14] If workers make complaints, liaison officers may discuss the complaint with employers, and the remedy may be to return the complaining worker to his or her country of origin.

Most Caribbean workers admitted under the SAWP are from Jamaica, which required SAWP workers to authorize Canadian employers to deduct 25 percent of their wages and send them to a Jamaican office in Canada, which kept 5 percent and forwarded 20 percent to the worker's account at home.[15] Some workers complained of delays in receiving these forced savings at home and the low exchange rate used to convert Canadian into Jamaican dollars. After January 1, 2016, the Jamaican government was allowed to deduct only C$5.45 a day from each worker's pay to cover the cost of liaison services, a policy shift that angered the Jamaican government.[16]

The Jamaican government's forced savings and deductions policy is an example of how some sending-country governments tax citizens who work abroad, reasoning that the government should collect some of the guest worker's foreign earnings. The issue of the Jamaican government's involvement went further when it was revealed that members of Jamaica's parliament are allowed to nominate workers for the SAWP work-ready pool, prompting complaints from Canadian farmers and a promise in 2004 to ensure that all Jamaicans in the work-ready pool have farm work experience.[17]

Guest Workers: Ag Stream

Farmers may also hire foreign workers under the agricultural stream,[18] which began as the Pilot Project for Occupations Requiring Lower Levels of Formal Training (National Occupational Classification [NOC] C&D Pilot) in 2002. The number of workers admitted under the NOC C&D Pilot more than doubled from 101,300 in 2002 to 251,200 in 2008, and most of the workers who were admitted filled year-round nonfarm jobs.

The NOC C&D Pilot and what later became the agricultural stream of the temporary foreign worker program admitted 7,100 workers in 2013 (NOC 8431, 8432, 8611, 8251, 8252, 8254, 8256). The agricultural stream involves mostly Guatemalans employed by Quebec farmers, while the SAWP involves mostly Mexicans employed by Ontario farmers. Foreigners admitted under the SAWP can return to Canada indefinitely, while foreigners admitted via the agricultural stream can stay in Canada up to 24 months.[19]

The SAWP is governed by bilateral MOUs, and recruitment is overseen by a government agency in the sending country. The agricultural stream, by contrast, is a unilateral program (similar to the US H-2A program) that allows Canadian employers to recruit guest workers from almost all countries.

The Guatemala-Quebec farm worker program was developed in 2003 with the help of the International Organization for Migration (IOM) to ensure clean recruitment. IOM's involvement ended in 2013 amid charges that Guatemalans had to pay high fees to be selected and had to deposit $500 with IOM Guatemala as a surety bond that was forfeited if the worker did not return at the end of the contract (Gabriel and Macdonald 2017, 1715). The Guatemalan government was supposed to take over the IOM-created clean recruitment system, but instead the former IOM director who developed the program created a private labor recruiter, Amigo Laboral, which dominates the sending of Guatemalan farm workers to Canada (Gabriel and Macdonald 2017, 1717).

There are many private recruitment agencies in Guatemala that collect fees and deposits from rural Guatemalans for nonexistent foreign jobs. The Guatemala-Quebec program, begun with good intentions, appears to be example of an initial success that led to a desire among rural Guatemalans to work abroad but left them with few honest and legal channels to obtain foreign jobs.[20]

The Guatemalan government wants to send more workers abroad. Guatemala signed a safe-third-country agreement with the United States in summer 2019 that requires Hondurans, Salvadorans, and other foreigners who pass through the country to apply for asylum in Guatemala rather than continue through Mexico and apply for asylum in the United States. In return, a US official suggested that the number of H-2A visas issued to Guatemalans could triple from the 4,000 issued in FY18. In September 2020, the United States and Guatemala announced the creation of a work-ready pool to expedite the recruitment of Guatemalans by US farm employers.

There have been complaints about the treatment of workers who arrive in Canada under the agricultural stream, especially workers who are employed by temp or staffing agencies that move them from one Canadian farm to another. A federal review in February 2018 found that farmers want access to guest workers streamlined, while unions emphasize the potential for recruitment fraud abroad and worker exploitation in Canada.[21]

The SAWP allows farm employers who pay for worker transportation to Canada to deduct half of the airfare from worker wages, and it requires employers to offer housing to workers at no charge. The agricultural stream allows employers to require guest workers to cover their transport costs to Canada. Employers using the agricultural stream can charge guest workers up to C$30 a week for employer-provided housing, which can be off the farm.

Table 1.1 shows the evolution of Labour Market Impact Assessments (LMIAs), which represent government agreement with employers that Canadian workers are not available, over the past decade for the SAWP and the agricultural stream, the programs that account for 99 percent of the 70,000 LMIAs. The SAWP accounted for about three-fourths of the 2018 farm-related LMIAs, and the agricultural stream another quarter, but the less-regulated agricultural stream expanded faster.

Table 1.2 shows SAWP and other temporary foreign worker admissions in 2019, and emphasizes two points. First, almost 90 percent of the guest

Table 1.1 SAWP and Ag Stream LMIAs, 2011–18

	SAWP	Ag Stream	Total
2011	28,835	2,156	37,945
2012	29,021	7,680	40,271
2013	34,042	8,480	45,361
2014	36,718	8,106	47,474
2015	41,702	9,977	53,298
2016	40,238	13,003	54,260
2017	44,742	14,608	60,578
2018	50,550	18,095	69,775
Change, 2011 to 2018	75%	739%	
Share of Total LMIAs	72%	26%	

Source: Government of Canada, "Temporary Foreign Worker Program Labour Market Impact Assessment Statistics 2015–2022," last modified March 22, 2023, https://open.canada.ca/data/en/dataset/76defa14-473e-41e2-abfa-60021 c4d934b#wb-auto-6.

Table 1.2 Guest Workers in Canadian Agriculture and Related Food
Industries, 2019

Province/ Industry	Transportation	Farm Labour	Fishing	Processing (Meat)	Processing (Seafood)	Processing (Other)	Total
NL	115	555	0	0	60	0	230
PE	85	370	0	0	535	0	990
NS	125	1,435	0	0	355	5	1,920
NB	230	235	0	10	1,020	0	1,495
QC	475	15,340	0	50	120	945	16,935
ON	210	23,920	0	155	0	555	34,845
MB	195	670	0	0	0	0	865
SK	35	485	0	0	0	0	520
AB	610	2,195	0	270	0	15	3,095
BC	1,375	11,395	5	50	20	80	12,930
Canada	3,450	56,110	5	540	2,100	1,610	63,830

Source: Falconer, 2020b, Table 2

workers associated with Canadian agriculture are employed in primary farm labor, that is, on farms. Second, almost 90 percent of all farm guest workers are in three provinces, Ontario, Quebec, and British Columbia.

Canada also admits foreign workers to do farm work under high- and low-wage programs. Figure 1.3 shows that there are four options for farm

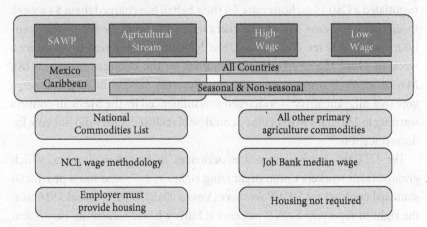

Figure 1.3 Canadian Guest Workers for Agriculture

employers to hire guest workers. The high-wage program is growing slowly, and involved 200 positive Labor Market Impact Assessments in 2018, while the low-wage program has shrunk in recent years to less than 1,000 LMIAs in 2018.

A 2018 review of the four guest worker programs or streams found worker advocates asking for more transparency in how the minimum wages that employers must pay are determined. Employers, on the other hand, requested the right to deduct some or more of the cost of housing from worker wages.[22] Some employers wanted to attest that they needed guest workers, eliminating the government review of whether local workers are available.

Canada: A Model?

Most farmers are satisfied with the SAWP and the agricultural stream, but the United Food and Commercial Workers (UFCW) union calls the SAWP "Canada's dirty little secret." The UFCW operates Agriculture Workers Alliance support centers for SAWP and other guest workers to inform them of their rights and to solicit their complaints.

The UFCW organized some SAWP workers, including those employed by Mayfair Farms in Portage la Prairie, Manitoba. Mayfair signed a three-year contract with UFCW Local 832 in June 2008 that linked future wage increases to the provincial minimum wage and provided a C$1-an-hour overtime premium for work done after 70 hours a week.

Mayfair's SAWP workers were dissatisfied, complaining that the UFCW negotiated a C$0.15 an hour raise on their behalf but charged them $4 a week in union dues. Some Mayfair workers wanted to work twelve-to-fourteen-hour-days and seven days a week, but Mayfair limited them to 70 hours a week to avoid the overtime pay required by the contract (Russo 2018). Mayfair's SAWP workers voted 26–0 to decertify UFCW in August 2009, a vote that migrant advocates charged was influenced by the Mexican consul's warning to Mayfair's workers they could be blacklisted if they did not vote for decertification.[23]

The UFCW also had mixed experiences in British Columbia, which granted farm workers union organizing rights in 1975 and has a provincial standard contract for SAWP workers (Vosko 2019). UFCW Local 1518 won the right to represent SAWP workers at Surrey-based Greenway Farms and Floralia Plant Growers in 2008, and at Mission-based Sidhu & Sons Nursery in 2010. The UFCW achieved collective bargaining agreements (CBAs) with Floralia and Sidhu by way of arbitration that included provisions specific to the SAWP workers, such as the right to return to their home country during the worker's contract if there was a death in the family and the right to store work and other equipment at their Canadian employer while SAWP workers were at home (Vosko 2018, 896–97).

The SAWP CBAs included seniority recall after completing the first season and speedy arbitration if a SAWP worker was fired, since losing a job in Canada normally requires a worker to return to her home country. Seniority recall may not be observed strictly because Canadians have priority to fill jobs, so some SAWP workers may not be recalled if the employer recruits more local workers. The Mexican government can block the return of particular SAWP workers named by Canadian employers.

This is what happened at Sidhu, where the UFCW complained that the Mexican government in 2011 blocked the return of some pro-union SAWP workers. The UFCW filed charges against the Mexican government with the British Columbia Labor Board. The Mexican government countered successfully that it was a sovereign immune from labor suits (Jensen 2014; Vosko 2018, 900–901; Vosko 2016). Workers at Sidhu voted to decertify the UFCW in an election that some workers said was tainted by Mexican labor attachés warning workers to vote out the UFCW in order to keep their jobs. Critics cite the Sidhu case as an example of the Mexican government acting on behalf of Canadian employers rather than Mexican SAWP workers.[24]

The North-South Institute supported several studies that evaluated the SAWP's impacts on Canada and sending countries. The overall conclusion is that the SAWP helps Canadian farmers to recruit and employ reliable low-skilled workers but allows Canadian farm wages to be depressed and working conditions to erode because SAWP migrants are vulnerable and do not complain (Verma 2002). Worker vulnerability was highlighted by Casey et al. (2019), who used the Ontario Ministry of Labor's Employment Standards Information System to determine that labor law enforcement depends on worker complaints, and SAWP workers rarely complain.

The Institute for Research on Public Policy interviewed 600 Mexican and Jamaican farm workers in 2012 and found that they worked in Canada for an average of eight seasons. Many noted their isolation on the Canadian farms where they worked, but two-thirds said they would like to return next season due to Canadian wages, which were much higher than they could earn at home. Many wanted to become Canadian immigrants (Hennebry 2012).

The SAWP is an example of a circular migration program that fills seasonal jobs with workers who return year after year. The Mexican government in a 2015 press release called the SAWP "a model of bilateral cooperation between the two countries, guaranteeing employment to farm workers and making it possible to maintain a temporary migration flow that is orderly, circular and secure, and above all, one that fully respects the workers' labor, social and human rights."[25] Worker advocates emphasize the vulnerability of guest workers who are dependent on Canadian employers to remain in Canada and to be recalled for next season (Choudry and Smith 2016).

Farmers benefit from the fact that over 85 percent of SAWP workers have been employed in Canada previously, which reduces training costs and ensures high worker productivity. Hennebry and Preibisch (2012) praise the cooperation between governments to regulate recruitment and employment, transparent processes for selecting workers, and the availability of health insurance for SAWP workers while they are in Canada. They note that there is no formal program to recognize worker qualifications in Canada or in the workers' home countries to acknowledge the skills guest workers acquire in Canada. But if the alternative to SAWP is illegal migration and contractors assembling crews of workers to fill seasonal farm jobs, as in the United States, the SAWP can be considered a "model despite flaws" (Basok 2007).

There is less evidence that the SAWP has promoted stay-at-home development in worker areas of origin, as may occur if returned workers invest their remittances to expand small farms and start small businesses. Most returned SAWP workers improved their housing and spent more on their children's health and education than similar families that did not receive remittances, but many household heads continue to migrate year after year to Canada.[26] Upward mobility may be intergenerational, as when the children of SAWP workers who obtain more health care and education due to their parents' remittances find good jobs in Mexico.

Migrant advocates recently persuaded the Canadian government to test new mechanisms to protect temporary workers (Weiler and McLaughlin 2019), including a pilot Migrant Worker Support Network launched in British Columbia in 2018 and an Agri-Food Immigration Pilot in 2019 that allows some temporary foreign workers who have been employed for at least a year in meatpacking, mushrooms, greenhouses, and livestock production to apply for permanent residence if they have a high school diploma, knowledge of English or French, and a Canadian job offer. The Canadian government is considering a visa portability plan that would grant occupation-specific rather than employer-specific work permits to allow low-skilled temporary foreign workers to move away from abusive employers.

The COVID pandemic of 2020 raised new tensions between farm employers and worker advocates. Mexico briefly suspended sending SAWP workers to Canada in March and April 2020 after several workers got sick and some died, and the Canadian government helped farm employers to cover the mandatory two-week quarantine of SAWP workers after their arrival. However, some SAWP workers complained when their employers prohibited them from having visitors or leaving the farm except during weekly trips for groceries organized by the employer; the workers complained of being "imprisoned" on the farms where they lived in employer-provided housing. The federal government in August 2020 reminded employers of SAWP workers that they may not limit their employees' freedom of movement when they are not working, but most SAWP employees followed employer instructions to stay on the farm to ensure that they would be invited to return in 2021.[27]

Canada's SAWP and other farm guest worker programs are considered models because they operate under the terms of government-to-government agreements, employers are involved in developing program regulations, and most guest workers employed by farmers directly rather than brought to farms by contractors. In comparison to the US H-2A program, which requires employers to pay all worker costs, Canadian farm employers may recoup some travel and housing costs in deductions from worker wages. The Canadian government has been willing to experiment with new programs and to modify program requirements in response to employer and worker requests, usually by adding new programs or streams for guest workers.

2

Mexico

Agriculture and Labor

Mexico developed a system of estates employing peasants until the 1910–17 revolution created the ejido system, which gave farmers land they could use but not sell. Mexican agricultural policies that offered high prices for corn and beans benefitted primarily large commercial farmers who had surpluses to sell rather than the more numerous subsistence farmers who farmed to feed their families, and worsening poverty on the ejidos in the 1980s prompted rising Mexico-US migration. NAFTA aimed to substitute trade for migration, to allow Mexico to export tomatoes rather than tomato pickers to the United States, and led to the creation of a farm export sector that provides 750,000 jobs for young Mexicans with little education, in which they earn two or three times Mexico's minimum wage. Export agriculture is a NAFTA success story that offers a first step up the job ladder for rural Mexicans and their families.

Agricultural Evolution

Mexico was a Spanish colony for over three centuries, and the Spanish government granted land to conquering soldiers and white settlers under the encomienda system, which obliged indigenous residents to live on and work for the owners of haciendas (large estates) in exchange for protection and instruction in Catholicism; Photo 2.1 shows the social distances between hacienda owners and peasants. Estates existed alongside subsistence farmers with communal land, but haciendas devoted to crop and livestock farming employed and housed most Mexican residents, producing food for urban residents as well as for the miners who accounted for most of colonial Mexico's exports.

After Mexico's independence in 1821, the haciendas expanded, taking land from small farmers and native communities that led to clashes in

Bracero 2.0. Philip Martin, Oxford University Press. © Oxford University Press 2024.
DOI: 10.1093/oso/9780197699973.003.0002

several Mexican states. The Liberals who came to power in 1855 wanted to create a middle class of farmers who owned the land they farmed. The Lerdo Law of 1856 broke up large landholdings, including land owned by the Catholic Church and the civil corporations under which some indigenous communities held property. However, flawed implementation of the Lerdo Law and contradictions between federal and state laws and practices allowed a relative handful of individuals to acquire ever more farmland, including Americans in northern Mexican states (Galindo 2019).

Peasants who lived on communal and church land were displaced and landownership become concentrated among a few families. By 1910, when Mexico had 15 million people, about 2,000 families owned 87 percent of Mexico's rural land, and peasants were worse off than they had been in 1855 (Hufbauer and Schott 2005, 334). There were some small farmers, but most rural residents were landless, so "land for the peasants" became a rallying cry of the Mexican revolution.

Photo 2.1 Peasants on Hacienda Peotillos, San Luis Potosí, late 1800s
Source: US Library of Congress

The Mexican Revolution of 1910–17 was fought in part to ensure that peasants had their "own" land.[1] Article 27 of the Mexican Constitution of 1917 allowed Mexico's agrarian reform ministry to redistribute large private land holdings to ejidos, or communal farms. Over 55 percent of Mexico's land went to ejidos, including some of the land that had been taken from indigenous communities under the Lerdo Law of 1856. Ejido members had the right to farm their plots of ejido land as long as they actively worked and lived on the ejido, and their heirs could inherit their ejido land. However, the government did not want peasants to lose their ejido land, so ejidatario farmers could not sell or rent their land, nor could they borrow money using ejido land as collateral.[2]

Mexico urbanized and its economy expanded between the 1940s and 1970s, requiring Mexican agriculture to feed the growing population with a smaller share of the workforce. In 1940, two-thirds of Mexican workers were employed in agriculture; by 1980, the share was 30 percent. However, a tripling of the population from 20 million to 67 million between 1950 and 1980 meant that total employment in agriculture rose by 50 percent even as the share of Mexicans employed in agriculture fell and real wages and productivity rose.

Farm output quintupled over four decades as large farmers using irrigation and modern seeds and technologies in Sinaloa and other northern Mexican states achieved the same yields as US farmers. Mexico was a leader in implementing Green Revolution technologies that raised yields and enabled Mexico to feed its rapidly growing population in the 1960s. Government agricultural policies after 1974 guaranteed high prices for corn and beans, and subsidized these staples for urban residents via CONASUPO stores, benefitting the large farmers who had the most crops to sell and Mexicans who shopped at CONASUPO stores.

Most of the 32,000 ejidos in 1990 included about 100 farmers and their families, and most of the 3.5 million ejidatario farmers had less than five hectares of land (Hufbauer and Schott 2005, 334).[3] Most ejidatario farmers and their families produced corn and beans without irrigation, often on several small and noncontiguous plots. Few ejidatario farmers produced a surplus to sell to the government for more than the world price for corn (this was the government's major anti-poverty policy in rural areas for most of the 20th century), so most were poor, highlighting the unequal sharing of the benefits of Mexico's agricultural revolution.

President Carlos Salinas, who proposed what became NAFTA in 1990, persuaded Mexico's Congress to amend Article 27 in 1992 to permit ejido land to be sold, rented, and used as collateral for loans. In the quarter century since, relatively little ejido land has been privatized, in part because a two-thirds majority of the ejidatario farmers must approve a sale during a meeting of ejido members with at least 75 percent participating. Many ejidatarios live in the United States or in Mexican cities, making the participation requirement difficult to satisfy and explaining why less than 5 percent of the 10 million hectares of ejido land was sold between 1992 and 2015. The ejido land that was sold often went to urban developers rather than staying in agriculture, with farming reorganized to raise productivity. Figure 2.1 shows Mexico's evolving land tenure system.

Mexico changed its agricultural policies in the 1990s, switching from subsidizing the price of corn to providing direct income support to poor farmers.[4] The theory behind this policy change was that some large private farmers would switch from corn to fruits and vegetables that could be sold in Mexico or exported, while poor farmers would get direct payments from the government as they and their children transitioned to nonfarm jobs. Under free trade, Mexico would import cheaper corn and grains from the United States and export labor-intensive fruits and vegetables, reflecting the comparative advantage of the two countries.

Agrarian system Features	Hacienda System 19th Century	Agrarian Reform 20th Century	Post-NAFTA 21th Century
Land tenure	Large estates	*Ejido*, land distribution policies	Private ownership and urbanization of communal and *ejido* land
	Ancestral communal land	Small private properties	
	Population concentrated in small villages and towns	Restrictions from *ejidos* regarding the open-land market	

Figure 2.1 Haciendas, Ejidos, and Private Farms in Mexico

Source: Melissa Schumacher et al., "Evolution and Collapse of Ejidos in Mexico—To What Extent Is Cosmmunal Land Used for Urban Development?," *Land* 8, no. 10 (2019): 146, https://www.mdpi.com/2073-445X/8/10/146/html.

Farm Structure and NAFTA

Mexico has many agricultures, including large and modern farms in the north and central states and subsistence farms in mountainous areas and in southern states. Modern farms in the north and center of Mexico rely on machinery rather than hired workers to produce corn and grains for the Mexican market, but an important subsector employs hired workers to produce fresh fruits and vegetables to export to the United States. Farms in southern Mexico are smaller, rely on rainfall to provide water for plants and animals, and produce mostly corn and grains for home consumption. There are exceptions to these generalizations in both northern and southern Mexico.

Corn occupies a special place in Mexico. Tortillas are a staple of the Mexican diet, and some 7.5 million hectares of land were devoted to corn in 2017, a fifth of Mexico's 22 million hectares of cropland. A third of Mexico's 1.5 million corn farmers were in the relatively poor states of Chiapas, Oaxaca, and Puebla, and they had an average 3.6 hectares of corn (Zahniser et al. 2019). Small farmers in southern Mexican states obtain yields of two to three tons per hectare, while large farms that irrigate corn in Sinaloa achieve yields of 10 tons per hectare.

Mexico produces 27 million metric tons of corn a year, 90 percent of that white corn. The United States, by contrast, produces 367 million metric tons of yellow corn a year, a third of global corn production of 1.1 billion metric tons. Mexican white corn is used mostly to make tortillas and other food products, while most US corn is used for ethanol fuel or animal feed.

The Mexican government budgets almost $20 billion a year for agriculture and rural development, but the budget for Mexico's equivalent of the USDA, the Secretaría de Agricultura y Desarrollo Rural (SADER), is less than $4 billion a year. A quarter of the SADER budget is for the Production for Well-Being (Producción para el Bienestar) program shown in Photo 2.2, which provides direct payments of $60 to $100 per hectare on up to 20 hectares of white corn, dry beans, and other staples produced by small- and medium-sized farmers. A second program sets minimum prices for basic grains, such as $290 per metric ton for white corn from rainfed land of up to five hectares in 2019, a premium of $100 a ton over the price of imported white corn, while a third program provides up to 600 kilograms of subsidized fertilizer to each qualifying small producer.[5]

Photo 2.2 Paying Small Mexican Farmers

Source: Gobernanza Mexicana, "Producción para el Bienestar 2022–2023: Registro y entrega de pagos," 2022, https://gobmx.org/apoyos-del-gobierno/produccion-para-el-bienestar/.

Mexican agriculture changed with the North American Free Trade Agreement, especially after most barriers to trade in farm commodities were eliminated in 2008. Imports of less costly US yellow corn, soybeans, and wheat, as well as imports of meat and dairy products, led many small Mexican farmers and their children to quit farming, as they realized they could not compete with lower-cost commodities imported from the United States. NAFTA accelerated the shrinking of Mexico's agricultural workforce as farmers and their children left rural areas for Mexican cities and the United States.

Many critics blame NAFTA for the Mexican flight from the land in the 1990s and 2000s, and some argue that US approval of NAFTA set the stage for unauthorized Mexico-US migration as well as urbanization and associated ills in Mexico. For example, Gálvez (2018) argues that imports of US corn drove small farmers into cities, where their low incomes encouraged them to buy cheap calories in the form of processed food instead of artisanal corn from small plots that was made into tortillas in multigenerational households in rural Mexico. With urbanized nuclear families earning cash wages and eating at McDonald's, obesity increased, leading Gálvez to attribute Mexican obesity to NAFTA's free trade in farm commodities.

NAFTA accelerated changes that were already occurring, including rising obesity and the movement of small farmers off the land in Mexico. Blaming NAFTA for obesity in Mexico ignores the fact that Pacific Island countries have the world's highest adult obesity rates, with more than half of adults having a body mass index above 30. The US obesity rate of 36 percent is higher than Mexico's 29 percent rate, but countries with which the United States does not have free trade agreements, including Turkey and Egypt, have obesity rates of 32 percent, higher than the Mexican rate.

Food romantics often picture poor families growing traditional crops in traditional ways, eating healthy foods, and living happily in villages until their lives are disrupted by free trade. But this is a misleading picture. Villages with residents speaking indigenous languages are mostly poor, but they are not free of the problems of most social groups, from jealousies to crime. Many youth want to escape from villages and their traditions, but they often lack the education needed to succeed in the cities to which they move.

Mexican leaders told Mexicans that NAFTA was part of a great leap forward, raising expectations for higher incomes and more opportunities. However, foreign investment was concentrated in northern Mexican states, far from the peasant villages of southern Mexico. Southern Mexicans had to "go north for opportunity" after NAFTA, and many continued on to the United States.[6] As Nobel Prize–winning economist Theodore Schultz pointed out in the 1940s and 1950s, the best way to help rural youth is to give them the education that allows them to flourish wherever they live. Food romantics may want to visit rural villages with small farmers engaged in artisanal food production, but many youth in such villages prefer to seek opportunity in cities.

Export Agriculture and Labor

The value of Mexico's agricultural output rose by an average 3.2 percent annually between 1994 and 2018, and rose faster after the 2008–9 recession, with the value of some fresh fruits and vegetables that are mostly exported rising over 10 percent a year. Mexico exported agricultural commodities worth $45 billion in 2021 and imported $35 billion worth of agricultural commodities. Canada, Mexico, and the United States have agricultural trade surpluses.

As Mexico's export-oriented fruit and vegetable agriculture expanded, exports of avocados, berries, tomatoes, and other fresh fruits and vegetables to the United States turned what had been a US agricultural trade surplus with Mexico into a deficit beginning in 2012. NAFTA shows comparative advantage at work, as Mexico imports grains and meat from the United States and exports labor-intensive fruits and vegetables to the United States.

Fruits and vegetables occupy 10 percent of Mexico's cropland but generate 40 percent of Mexican farm sales. Figure 2.2 shows that fruit and vegetable exports to the United States of $11 billion in 2016 were almost half of Mexico's $23 billion in farm exports, making Mexico's farm exports comparable in value to remittances and tourism receipts. Mexico's $18 billion in farm imports from the United States were dominated by corn and soybeans, meat, and dairy products. Mexico has both an overall trade surplus and an agricultural trade surplus with the United States.

Few of Mexico's 3.6 million farms export fruits and vegetables to the United States, for several reasons. First, most Mexican farms are small. Over 70 percent of Mexican farms have less than five hectares, and half have less than two hectares. At the other end of the size spectrum, the 25,000 Mexican farmers who have more than 100 hectares of farmland have 30 percent of

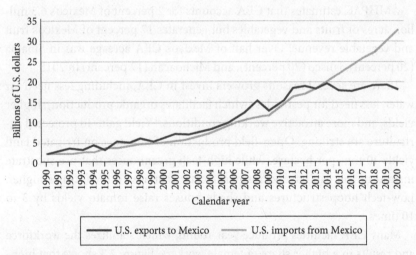

Figure 2.2 Mexico Has Had an Agricultural Trade Surplus with the United States Since 2012

Source: US Department of Agriculture, Economic Research Service, "Mexico: Trade and FDI," last updated March 14, 2023, https://www.ers.usda.gov/topics/international-markets-u-s-trade/countries-regions/usmca-canada-mexico/mexico-trade-fdi/

all Mexican cropland and produce most of Mexico's farm output. Second, producing fresh fruits and vegetables to export requires capital, management ability, and infrastructure that most small farmers lack. Banks are reluctant to lend to small farmers because of historically high default rates and frequent government intervention to forgive farm debts (Hufbauer and Schott 2005, 336).

Mexico is a world leader in controlled environment agriculture, including glass greenhouses and other structures that fully or partially protect growing plants. There are three major types of protective structures: high-tech greenhouses, low-tech structures that use metal hoops covered with plastic to enclose and protect plants, and open-sided shade houses that protect plants from rain and sun. Medium-tech protective structures are a mix of hoop and shade structures.

The Mexican Association of Protected Horticulture (AMHPAC) reported that Mexico's CEA acreage expanded from 330 acres in 2003 to 106,000 acres in 2018, including 27 percent in greenhouses, 29 percent in hoop or macro tunnels, and 45 percent in shade houses.[7] About 70 percent of Mexico's CEA acreage in 2015 was devoted to tomatoes, 16 percent to bell peppers, and 10 percent to cucumbers. Over 80 percent of the vegetables produced under CEA were exported to the United States (Pratt and Ortega 2019, 4).

AMHPAC estimates that CEA accounts for 2 percent of Mexico's 6.3 million acres of fruits and vegetables but generates 17 percent of Mexico's fruit and vegetable revenue. Over half of Mexico's CEA acreage was in Sinaloa (20 percent), Jalisco (20 percent), and Michoacán (17 percent) in 2015.

There are several reasons growers invest in CEA, including less need for water, less need for pesticides (which facilitates organic production), higher yields, and more attractive working conditions.[8] Yield gains in protected agriculture are striking. Open-field production of tomatoes on irrigated land yields 40 tons per hectare, while high-tech greenhouses that use substrate instead of soil can have yields per hectare that are 10 to 30 times higher. Low-tech hoop structures and shade houses raise tomato yields by 3 to 10 times.

Many CEA facilities produce year-round, which stabilizes the workforce and results in a higher share of female workers. Figure 2.3 shows that high-tech greenhouses use fewer workers per hectare, 10 compared with 20 or more in open fields and low-tech greenhouses, and almost always enroll their workers in Mexico's safety net program (Instituto Mexicano del Seguro

Variable	BAU (open-field)	High-tech	Low-tech	Shade house	Medium-tech
Workers per hectare at full operation	21–30	10	21	21	14
Work type	Hard manual, low-skilled field labor	Resembles manufacturing; semi-skilled	Same as BAU	Same as BAU. In year-round production, the labor requires some skill	Resembles manufacturing; some skill
Labor term	Not year-round, not permanent/ Frequently daily or piece rate	Permanent, year-round, usually social benefits included	Same as BAU	Seasonal or year-round	Frequently year-round and permanent
Safety	Low injury rate due to lack of machinery Extensive exposure to high-risk agro-chemicals	Low injury rate due to lack of machinery Indoor working conditions Limited exposure to relatively low-toxicity chemicals	Low injury rate due to lack of machinery Extensive exposure to high-risk agrochemicals	Low injury rate due to lack of machinery Exposure to chemicals could be high or low depending on market orientation	Low injury rate due to lack of machinery Mostly indoor work Exposure to chemicals could be high or low depending on market orientation
Gender	Nature of work apt primarily for men	Most jobs appropriate for women	Nature of work apt primarily for mén	Nature of wok apt primarily for men	More work for women than BAU

Figure 2.3 Labor Conditions in Protected and Open-Field Tomatoes
Source: Pratt and Ortega 2019

Social, IMSS), and use payroll taxes to cover the cost of health care and child care as well as pensions (Pratt and Ortega 2019). There is often less exposure to toxic chemicals in CEA than in open-field agriculture, and safety and labor compliance protocols are more likely to be followed in CEA facilities that export fresh produce.

Avocados, Berries, and Tomatoes

The three leading fresh fruits and vegetables exported from Mexico to the United States are fresh avocados, worth $2.2 billion in 2020; fresh berries, worth $3 billion; and fresh tomatoes, worth $2.4 billion. These three commodities account for over half of the value of Mexico's fresh fruit and vegetable exports to the United States (Zahniser 2022). Mexico's major competitive advantage is a climate that permits production during the winter and spring months, when there is little US production of competing fruits and vegetables. Lower labor costs and latecomer advantages, such as producing berries and vegetables under protective structures, should help Mexican producers to continue to increase their share of US fruit and vegetable sales.

Avocados

Mexico is the world's largest producer and exporter of alligator pears or avocados, producing about 2.5 million metric tons during the July–June marketing year, almost a third of global production. Avocados are harvested in Mexico year-round, but production peaks between October and February. Yields from the 230,000 hectares of Mexican avocados average over 10 metric tons per hectare, and almost all are the Hass variety. Avocados are the smallest share of the world's four major tropical fruits, accounting for 5 percent of total tropical fruit production, compared with 52 percent for mangoes, 28 percent for pineapples, and 15 percent for papayas.

Mexicans consume an average 7 kilograms of avocados per person per year, or 1 million metric tons a year. Mexico exports 60 percent of its avocados, three-fourths to the United States,[9] in the past only from Michoacán but also from Jalisco since 2022. Mexican avocado producers prefer to export their avocados in order to obtain higher prices.

The Association of Avocado Producers and Packers and Exporters of Mexico (APEAM) reported 29,000 registered avocado producers in Michoacán, most of whom have 5 to 10 hectares. The four largest avocado packing houses, Calavo de México, Misión de México, Frutas Finas de Tancítaro, and Empacadora Agroexport, account for a third of avocado exports (UNCTAD 2014, 113).

Figure 2.4 shows that Uruapan, Michoacán, is Mexico's avocado capital and a place where criminal gangs levy taxes on some avocado farmers of about $250 per hectare for "protection." Mexico's war against drug kingpins began in Michoacán in 2006, splintering some drug cartels into smaller groups that are more likely to extort money from local residents than to smuggle drugs to the United States. Four gangs, the Jalisco Cartel New Generation, the Nueva Familia Michoacana, the Tepalcatepec Cartel, and the Zicuirán Cartel, compete to tax avocado producers, and some growers complain of state and local government fees as well as assessments for nonexistent services.

Avocado producers near the city of Tancítaro (population 30,000) pay a per-hectare fee to support the Tancítaro police and their own security force, a reaction to the burning of two packing plants.[10] Gang-linked violence and illegal deforestation to plant more avocado trees have prompted some to call Mexican avocados a "conflict commodity" associated with "killings, modern slavery, child labor and environmental degradation."[11]

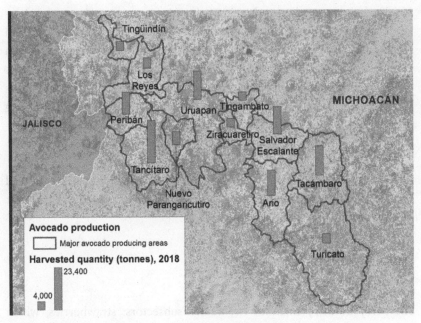

Figure 2.4 Avocado Production Areas in Michoacán

Source: "Mexico: Leading Producer and Exporter of Avocados," *Rural Migration News* blog, January 16, 2020, https://migration.ucdavis.edu/rmn/blog/post/?id=2394

Most Jalisco avocado farms are larger than those in Michoacán, and half of Jalisco's avocado acreage is controlled by 15 to 20 growers, suggesting 1,000-acre avocado farms. The picture of larger-scale avocado production in Jalisco is further strengthened by the fact that 85 percent of Jalisco avocados are irrigated, versus 40 percent in Michoacán.

There are three major entities involved in the production of avocados: farmers, harvest workers, and packing houses. Farmers and their hired workers prune, fertilize, and care for trees during the year. Harvest crews coordinate with packing houses to determine where and how much to harvest, and packing houses sort, pack, and market the fruit.

Harvesting avocados in Michoacán pays well, an average $450 a month—the highest farm worker wages in nonborder areas of Mexico.[12] However, most employers do not enroll avocado harvesters in the IMSS system, which provides health, retirement, and other benefits, largely because harvesters are hired by the day or for a few days rather than for weeks or months.

California produces 175,000 tons of avocados a year, 85 percent of US production, and production peaks during the summer months. California's

50,000 acres of avocados produce an average 4 tons per acre (10 tons per hectare), making US yields similar to those of Mexico. The cost of picking and hauling avocados was $0.20 a pound in 2011, when the grower price was $1 a pound, suggesting harvest costs of 20 percent of grower revenue. Harvesters pick avocados into bags that are dumped into bins. Most avocado orchards are picked three times, twice for size and a third time to strip the remaining fruit. It takes 60 avocados that each weigh less than 7.5 ounces to fill a 25-pound box and 48 avocados that each weigh 7.5 to 9.5 ounces to fill a 25-pound box.

Avocado prices rose sharply in recent years, so California farmers received over $2 a pound for avocados in 2022. US farm-level avocado prices peak during the summer months.

Berries

The berry industry includes two major subsectors: strawberries, which usually are planted each year, and perennial blueberries, raspberries, and blackberries, which can produce fruit for more than a decade, although most farmers replant after three or four harvests. Demand for fresh berries has been rising because of their health benefits as well as rising incomes, year-round availability, and convenient packaging. Berries are the highest-revenue fresh produce item sold in US supermarkets, which get half of their berry revenue from strawberries, a quarter from blueberries, and 15 percent from raspberries.

Mexico's export-oriented berry industry is expanding. The Mexican National Berry Export Association (Aneberries) projects exports of almost 600,000 metric tons of berries worth over $3 billion in 2022, with 95 percent headed to the United States. About 40 percent of Mexican berry exports by value are raspberries, with the other 60 percent divided almost equally between strawberries, blueberries, and blackberries. Aneberries estimates that 120,000 people are employed in Mexico's export-oriented berry industry, including those packing raspberries for export in Photo 2.3.

Mexico's major berry production areas are Irapuato, Guanajuato (mostly strawberries that are often frozen), Michoacán (mostly strawberries and blackberries), and Jalisco (mostly blueberries and raspberries). Baja California also produces organic strawberries and raspberries on its sandy soils with desalinated water (Zlolniski 2019). Mexico is the world's largest

Photo 2.3 Sorting Harvested Raspberries in Jalisco
Source: Philip Martin

producer and exporter of blackberries, and it is poised to become the largest producer of raspberries, which often are picked every day during the peak season.[13]

Most Mexican berries are produced under CEA, usually plastic-covered hoop structures that protect five to seven rows of berries from birds and weather. Since most berries are eaten raw, food security is a major concern. Berry farms are fenced, and entries and exits are checked. Most berry farms transport workers between their housing and the fields in buses, so there are no worker cars on site, and toilets and hand-washing facilities are readily available.

The United States is also a major producer of strawberries. California produces 90 percent of US strawberries; Florida dominates US production during the January–March winter months, when the United States also imports strawberries from Mexico. Strawberries are a high-value and high-cost crop, requiring up to $100,000 an acre in production and harvesting costs, making them risky for smaller growers with limited capital who may be unable to survive weather or disease events that reduce yields or production during their peak periods of production.

Many Mexican-born farm workers in the United States want to become strawberry farmers, which they can do with little capital by leasing land and plants and delivering the harvested berries to marketers, who deduct their costs and forward the balance to the grower. Strawberries may be the only California commodity with mostly Hispanic growers, although their typically smaller farms mean that Hispanic growers do not account for most of the state's acreage. Chapter 7 examines alternatives to hand labor in strawberries.

Tomatoes

Mexico produces over 3.5 million metric tons of tomatoes each year and exports almost 2 million metric tons (or 60 percent of its tomatoes), almost all to the United States. Mexico produces tomatoes year-round, but production for export peaks between December and April, when Sinaloa is the main tomato producer. Production for both the domestic and export markets peaks from May through November, with production led by San Luis Potosí and Michoacán, but other states produce tomatoes as well.

Mexico is the world's largest exporter of fresh tomatoes due to its embrace of CEA, which includes greenhouses, shade, and tunnel structures that protect growing plants. Figure 2.5 shows that two-thirds of the Mexican tomatoes that are exported to the United States are from CEA, which raises yields, lengthens seasons, and facilitates organic production.

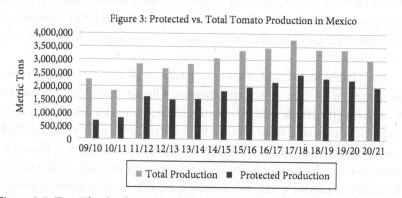

Figure 3: Protected vs. Total Tomato Production in Mexico

Figure 2.5 Two-Thirds of Mexican Tomatoes Are from CEA

Source: https://apps.fas.usda.gov/newgainapi/api/Report/DownloadReportByFileName?fileName=Tomatoes%20and%20Products%20Annual_Monterrey%20ATO_Mexico_MX2022-0035.pdf

Mexican tomato production for export began in Sinaloa in the 1970s, as well-capitalized farmers organized themselves into the Confederación de Asociaciones Agrícolas del Estado de Sinaloa (CAADES) to develop dams and irrigation systems and to control the licenses that were then needed to export farm commodities. Some 40 to 80 agribusinesses dominated Sinaloa tomato exports in 2000, growing and packing fresh tomatoes and providing housing for the internal Mexican migrants they employed (Mines 2010).

The CEA structures used to produce tomatoes vary from high-tech Dutch greenhouses to low-tech shade structures adapted from Spain, whose mild climate does not require steel-framed structures. The CEA structures used to produce tomatoes in Mexico can be covered by plastic or glass, may have passive or active environmental controls to regulate temperature and light, and grow plants in soil or use hydroponics (in which ground-up rock provides mechanical support for plant root systems and drip irrigation tubes provide water and nutrients). Glass greenhouses with active environmental controls and hydroponics are the most expensive structures to build and operate, and are most common in Canada and the United States. Many Mexican tomatoes are grown under less expensive CEA structures.

Canadian farmers in the mid-1990s adopted Dutch-developed greenhouses to produce what were then called hothouse tomatoes. Central Mexican tomato growers relied on a temperate climate and the extensive light available at high altitudes to produce tomatoes for the Mexican market, and built CEA facilities to produce premium and certified-safe fruits and vegetables, as with the greenhouses developed with Israeli technology in Querétaro.

CEA or hothouse tomatoes are picked when they are red and ripe, a contrast with the mature green tomato industry of California and Florida, which picks ripe tomatoes when they are green and turns them red with ethylene. Americans are willing to pay premium prices for CEA tomatoes and other vegetables such as bell peppers and cucumbers.

Florida's winter vegetable industry expanded after the US embargo of Cuban trade in 1961 and competes with tomato imports from Mexico during the winter and spring months. Florida growers stake their tomato plants to support the vines as they develop tomatoes, and their acreage is shrinking in the face of rising imports from Mexico. Harvest workers in Florida pick green tomatoes into five-gallon buckets and take them to dumpers stationed on trucks, who dump the full buckets into gondolas and give workers a token for each bucket picked, typically $0.50 to $0.75 for a bucket with 30 to 35 pounds of tomatoes. Harvest workers pick an average of 20 to 30 buckets an hour, depending on yields and how far they must walk to dump full buckets.[14]

Florida growers periodically accuse Mexicans of "dumping," or selling tomatoes in the United States at less than their cost of production. The US-Mexico tomato trade dispute resulted in a series of tomato suspension agreements since 1996, and the Florida growers' suit remains suspended if Mexican producers sell tomatoes in the United States for at least the minimum or reference price stipulated in the agreement. By requiring Mexican growers to sell at the reference price or more, Florida growers established a minimum price for tomatoes that in turn facilitated investment in CEA in Mexico and accelerated the shrinking of the Florida tomato industry. The US trade representative, Katherine Tai, refused to launch the Section 301 investigation requested by southeastern growers in October 2022 into rising fruit and vegetable imports from Mexico, promising instead to consult industry leaders to help farmers in the southeastern states to better compete with Mexican imports.

3

United States

Agriculture and Labor

American farmers produce food and fiber for over 330 million Americans and export almost 40 percent of the $400 billion worth of crops and livestock they produce each year.[1] Most US farms are operated by families to produce grain and livestock, but most US-produced fresh fruits and vegetables are from large commercial enterprises that each employ hundreds or thousands of seasonal workers, 70 percent of whom were born in Mexico. The settled Mexican-born workforce that arrived illegally in the 1990s is aging and being replaced by younger Mexicans, promising a new era of dependence on legal Mexican guest workers to fill seasonal farm jobs. The bracero programs, begun during World War I and World War II, usually involved workers who lived on and were employed by the farms where they worked. Many H-2A guest workers today are brought to farms by nonfarm employers such as labor contractors and housed in motels in urban areas.

Agricultural Evolution

The United States was settled largely by European immigrants seeking their own farmland. The economies of the North American colonies in the 17th and 18th centuries were dominated by agriculture and the concerns of farmers. Three distinct farming systems evolved to obtain seasonal farm labor: family farms that relied on family labor in the northern colonies, plantations reliant on slaves in the southern colonies, and large farms dependent on newly arrived immigrants in the western states.

Most farms in the northern colonies in the 1700s were operated by families that produced crops and livestock to satisfy their own needs.

Bracero 2.0. Philip Martin, Oxford University Press. © Oxford University Press 2024.
DOI: 10.1093/oso/9780197699973.003.0003

These subsistence farms had little reason to produce a surplus to sell because colonial cities were small,[2] transport costs were high, and European countries produced the same commodities. After the completion of the Erie Canal in 1825, the construction of railroads, and the growth of cities, family farmers moved west and operated larger farms with the help of labor-saving machinery to produce a surplus for residents of growing East Coast cities.

Agriculture in the southern colonies of Virginia and the Carolinas was different. Many US histories distinguish between northern colonies founded to allow religious minorities to practice their religion, southern colonies that sought to extract profits from exports of cotton and tobacco, and the tolerant Pennsylvania colony open to all peoples and religions that became the model for the United States (Martin, Susan 2021).

Southern farming was dominated by plantations that produced commodities that could not be grown in Western Europe, including cotton and tobacco. Plantations required more seasonal labor than large farm families could provide, so they relied on slaves because free workers were unwilling to work seasonally for low wages when they had the opportunity to operate their own farms. Cotton and tobacco are relatively long-season crops, and plantations provided food and housing for slaves year-round to ensure that workers were available for the six to eight months involved in planting and harvesting cotton and tobacco.

The price of land used to grow cotton and the price of slaves rose with cotton prices before the US Civil War in the 1860s. Areas with less productive land such as Virginia specialized in producing slaves for areas where cotton acreage was increasing, as in Louisiana and Texas. Conrad and Meyer (1958) concluded that slavery became more profitable as Virginia plantations specialized in producing slaves and farmers in Texas bought slaves to produce cotton.

After slavery ended in the 1860s, plantations employed ex-slaves as sharecroppers—that is, tenant farmers who grew and harvested cotton on land owned by the plantation in exchange for housing and a share of the revenue from the sale of the crop. Labor-saving mechanization in the 1930s reduced the need for hand labor to produce cotton, encouraging many Black farm families to migrate north to Chicago and other cities in search of nonfarm jobs. Tobacco remains a major labor-intensive crop in southeastern states, where it is produced on fewer and larger farms with the help of Mexican guest workers (Gale, Foreman, and Capehart 2000).

Waves of Migrants

Agricultural and farm labor systems in the western states evolved later and differently. Spain and later Mexico granted large tracts of land in what became California and the southwestern states to favored elites and to the Catholic Church for missions, often 50,000 acres or more for ranchos and missions that grazed cattle and produced wheat. Many of these large ranchos were bought by Americans after California became a state in 1850, ushering in an era of cattle grazing for meat and hides and "bonanza" wheat farming. Just as finding gold was uncertain, the often absentee owners of large California farms planted wheat in the fall and hoped that winter rains would bring a bonanza harvest in the spring.

After the transcontinental railroad was completed on May 10, 1869,[3] it became easier and cheaper for small farmers to move west and for western farm commodities to travel east. California's Mediterranean climate was ideal for producing fruit, and the development of an irrigation infrastructure and lower transportation costs encouraged a switch from wheat farming to citrus and other fruits. Fruit farming requires more seasonal workers than wheat farming, and contemporary observers believed that large farms would have to be broken into family-sized units in order to obtain seasonal workers. The expectation was that the family farm system of Iowa would come to California, and that farmer-owned cooperatives would emerge to market the fruit produced by family farmers.

However, large farms did not have to be subdivided into family-sized units to obtain seasonal workers because workers with no other job options were available. Over 15,000 Chinese workers were imported from Guangdong by the Central Pacific Railroad to build the transcontinental railroad from west to east through the Sierra Nevada for wages of $1 a day.[4] When the railroad was completed, the Chinese workers were laid off, and most moved to Sacramento, San Francisco, and other cities rather than returning to China (Chang 2019).

The transcontinental railroad brought cheaper manufactured goods to California, which bankrupted many of the smaller and less efficient factories that had supplied goods for the small California market. White workers who lost factory jobs blamed the Chinese, accusing them of working for low wages, and many of the Chinese were driven out of California cities. Farmers hired Chinese workers, paying them when they were needed and leaving them to fend for themselves in the off-season, creating a just-in-time seasonal farm labor system that offered relatively high hourly or daily wages but low annual earnings (Martin 2003, ch. 2).

Relatively low labor costs, made possible by paying seasonal workers only when they were needed, raised the value of California farmland, making it harder for small farmers to buy land. Since discrimination limited job options for Chinese workers, farmers who did their own farm work earned the equivalent of what Chinese workers could earn, discouraging most from becoming fruit farmers. Meanwhile, large farmers feared labor shortages, since the southern and Eastern European immigrants arriving at Ellis Island in the late 19th and early 20th centuries wanted to become farmers or factory workers, not seasonal farm workers.

Large California farmers needed new arrivals who saw seasonal farm work as a step up the economic ladder, and found this workforce in the waves of immigrants without other US options that arrived in the western states. The Chinese were followed by the Japanese in the 1880s, South Asians early in the 20th century, Mexicans during the 1920s, Dust Bowl migrants in the 1930s, and rural Mexicans since World War II. These newcomers accepted seasonal farm jobs for a decade or two before finding nonfarm jobs, and their children, educated in the United States, rarely followed their parents into the fields.

The result was an agricultural labor treadmill. As seasonal farm workers climbed the US economic ladder and their children shunned seasonal farm work, farmers complained of labor shortages and sought new sources of workers. Reformers opposed bringing newcomers into the state, arguing in the 1930s that the better policy would be to break up large farms into family-sized units. However, instead of land reforms, large farmers found another source of seasonal farm workers in rural Mexico.

Braceros

Rural Mexico has been the major source of new US farm workers for almost a century. Several bracero programs set migration from rural Mexico to US agriculture in motion, and networks combined with push and pull forces to expand migration flows over time. With the country's history as a nation of immigrants, the US government favored the admission of immigrants or green card holders,[5] who are foreign nationals with visas that allow them to live and work in most US jobs and, after five years, to become naturalized

US citizens. Legal immigrants may change employers or be jobless without losing the right to be in the United States, emphasizing their status as intending Americans.

There were exceptions to this immigrant-with-freedom-in-the-labor-market concept, including slavery and contract workers.[6] Contract workers were foreigners who pledged to work one or more years for the US employer who paid for the migrant's transportation to the United States. During the 1861–65 Civil War, the Union government enacted the Contract Labor Law (Act to Encourage Immigration) of 1864 to help private firms to recruit contract workers in Europe. US employers paid for the passage of contract workers, and they were obliged to work at least 12 months for the US employer who paid their passage.[7] At the behest of unions worried about having to compete with "indentured workers," the Contract Labor Law was repealed in 1868, and US immigration law was amended by the Foran Act in 1885[8] to prohibit the entry of contract migrant workers who were required to work for a particular US employer upon arrival (Briggs 1992, 49–50).

The federal government made several exceptions to US immigration law and admitted foreign guest farm workers who were tied to a particular US employer in the 20th century. Three themes recur in analyses of World War I and World War II farm guest worker programs, also known as the bracero programs (Rasmussen 1968; Vialet and McClure 1980). First, government regulators found it hard to determine if foreign farm workers were truly needed. For example, when farmers complained of labor shortages during World War I, Assistant Secretary of Labor Louis Post said: "The farm labor shortage is two-thirds imaginary and one-third remedial," meaning that farmers could find US workers by offering higher wages and better housing (Martin 2008, 5). Government agencies found it difficult to agree on the minimum wage that must be paid to guest workers and on what mechanisms to use (such as regulating productivity standards) to prevent guest workers from adversely affecting similar US workers.

Second, the US Department of Labor (DOL) sometimes loosened wage and work requirements to encourage employers to hire legal rather than unauthorized workers. After Operation Wetback removed over 1 million unauthorized Mexicans in 1954, DOL made it easier for farmers to hire legal braceros. However, DOL reversed course in the late 1950s, raising minimum wages and stepping up its enforcement of housing and other work-related regulations after the harvesting of major crops such as cotton and sugar beets was mechanized.

Third, the accordion-like loosening and tightening of bracero wages and labor standards obscured the cumulative effects of foreign on US workers. Careful studies of labor markets with significant numbers of braceros found that they did not experience the wage increases enjoyed by farm workers in areas without braceros and in nonfarm labor markets.[9] In response, DOL in May 1962 developed an Adverse Effect Wage Rate (AEWR) for each state where braceros were employed, and required farmers to pay this AEWR to braceros and similar US workers to prevent the presence of the guest workers from depressing farm wages.

Seasonal farm workers were often in the news in the early 1960s. The CBS television documentary *Harvest of Shame*, which aired just after Thanksgiving in 1960, sparked a national conversation about the plight of farm workers by quoting a farmer who said during a day labor market: "We used to own our slaves; now we just rent them."[10] Both houses of Congress had subcommittees on migrant farm labor, and these committees held hearings and produced reports calling for policy reforms, keeping migrant farm workers in the news.[11]

Today there are fewer hired farm workers, most are foreign-born and do not speak English, and many are unauthorized, making it harder for journalists to report on farm workers and perhaps reducing legislative interest in workers who are not US citizen. Farm labor has shifted from a general concern to a more specialized issue of interest to farm employers, federal and state agencies, and worker advocates.

There are several concepts central to all guest worker programs, including the recruitment efforts that employers must undertake before being certified to hire legal foreign workers and the minimum wages and working conditions that must be offered to guest workers and US workers employed alongside them. Table 3.1 explains the concepts that were developed to implement the Mexican bracero programs of World War I and World War II, and they have changed little over the past century.

World War I Braceros

There was no statutory basis for the admission of temporary foreign workers between 1885 and 1952, but exceptions to immigration laws were made to admit foreign farm workers. For example, the Immigration Act of 1917 required foreigners 16 and older to pass a literacy test and pay a head tax of $8

Table 3.1 Bracero and H-2A Concepts

World War I	Source/Issue	Implementation	Comment
DOL must certify employer need for braceros	DOL order, June 12, 1918	Local Employment Service office must certify that local workers are unavailable	Braceros could shift between certified employers
Minimum standards for worker contracts	DOL order, June 12, 1918	Bracero contracts must offer the same wages and working conditions as paid to US workers	Six-month bracero contracts could be renewed
Braceros must return to Mexico "at no cost to the US government" after contract ends	DOL order, June 12, 1918	Employers must pay the cost of return transportation	72,862 Mexicans admitted between 1917 and 1921, and 34,922 (48 percent) returned as required
World War II			
US government was employer, 1942–47, with farmer as subcontractor to government	US-Mexico government agreement and PL 45 (1943)	Bracero contracts guaranteed $0.30 an hour, and employer provided transportation, housing, and work for three-quarters of contract period	US farm workers did not have contracts and did not have to be paid a minimum wage
Bracero and H-2 programs	PL 78 (1951) and PL 82-414 (1952)	DOL certified that US workers were not available and that guest workers would not adversely affect US workers	Employers must try and fail to recruit US workers
Bracero experience I	1950s surge in unauthorized migration; farmers saved transportation costs and minimum wage requirements	Operation Wetback in 1954–55 deported unauthorized Mexicans; DOL made it easier to hire braceros	Bracero admissions peaked at 445,200 in 1956

(continued)

Table 3.1 Continued

World War I	Source/Issue	Implementation	Comment
Bracero experience II	Prevailing wages and Adverse Effect Wage Rates	1958: DOL set prevailing wages that must be paid 1962: DOL set AEWRs (AZ, $0.95 an hour; CA, $1; CO, $0.90; KS, $1; NM, $0.75; TX, $0.70)	Farmers had to pay braceros, but not US workers, at least prevailing or minimum wages
H-2	1948 agreement between DOL and INS required DOL to certify an employer's need for H-2 workers	H-2 terms and conditions negotiated by Caribbean governments and US employer associations	Western growers planned to switch to H-2 workers in 1964 but were deterred by DOL's December 19, 1964, regulations and AEWRs

Source: Author's elaboration

to enter the United States, but the Bureau of Immigration (then housed in the US Department of Labor) waived these requirements on May 23, 1917, "to admit temporarily otherwise inadmissible aliens" to work in US agriculture and on US railroads.[12]

DOL's action to admit Mexican farm workers was opposed by the chair of the House Committee on Immigration and Naturalization, who did not think DOL had the power to unilaterally suspend the bar on the admission of contract workers. DOL defended its decision by emphasizing that the alternatives to Mexican braceros would be worse, including a repeal of the Chinese Exclusion Act that would lead to more Chinese farm workers (Vialet and McClure 1980, 9). The Bureau of Immigration reported that with ample supplies of workers, "large acreages were planted and record crops harvested throughout the Southwest" in 1917 (quoted in Vialet and McClure 1980, 7).

A DOL order issued June 12, 1918, required employers to provide proof to their local Employment Service office that there were not sufficient US workers to fill the seasonal farm jobs they offered. Once certified, employers made written offers of "wages, housing conditions, and duration of employment" to Mexican workers that were to be the same as those "for similar labor in the community in which the admitted aliens are to be employed" (DOL order, April 18, 1918, quoted in Vialet and McClure 1980, 10). Bracero housing had to satisfy state laws or, if there were no state laws governing farm worker housing, standards set by DOL. Foreign workers were given ID cards and admitted for six months, with a six-month extension allowed, and were required to leave the United States, at no cost to the US government, when their contracts ended. Some bracero wages were withheld and deposited with the US Postal Savings Bank, to be repaid to workers in Mexico.

The program that admitted Mexicans to work on US railroads ended at the behest of US unions in 1918, but the farm worker program continued until March 2, 1921, with some exceptions afterward for "particularly meritorious cases" (Vialet and McClure 1980, 6). Otey Scruggs, the leading authority on the use of Mexican labor in southwestern agriculture during this first bracero era, emphasized that "Mexican immigrants had begun to form a reservoir of 'cheap' labor for the railroads and farms of the Southwest," and they were "the principal work force in many southwestern farming areas . . . by the early 1920s" (Scruggs 1960, 319).

The World War I bracero program found it hard to enforce returns. The annual report of the Bureau of Immigration for 1921 reported that 72,862 aliens were admitted between 1917 and 1921, but 21,400 absconded and "15,632 are still in the employ of their original importers," meaning that they did not return to Mexico at the end of their contracts (quoted in Vialet and McClure 1980, 11). Only 48 percent of the Mexican contract workers returned to Mexico as required, which the El Paso immigration supervisor attributed to many farmers refusing to cover the cost of return transportation. Scruggs concluded that the "basic weakness of the program was the lack of adequate enforcement machinery," so neither workers nor employers felt they had to abide by the contracts they signed (Scruggs 1960, 324).

The Mexican government was ambivalent about this first bracero program. The 1910–17 Mexican revolution damaged the haciendas on which many peasants lived and worked, leaving rural Mexicans eager to migrate to the United States for jobs. The Mexican government expressed concerns about the treatment of Mexicans in Texas, where signs reading "No Dogs or Mexicans" were common as seen in Photo 3.1. Some braceros returned to Mexico with few savings because of charges they incurred at farmer-owned stores in the camps where they lived (Fuller 1991).

Legal and illegal Mexican immigration surged in the 1920s. There were few US border entry stations, and the Border Patrol was not created until 1924, so illegal entry meant entering the United States without paying the head tax at one of the border entry stations or between them.[13] George Kiser

Photo 3.1 Sign Reading "No Dogs, Negros, Mexicans"
Source: US Library of Congress

argued that one reason for continued Mexico-US migration during the 1920s was US government agencies' tolerance of illegal Mexico-US migration in order to satisfy farm employers. He concluded that instead of "reducing the number of Mexican workers, the end of the emergency program [in 1921] marked the beginning of a decade which brought Mexican workers to the US in vastly increased and unprecedented numbers" (Kiser 1973, 136).

World War II Braceros

The 1930s were marked by farm labor surpluses in California and other western states. As the US unemployment rate rose toward 25 percent in 1932, some of the 300,000 Mexicans who immigrated to the United States during the 1920s, as well as their US-born children, were "repatriated," or returned to Mexico, between 1930 and 1933 to open jobs for US workers. The Mexican government cooperated with this repatriation, hoping to benefit from the return of citizens who had gained agricultural and industrial expertise in the United States.

California had 5.7 million residents in 1930, and Dust Bowl migration between 1935 and 1940 brought 1.3 million midwesterners to California. Many of these Okies and Arkies sought work in agriculture, hoping become farmers by first working as a hired hand on a California fruit farm and then operating a family-sized fruit farm of their own. Some Dust Bowl migrants drove to California farmhouses seeking work, but they soon learned that California's commercial farms hired crews of seasonal workers when they were needed, not year-round hired hands. Many Dust Bowl migrants wound up in informal camps known as Hoovervilles, and their plight was memorialized by Dorothea Lange's photo of Florence Owens Thompson and her children in Nipomo, California in Photo 3.2.

Pictures of farm worker children leaving Hooverville camps to go to school led to an outcry and the creation of federal farm worker housing centers, one of which served as the background for John Steinbeck's 1939 novel, *The Grapes of Wrath*.[14] The late 1930s proved to be a unique period in the history of the waves of immigrants who dominated among western farm workers because that was the only time that the majority of seasonal farm workers were white US citizens (in this case, Dust Bowl migrants).

Senator Robert La Follette Jr. (R-WI), who chaired the Senate Committee on Education and Labor's Subcommittee Investigating Violations of Free

Photo 3.2 Dorothea Lange's *Migrant Mother* (1936)
Source: US Library of Congress, Prints & Photographs Division, Farm Security Administration/Office of War Information Black-and-White Negatives.

Speech and the Rights of Labor, held hearings and issued reports between 1936 and 1942 that highlighted examples of California farmers and their allies in law enforcement routinely violating the rights of farm workers (Senate Committee on Education and Labor 1940). La Follette recommended that federal labor laws be extended to cover all farm workers, or at least those employed on farms that received federal subsidy payments (Senate Committee on Education and Labor 1942).

The United States declared war on the Germany and Japan in December 1941, and a federal interagency committee in May 1942 predicted that supplemental foreign farm workers would be needed for the fall harvest. Despite protests from US unions and Mexican American groups that there were no farm labor shortages,[15] the committee drafted a guest worker agreement that the Mexican government modified and signed on July 23, 1942.[16] The first of 4,189 Mexican braceros entered the United States on September 27, 1942, and went to work in the sugar beet fields near Stockton, California, for $0.30 an hour.[17]

Western farmers recruited Mexican braceros, while Eastern farmers recruited guest workers from the British West Indies under MOUs with the Bahamas (March 16, 1943), Jamaica (April 2, 1943), and Barbados (May 24, 1944). Some 4,698 residents of the Bahamas and 8,828 Jamaicans were admitted in 1943, mostly to work in Florida.[18] A total of 310,000 foreign farm workers were admitted between 1942 and 1947, including 220,000 Mexicans, 71 percent of the total. Admissions peaked in 1944, when 84,340 foreign farm workers were admitted, half to California; of these, 74 percent were Mexicans and 19 percent were Jamaicans.

The Mexican government insisted that the US government be the employer of braceros, so the Farm Security Administration (FSA) signed bracero contracts and paid the transportation costs of braceros to US farms, where the US farmer became a subcontractor to the FSA. Braceros were guaranteed work for at least three-quarters of the contract period and were entitled to $3 for each day on which the three-quarters guarantee was not met (Vialet and McClure 1980, 16).[19] US employers withheld 10 percent of bracero earnings and deposited them with Wells Fargo Bank, which sent these forced savings to the Bank of Mexico and then to the Banco de Credito Agricola, where they were lost.[20]

The World War II bracero program was authorized under Public Law 45, the first of what came to be known as the farm labor supply appropriations acts. PL 45 explicitly stated that minimum wages applied only to foreign farm workers, not US workers: the US government could not "fix, regulate, or impose minimum wages or housing standards" on employers of US farm workers (Vialet and McClure 1980, 18).[21]

The late 1940s witnessed rising unauthorized Mexico-US migration (Kim 2004).[22] Some Mexican workers crossed the border illegally to avoid paying bribes in Mexico to get on recruitment lists, and some US employers hired unauthorized workers to avoid paying the minimum wage that was mandated for bracero workers. President Harry S. Truman's Commission on Migratory Labor studied the effects of wartime braceros on US workers and concluded that braceros had "depressed farm wages and, therefore, had been detrimental to domestic labor." The Truman Commission was especially critical of what it called the "drying out of wetbacks," the process of apprehending unauthorized Mexicans inside the United States, returning them to the Mexico-US border, and then admitting them with bracero contracts and visas.

Table 3.2 shows that bracero admissions fell and apprehensions surged in the postwar years, with 10 apprehensions per admission in 1947.[23] Between 1947 and 1949, 74,600 Mexican braceros were admitted and "142,000 wetbacks already in the US were legalized by being put under contract."
Like La Follette's Senate subcommittee, the Truman Commission recommended that farm workers be covered by the Fair Labor Standards Act, which establishes minimum wages, and the National Labor Relations Act, which gives private sector workers union organizing rights. The Truman Commission also recommended that the federal government fine or sanction US employers who hired unauthorized workers.

Congress rejected the Truman Commission's recommendations and instead enacted the Migratory Labor Agreement (PL 78) in July 1951, which is often considered *the* bracero program because it accounted for the most braceros. PL 78 required minimum wages only for braceros,[24] and Congress rejected employer sanctions the next year via the so-called Texas Proviso, a provision in the Immigration and Nationality Act of 1952 (also called the McCarran-Walter Act) that made "illegally harboring or concealing an illegal entrant" a felony but excluded from this the employing of unauthorized workers.

Bracero admissions stabilized at 200,000 in the early 1950s as apprehensions of unauthorized foreigners topped 500,000 a year (Hawley 1966). Attorney General Herbert Brownell visited the Mexico-US border in August 1953, called the level of unauthorized Mexico-US migration

Table 3.2 Mexican Braceros and Apprehensions, 1942–64

Year	Braceros	Apprehensions	App./Bracero	Immigrants
1942	4,203	11,784	2.8	2,378
1943	52,098	11,175	0.2	4,172
1944	62,170	31,174	0.5	6,598
1945	49,454	69,164	1.4	6,702
1946	32,043	99,591	3.1	7,146
1947	19,632	193,657	9.9	7,558
1948	35,345	192,779	5.5	8,384
1949	107,000	288,253	2.7	8,803
1950	67,500	468,339	6.9	6,744
1951	192,000	509,040	2.7	6,153
1952	197,100	528,815	2.7	9,079
1953	201,380	885,587	4.4	17,183
1954	309,033	1,089,583	3.5	30,645
1955	398,650	254,096	0.6	43,702
1956	445,197	87,696	0.2	61,320
1957	436,049	59,918	0.1	49,321
1958	432,857	53,474	0.1	26,721
1959	437,643	45,336	0.1	22,909
1960	315,846	70,684	0.2	32,708
1961	291,420	88,823	0.3	41,476
1962	194,978	92,758	0.5	55,805
1963	186,865	88,712	0.5	55,986
1964	177,736	86,597	0.5	34,448
1942–64	4,646,199	5,307,035	1.1	545,941

Source: Vialet and McClure (1980)

"shocking," and ordered Immigration and Naturalization Service (INS) commissioner and former general Joseph Swing[25] to mount Operation Wetback, which involved federal, state, and local police sweeping areas with significant numbers of Mexicans and Mexican Americans to apprehend and remove any who were unauthorized (Vialet and McClure 1980, 40). The 1955 INS annual report noted that these police sweeps encouraged tens of thousands of Mexicans to leave "on their own accord," a repeat of the early 1930s repatriations, when unauthorized and legal Mexicans, as well as their US-born children, returned to Mexico.

The combination of more border enforcement and less enforcement of bracero regulations increased the employment of braceros and reduced illegal migration. The Bracero workers in Photo 3.3 quickly dominated the harvesting of particular commodities, especially citrus and tomatoes; in the late 1950s over 70 percent of harvest workers in these commodities were braceros (Lloyd, Martin, and Mamer 1988).[26]

President Dwight D. Eisenhower's labor secretary James Mitchell played a major role in ending the bracero program by appointing four consultants to study its effects. They issued a report in 1959 concluding that braceros adversely affected US farm workers: "Wage levels tend to become fixed in areas and activities where Mexicans are employed" (US Department of Labor 1959, 273). The consultants, who noted that over 60 percent of braceros "work in crops which are in surplus supply," including cotton and sugar (US Department of Labor 1959, 272–73), recommended that DOL determine a wage "rate necessary to avoid adverse effect on domestic wage rates" in crops and areas dominated by braceros, what became the Adverse Effect Wage Rate in 1962 (US Department of Labor 1959, 283).

The bracero program ended after 22 years on December 31, 1964. Farmers planned to continue to employ Mexican workers as H-2 guest workers, but on December 19, 1964, DOL published regulations that required employers of H-2 workers to offer and pay their US workers the DOL-determined AEWR and to provide their US workers with the same housing and transportation

Photo 3.3 Mexican Braceros Entering the United States in Texas in 1959
Source: US Library of Congress

benefits provided to guest workers (Vialet and McClure 1980, 65). Most farmers found the AEWR to be too high and did not want to house US workers, so 1965 and 1966 became years of adjustment as farmers sought alternatives to braceros.

Bracero Legacies

The bracero program was ended for many reasons, including the mechanization of cotton and sugar beet harvesting, which reduced the demand for hand workers; evidence that the presence of braceros reduced the wages of US farm workers; and political agreement that ending competition in the fields between braceros and US farm workers would benefit Mexican Americans. Braceros left three major legacies in Mexico and the United States: maquilas, mechanization, and unions.

First, the bracero program changed Mexico's rural economy by encouraging rural Mexicans to move to the US border to increase the chance that they would be selected by US employers; farmers had to pay worker transportation costs, which were lower for workers recruited in border areas. When the bracero program ended, thousands of Mexicans living along Mexico's northern border lacked jobs. In response, Mexico and the United States agreed under the Border Industrialization Program to create the maquila program in 1965, which invited US investors to create factories in northern Mexico that imported components, assembled them into products, and reexported them, paying taxes only on the value added in Mexico, primarily Mexican wages.

Mexico in the 1960s had a protectionist and inward-oriented trade policy, and the maquila program was designed to use US investment to create jobs for ex-braceros. However, this trade-in-place-of-migration strategy failed because US investors were slow to invest, and when they did, maquilas hired mostly young women, not the older men who had worked on US farms. The maquila program backfired as a policy to discourage illegal Mexico-US migration because it drew even more Mexicans toward the US border.

Second, the end of the bracero program spurred labor-saving mechanization and management changes, so farm workers were used more efficiently. When workers were plentiful, farmers often picked fruit into 50- or 60-pound boxes or lugs to minimize damage. With fewer farm workers available, farmers switched to 1,000-pound bins into which workers dumped bags or buckets, and the bins were moved by forklifts; that is, farmers accepted more damage to fruit at the bottom of bins in exchange for fewer workers needed to handle picked fruit in fields and orchards.

Growers and processors cooperated to embrace machines to harvest and handle commodities such as processing tomatoes and wine grapes. As we will see in Chapter 6, mechanization in fruits and vegetables is a process rather than an event, as biologists modify plants and trees, engineers develop machines to harvest commodities, and packers and processors cooperate with growers to accept machine harvesting, which may mean more sorting and discarding of machine-harvested produce in their plants.

Braceros were in the United States and were often housed on or near the farm where they worked, so they could be called on to work when needed. Without braceros on standby, some farm employers hired personnel managers to rationalize seasonal farm work, including requiring better communication between growers and packers to predict the demand for labor and improved communication with fewer and more productive workers. A Ventura lemon growers' cooperative reduced the number of seasonal workers hired from over 7,000 to less than 2,000 to pick the same quantity of lemons. The annual earnings of the fewer workers were three times higher because they worked more hours (Lloyd, Martin, and Mamer 1988; Mamer and Rosedale 1975).

Third, the end of the bracero program facilitated the rise of the United Farm Workers (UFW) union. During the 1950s, strikes called by unions were often broken by braceros. Grape farmers in 1965 tried to reduce the standard wage of US workers from the bracero-mandated $1.40 an hour to $1.25, prompting a strike by Filipinos that was eventually led by Cesar Chavez. After a boycott and a march from Delano to Sacramento in spring 1966, liquor firm Schenley agreed to raise the wages of workers on its California grape farms from $1.25 to $1.75 an hour, a 40 percent increase that was matched by other table grape growers in 1970 (Martin 2003, ch. 3).

The UFW adopted the winning strategy to pressure growers who produce commodities for which demand is inelastic, meaning that consumers buy about the same quantity of grapes whether prices are high or low (Fuller 1967). The strikes called by unions in the 1950s tried to reduce the supply of labor, and failed when braceros who could be deported if they went on strike were used as strikebreakers. Reducing demand by persuading up to 15 percent of Americans not to buy grapes, on the other hand, reduced grower prices, and growers had to hire farm workers to obtain this lower price. When demand is inelastic, a boycott can shift most of the cost of worker protests from workers to growers.

The bracero program had many other effects. The availability of braceros allowed labor-intensive agriculture to expand in California and other western states without raising real wages significantly, hastening the separation of the production and consumption of fresh fruits and vegetables and allowing California to replace New Jersey as the US garden state (Fuller and Mason 1977). Competition with braceros in the fields had encouraged Mexican Americans to move from rural areas to cities such as Los Angeles and San Jose in the 1940s and 1950s, a rural-urban migration that slowed during the 1960s.

In Mexico, the bracero program created knowledge and experience to link rural Mexicans to US farmers. Furthermore, during the late 1960s, a US job offer was sufficient to get an immigrant visa, so many farmers sponsored their supervisors and skilled workers for immigrant visas. These so-called green-card commuters lived in Mexico and worked seasonally in the United States, and were well placed to recruit unauthorized Mexican workers in the 1970s and 1980s.

Farm Employment and Farm Workers

The legacy of braceros is evident in farm employment and farm workers today. The United States has 2 million farms.[27] Most are small, money-losing hobby and retirement operations, while most US-produced farm commodities are from the largest 3 percent of US farms, about 60,000 farms that each had sales of $1 million or more. Using averages derived from all farms can be misleading because of the large number of small farms.[28]

The North American Industry Classification System (NAICS) divides the agricultural industry into three major sectors: crop production (NAICS 111), animal production (NAICS 112), and support activities for agriculture (NAICS 115).[29] The values of US crop and animal commodity sales are roughly equal, about $200 billion each, but crop agriculture employs three-fourths of farm workers because crops include more labor-intensive fruits and nuts (NAICS 1113), vegetables and melons (NAICS 1112), and horticultural specialties such as greenhouse and nursery crops (NAICS 1114)—collectively known as FVH commodities. These FVH commodities account for three-fourths of wages and employment in crop agriculture.

The US Department of Agriculture (USDA) has developed several measures of farm size, including gross cash farm income and the market value of agricultural products sold. In 2015, some 65,300 US farms each had gross farm cash income of $1 million or more, and they collectively accounted for over half of total cash farm income. On the other end of the spectrum, half of US farms had less than $10,000 in sales each, and they collectively accounted for less than 1 percent of gross farm cash income. The median gross cash income of US farms in 2015 was $11,000, meaning that half had sales of more than $11,000 and half had sales of less than $11,000, demonstrating the limited usefulness of data from all farms.[30]

A second measure of farm size is the market value of agricultural products sold, the measure used in the Census of Agriculture (COA). Almost 80,000 US farms sold agricultural products worth $1 million or more in 2012 (MacDonald, Hoppe, and Newton 2018, tab. 1 and 3), meaning that less than 4 percent of US farms had $1 million or more in farm sales. These large farms produced corn and grain (43 percent), poultry (16 percent), specialty FVH crops (10 percent), and milk and hogs (7 percent each). Specialty crop FVH farms were 30 percent of the farms with $10 million or more in sales in 2012, followed by dairies (22 percent of $10 million or more farms), cattle feed lots (16 percent), poultry (12 percent), and hogs (8 percent).

These data suggest that fewer than 100,000 large farms account for most US farm production, including 10,000 large specialty crop farms that employ over half of US farm workers directly or indirectly, as when they rely on farm labor contractors (FLCs) and other intermediaries to bring workers to their farms. Farms producing FVH commodities account for almost 80 percent of average employment in US crop agriculture, and most of the workers who are brought to farms by support service firms such as FLCs are also employed on FVH farms.[31] It is true that there are many farm employers, about 100,000 according to the Quarterly Census of Employment and Wages (QCEW) and 500,000 according to the COA, but the 10,000 large FVH farms are most important for farm labor.[32]

FVH commodities include everything from avocados to zucchini, but the category is dominated by a relative handful of commodities. Americans have 115 pounds of fresh fruit available per person per year, and three-fourths of this fresh fruit involves seven items: 28 pounds of bananas, 17 pounds of fresh apples, and 8 pounds each of fresh avocados, grapes, oranges, pineapples, and strawberries.

Americans consume an average 156 pounds of fresh and processed vegetables each year, led by 48 pounds of potatoes and 29 pounds of tomatoes. Most of the potatoes and tomatoes are processed rather than fresh, as with french fries or tomato sauce. The other major vegetables, onions, lettuce, and carrots, are usually consumed fresh.

Some of these fresh fruits and vegetables are imported. All of the bananas and pineapples, and over 85 percent of the fresh avocados, are imported, as are half of the fresh grapes, 20 percent of the fresh oranges, 15 percent of the fresh strawberries, and 6 percent of fresh apples. A third of the fresh vegetables available to Americans are imported, including over half of the tomatoes.

The United States generally has an agricultural trade surplus, exporting farm commodities worth more than the value of the farm commodities that are imported. However, Figure 3.1 shows that the United States has a deficit in fresh fruit and vegetable trade: exports of fresh produce were worth $7 billion in 2019, a third of the $21 billion worth of fresh fruit and vegetable imports.

FVH commodities vary in their need for workers. The production of some commodities is largely mechanized, including potatoes, processing tomatoes (used to make salsa and catsup), tree nuts, and wine grapes. However, lettuce, apples, and strawberries are mostly hand harvested. There are 1.1 million

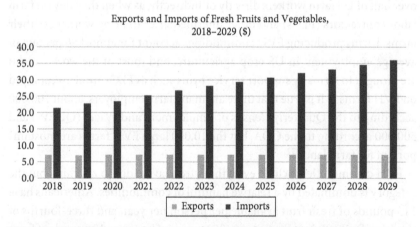

Exports and Imports of Fresh Fruits and Vegetables, 2018–2029 ($)

Figure 3.1 US Exports and Imports of Fruits and Vegetables, 2018–29

Source: US Department of Agriculture, Economic Research Service, "USDA Agricultural Projections to 2029," February 2020, https://www.ers.usda.gov/publications/pub-details/?pubid=95911

year-round-equivalent jobs on US crop farms, and 80 percent are on FVH farms. About 60 percent of FVH jobs involve workers who are hired directly by farm operators; 40 percent involve workers who are brought to farms by labor contractors and other nonfarm employers.

Most farms that produce FVH commodities are small, but most farm workers are employed on the relative handful of large farms that specialize in one or a few commodities. There are no data that report the share of lettuce, broccoli, or other commodities produced by the 10 largest farms that grow and pack these commodities, but industry insiders believe that the 10 largest growers account for half or more of the total US production of lettuce, broccoli, and many other fresh vegetables.

The large farms that produce most FVH commodities require large investments. Planting an acre of grapes or tree fruits can cost $30,000 to $50,000, and farmers who plant orchards or vineyards must wait two or three years for a first crop, forcing them to commit to a particular commodity and invest in specialized machinery. Farms that specialize in the production of leafy green annual crops such as lettuce or broccoli rarely change to other commodities, instead electing to adjust the number of acres planted in response to changing market conditions.

There are several sources of data on farm employment, each collected by a different agency and for a particular purpose. The farm labor market's employers, workers, and intermediaries are sometimes described collectively as a room of unknown size and shape, with each data source opening a window that varies in size and clarity or reliability. Three major employer-reported surveys open three windows into the farm labor market.

COA: Labor Expenses

The Census of Agriculture obtains data from US farmers for years ending in 2 and 7 and reported that 513,100 of the 2.1 million US farms had $31.6 billion in farm labor expenses for directly hired workers in 2017. Some 195,800 US farms, often the same farms that had expenses for directly hired workers, reported $7.6 billion in contract labor expenses, so direct-hire and contract farm labor expenses totaled $39.2 billion.

Farm labor expenses are concentrated in three interrelated ways: by size of farm, commodity, and geography. Large farms growing fruits and vegetables in the western and southeastern states hire most farm workers, whether directly or indirectly (as when they incur contract labor expenses to have workers brought to their farms).

The COA found that 10,000 US farm employers accounted for 52 percent of US direct-hire labor expenses in 2017, and 2,600 California farm employers accounted for 74 percent of California's direct-hire labor expenses.[33] Contract labor expenses are also concentrated. The 10,000 US farms with the most contract labor expenses accounted for 72 percent of the US total, and the 4,400 California farms with the most contract labor expenses accounted for 90 percent of the state's total. California accounted for 22 percent of US direct-hire labor expenses and 51 percent of US contract labor expenses.

Eight states had total farm labor expenses of $1 billion or more in 2017, including direct hire and contract. California's total farm labor expenses were $10.8 billion, Washington $2.4 billion, Texas $2 billion, Florida $1.8 billion, Oregon $1.2 billion, and Wisconsin, North Carolina, and Michigan $1.1 billion each. These eight states collectively accounted for 55 percent of US farm labor expenses. Another 14 states each had direct hire plus contract farm labor expenses of $600 million to $1 billion, each accounting for about 2 percent of US farm labor expenses. Many of these 2-percent states were in the Midwest (including Iowa and Illinois), the mid-Atlantic (including New York and Pennsylvania), or the West (Arizona and Idaho).

The COA asks farm operators to report how many workers they hired, how many workers were employed on their farms for more than 150 days, and how many were employed for less than 150 days. Some 513,100 US farm employers reported hiring 2.4 million workers directly in 2017, including two-thirds who were employed for less than 150 days on the responding farms.[34] Over 90 percent of farm employers hire fewer than 10 workers, and these small farm employers collectively account for less than half of the direct farm worker hires. At the other end of the number-of-workers-hired spectrum, the 7 percent of farm employers, about 35,000, that hire 10 or more workers account for over half of all hires.[35] Census data emphasize that agriculture includes about 5 percent of the 10 million US employers, but farm workers are less than 1 percent of the 162-million-strong US labor force.

The COA reports that a quarter of US farms have expenses for hired labor, and 10 percent of all farms pay labor contractors to bring workers to their farms. COA farm labor expenses are very concentrated, which emphasizes that most *workers* can be employed on farms that comply with labor laws even if most *farms* are not in compliance. This axiom that most workers are employed on compliant farms while most farms are not in compliance holds not just for the United States but also for farming systems in many other countries. Most large farms have management systems that aim to comply with labor laws, while some small farms and labor contractors have business models that depend on violating labor laws. When large farms violate labor laws, it is often because a supervisor did not follow protocols and procedures and the farm remains in business. When violations are found on small farms and with FLCs whose business models depend on violations, the result often is going out of business.

QCEW: Average Employment

Another window into the farm labor market is provided by DOL's Quarterly Census of Employment and Wages, which collects employment and wage data from employers as they pay the taxes that provide unemployment in-surance benefits to laid-off workers. UI coverage regulations vary by state, so QCEW data open different-sized windows into state labor markets.[36] States such as California and Washington require all farm employers to pay UI taxes on the wages of all of their employees, while Florida and many south-eastern states exempt small farm employers and H-2A guest workers from UI taxes.[37] DOL estimates that the QCEW covers 80 percent of agricultural employment.

The QCEW reports employment for the payroll period that includes the 12th of the month. Farm workers are usually paid weekly, so average employ-ment includes workers on the payroll during one week of the month. If these weekly payroll numbers are summed and divided by 12 months, the result is average employment or a measure of year-round-equivalent jobs.

Some 104,445 US agricultural employers (NAICS 11) paid $44 billion to an average 1.3 million workers in 2017—that is, the QCEW reported only a fifth as many employers as the COA, but 10 percent more wages paid. California accounts for a third of QCEW agricultural employment, as 16,252 California agricultural employers (NAICS 11) paid $14 billion to an average 422,000 workers in 2017. The COA is conducted every five years, with data available a year after collection, while the QCEW collects data continu-ously, with the data available within six months. Some 110,400 US agricul-tural establishments employed an average 1.3 million workers and paid total wages of $52 billion in 2021, a 20 percent higher wage bill than in 2017.

QCEW data highlight the growing importance of nonfarm employers who bring workers to farms. Table 3.3 shows that average direct-hire crop employment fell slightly across the United States over the last two decades, while average crop support employment rose by 25 percent; farm labor contractors and other nonfarm employers now account for 40 percent of total employment on US crop farms. This shift from hiring workers directly to relying

Table 3.3 US and California Crop and Crop Support Employment, 2001–19

	US Crop	US Crop Support	Calif. Crop	Calif. Crop Support
	(NAICS 111)	(NAICS 1151)	(NAICS 111)	(NAICS 1151)
2001	563,580	274,652	189,192	156,136
2002	555,075	266,888	186,335	151,334
2003	555,926	270,101	184,247	156,615
2004	555,437	268,106	178,844	153,778
2005	548,715	280,336	177,003	166,012
2006	540,682	283,589	172,267	169,717
2007	538,528	287,457	172,222	175,985
2008	536,507	290,855	174,697	178,862
2009	531,096	279,642	170,041	166,885
2010	528,867	287,480	170,068	177,168
2011	531,245	294,081	170,333	182,280
2012	543,075	305,784	171,501	191,025
2013	550,459	315,433	174,776	201,220
2014	557,083	321,058	175,127	204,599
2015	561,016	323,757	176,537	208,857
2016	560,049	330,901	172,847	215,512
2017	554,994	334,480	169,095	216,652
2018	549,393	338,780	165,014	221,664
2019	546,211	342,057	162,466	224,853
Change 2001–10	-6%	5%	-10%	13%
Change 2010–19	3%	19%	-4%	27%
Change 2001–19	-3%	25%	-14%	44%

Source: US Department of Labor QCEW

on nonfarm employers to bring workers to farms was more pronounced in California, where direct-hire employment fell 14 percent while crop support employment rose 44 percent since 2000. This means that more farm workers are brought to farms by nonfarm employers in California than are hired directly by crop farmers.

The QCEW data are often used to study the structure of industries, such as the interaction of general and specialty contractors in the construction industry, and they emphasize the growing importance of crop support establishments that bring farm workers to farms. Outsourcing the hiring of farm workers to labor contractors is most pronounced in oranges and other tree fruits, where most harvest workers work several weeks on a farm and are paid piece rates per bin or lug of fruit picked. Strawberry, apple, and tree nut farms, as well as greenhouses and nurseries, are more likely to hire workers directly rather than rely on contractors to bring workers to their farms.

The data also highlight the wage hierarchy in agriculture. DOL divides total wages paid by average employment to generate average weekly wages, which were $805 for the average worker employed in US agriculture in 2021, including $770 in crops, $855 in animals, and $740 in crop support. In more detailed industries, directly hired workers in oranges, tree nuts, mushrooms, and dairies earned over $800 a week, while workers employed in apples, in non-citrus tree fruit, and by contractors earned $600 a week. A worker employed 25 weeks would earn $20,000 at $800 a week, and $15,000 at $600 a week.

California data permit analysis of two important issues: the distribution of farm employment between large and small employers, and the annual earnings of farm workers. Agriculture is often considered an industry of small employers, each hiring only a few workers. Most farm employers *are* small, but most *farm workers* are employed on the relatively few large farms.

California's agricultural employment is *more* concentrated in large businesses than nonfarm employment is. California had almost 17,000 agricultural establishments (NAICS 11) registered with the state's Employment Development Department during the second quarter of 2019, the only quarter for which there is size-of-employer data. Over half or 53 percent of these establishments had fewer than 5 employees, while 135 had 500 or more employees. The agricultural establishments with fewer than 5 employees accounted for 3 percent of second-quarter agricultural employment of 458,000, while the 135 large agricultural establishments that each had 500 or more employees accounted for 30 percent of agricultural employment.

This means that most farm workers are employed on a relative handful of the state's farms. Less than half of the California's total (farm and nonfarm) employment is in establishments with 100 or more employees, compared to the two-thirds of the state's agricultural employment that is on farms with 100 or more employees.[38]

Data by commodity show the same pattern of a relative handful of large farms accounting for most farm employment. For example, 60 percent of California's 9,300 crop businesses (NAICS 111), 50 percent of the 2,600 animal businesses (NAICS 112), and 40 percent of the 4,500 agricultural support businesses (NAICS 115) had fewer than five employees in the second quarter of 2019, and these small farm establishments hired relatively few workers. Only 5 percent of the average 173,300 California crop employees were hired by the smallest establishments (fewer than five employees), as were 8 percent of the average 28,400 animal employees and 1 percent of the average 253,300 support employees. On the other hand, the largest 40 California crop establishments each had 500 or more employees and accounted for 25 percent of all crop employees, while the 95 largest agricultural support establishments employed 38 percent of the support employees.

The reports of the Senate's Subcommittee Investigating Violations of Free Speech and the Rights of Labor emphasized the day-and-night differences between the mass of small farm employers and the relatively few large employers who employ most farm workers. The subcommittee documented the efforts of California's largest farmers and their allies to block the extension of labor law protections to farm workers. Congress agreed to exempt agriculture from many labor laws, bolstering the argument for agricultural exceptionalism—the idea that groups of small farmers selling perishable commodities in competitive markets and hiring workers only seasonally would be unable to comply with labor laws modeled on protecting workers employed in large factories. Carey McWilliams (1939) and others countered that large farms were factories in the field, but agricultural exceptionalism triumphed and remains a feature of many federal labor laws today.

The California data can be used to compare the total number of workers employed sometime during the year with average employment, and finds that the number of unique farm workers is twice average employment. This daunting computer task begins with identifying the valid social security numbers (SSNs) reported by farm employers among the 20 million SSNs in the California database, determining the commodity and county of the employer where each worker had maximum farm earnings, and then examining

Table 3.4 Total Farm Workers and Average Agricultural Employment, 2018–21

	2018	2019	2020	2021	Average
Total workers	874,314	900,279	894,691	858,690	881,994
Average ag. employ.	419,800	420,100	404,300	407,800	413,000
Ratio	2.1	2.1	2.2	2.1	2.1

Source: Martin et al. 2023

the employment and earnings of primary farm workers or those whose maximum earnings were from farm employers.[39]

Table 3.4 shows that an average 882,000 workers were reported by California agricultural employers between 2018 and 2021, an average 2.1 workers for each average job. This does not mean that each worker was employed for six months. Instead, many did a few weeks or months of farm work, while fewer worked year-round. The largest groups of workers were in the categories of less than 1 month, 7 or 8 months, and 12 months (Martin et al. 2023).

All workers had to have at least one agricultural employer, and most had only one farm employer. Workers with two or more employers were assigned to the commodity of the employer where they had their highest earnings, a procedure that found 724,000 or 82 percent of all workers with at least one farm employer had their highest-earning job with a farm employer, while the other 18 percent of workers had their highest-earning job with a nonfarm employer.

These primary farm workers included 62 percent employed by crop support employers (NAICS 1151) in 2021, a third employed by crop employers (NAICS 111), and 5 percent employed by animal establishments (NAICS 112). Far more primary farm workers, over 333,000, were employed by FLCs than were hired directly by crop and animal establishments, with a total of 275,000.

The distinction between total workers and average employment highlights another issue: why US workers don't accept farm jobs that pay an average $41,000 a year, the average annual pay reported for a full-time worker in California agriculture in 2021 (Kitroeff and Mohan 2017). The answer is that two workers are typically sharing this $41,000-per-average-job pay, so average earnings are closer to $20,000 for primary farm workers.

Table 3.5 highlights average earnings by commodity. The average earnings of workers whose highest-earning job was in crops was $22,100 in 2021, and ranged from a low of $15,000 for direct-hire strawberry workers to $27,000 for direct-hire vegetable workers. Annual wages in animal agriculture were higher, over $31,000 a year for dairy employees. However, the largest gaps between full-time and actual pay were in crop support. The often skilled and specialized workers who were employed by nonfarm postharvest crop support firms (NAICS 115114) earned three times more than the many more workers who were employed by labor contractors (NAICS 115115).

Seasonal farm jobs offer few opportunities for lifelong careers. Almost half of farm workers earn less than $10,000 a year, explaining why the seasonal farm labor market is an exit market similar to fast-food restaurants and other sectors that experience high worker turnover. A McDonald's restaurant with 20 job slots may hire 40 workers sometime during the year to fill them, just as a farm with 100 year-round equivalent jobs may hire 200 or more workers

Table 3.5 Primary Farm Worker Earnings, 2018–21 ($/year)

	2018	2019	2020	2021	Average
Crops (NAICS 111)	21,776	22,781	23,922	19,956	22,109
Vegetables (111219)	26,623	28,148	30,485	24,793	27,513
Grapes (111332)	19,953	21,968	23,719	18,875	21,129
Strawberries (111333)	16,099	15,894	16,099	13,582	15,418
Other berries (111334)	16,314	16,599	18,244	15,246	16,601
Tree nuts (111335)	21,341	22,836	25,006	19,816	22,250
Non-citrus fruit (111339)	17,004	16,185	16,648	13,672	15,877
Nursery (111421)	26,233	27,882	29,095	24,704	26,979
Misc. crops (111998)	23,479	25,164	23,775	19,927	23,086
Animals (NAICS 112)	30,928	32,458	34,862	27,688	31,484
Beef cattle (112111)	30,616	29,786	31,295	24,845	29,135
Dairy (112120)	31,006	32,488	35,034	26,864	31,348
Support (NAICS 115)	12,712	12,876	13,643	11,161	12,598
Postharvest crop (115114)	22,888	24,126	26,947	22,557	24,129
FLCs (115115)	8,664	8,778	9,220	7,620	8,570

Source: Martin et al. 2023

sometime during the year to fill its jobs. The farm differs from the restaurant because there may be 150 jobs during the harvest peak and 25 jobs during the winter trough, while the restaurant may offer 20 jobs each day.

Agriculture differs from fast food in other ways as well. First, there may be more potential for labor-saving changes in farming. Machines have replaced hand workers in a wide range of farming tasks over the past century, a phenomenon often defying those who asserted that a particular farm task could never be mechanized. Second, farm commodities can be imported, while fast-food restaurants need employees in places where they are serving consumers.

ALS: Average Hourly Earnings

An employer survey that figures prominently in farm labor discussions is USDA's Agricultural or Farm Labor Survey (ALS), which collects data from a sample of 6,000 farm employers on the earnings and hours worked of various types of farm workers for the week that includes the 12th of the month in January, April, July, and October. The survey is mailed to about 12,000 farms, and half respond.[40] Employers report the total wages paid during the survey week and the number of hours worked by directly hired workers, including paid family members.

Employers complete a table with rows for 16 types of workers, such as crop, nursery and greenhouse farmworkers, reporting the total hours worked and the gross weekly wages paid to this type of worker during the survey week and separating base wages from bonus and overtime wages.[41] Section 3 collects data on peak employment and asks whether the farm had any H-2A workers during the previous year, while Section 4 collects data on the farm's sales during the previous year by category, such as over $5 million, the farm's acres of various crops, and the share of the farm's sales accounted for by fruits, nuts, and berries, vegetables and melons, and corn and grains (but not data on sales of individual commodities). Sections 5 and 6 collect data on farm operators.[42]

The ALS publishes data by region and farm sales and reports that hourly earnings are lowest on farms that have farm sales of less than $100,000 a year and highest on farms that have farm sales of $100,000 to $250,000 a year. Some 50 to 55 percent of field and livestock workers are employed on "other crop" farms, meaning FVH farms, followed by 30 percent employed on animal agriculture farms and 15 percent on field crop farms. US farms with sales of $1 million or more account for 55 to 60 percent of all directly hired farm workers, while US farms with 51 or more workers account for a third of US hired farm workers. Regional data on employment by size of farm are not published.

The ALS publishes average hourly earnings by type of worker for 18 regions, all of which are multistate except California, Florida, and Hawaii. The average hourly earnings of field and livestock workers were $14 an hour in 2019, and ranged from a low of $12 in the Appalachian II region (Kentucky, Tennessee, and West Virginia) to $16 in the Pacific region (Oregon and Washington).[43] DOL uses the earnings of field and livestock workers to set the Adverse Effect Wage Rate, the minimum wage that farm employers must pay to H-2A guest workers and any US workers in similar employment.

The sample of farmers who report data to the ALS is small, which means there can be large changes in average hourly earnings from year to year. For example, the average hourly earnings of hired farm workers in the Mountain II region (Colorado, Nevada, and Utah) rose over 20 percent between 2017 and 2018, and they were up 15 percent in the Mountain I region (Idaho, Montana, and Wyoming). Between 2014 and 2017, the average hourly earnings of all hired workers in the Mountain II states were flat or falling.[44]

DOL tried to deal with small ALS samples and sharp year-to-year changes in average hourly earnings by proposing to set AEWRs by job title rather than by state.[45] DOL's proposal would require employers to specify the job title or occupation to be filled, and DOL would use the ALS to set an AEWR for that occupation. However, if the ALS does not generate an hourly wage for a particular occupation, such as truck driver, DOL would turn to DOL's Occupational Employment and Wage Statistics (OEWS) to set the AEWR.[46]

The current ALS-based system generates AEWRs for 18 states and multistate regions, creating a small table, while DOL's proposed methodology would result in a 10-page table with AEWRs in each state for 10+ occupations.[47] The major effect of setting AEWRs by job title or occupation would be, to raise the AEWR of supervisors and equipment operators and reduce the AEWR for crop workers.[48]

The ALS interviews only farm employers, while the OEWS interviews only nonfarm employers who bring workers to farms such as labor contractors. The OEWS provides far more wage and employment data than the ALS, including employment for 830 detailed occupations and mean and median wages. The data are reported by job title for each state and for 530 metro and non-metro areas within states, so that the 2021 average hourly wage of crop workers in California varied from less than $15 an hour in the San Joaquin Valley to over $18 in Napa and Sonoma.

There are three major lessons from efforts to establish an AEWR minimum wage to protect US farm workers. First, no single source provides reliable data on the average hourly earnings of workers on farms. The USDA survey has been collecting employment and earnings data from farmers for over a century, but it does not survey the employers of crop support service workers, who account for 40 percent of average employment in US crop agriculture and 60 percent in California. Second, efforts to use USDA and DOL surveys to set AEWRs for state and substate areas inevitably mean small samples and large changes from year to year, drawing protests from employers when the AEWR rises sharply.[49] Third, there is no agreement on whether an AEWR is needed to protect US workers, nor on how it should be calculated and enforced.

Farm Labor Markets

Labor markets are exchanges where employers find workers and workers find jobs. Labor markets perform three essential functions (the 3 Rs): recruitment, or matching workers with jobs; remuneration, or paying wages and benefits to motivate workers to provide effort in exchange for reward; and retention, to retain experienced workers.[50] Each of these 3 Rs operates differently in farm labor markets.

Recruitment

Most nonfarm employers develop job descriptions laying out the qualifications required to perform a job, advertise for candidates, and screen and interview applicants to find the best person to fill a particular job. Farmers often use job ads and interviews to recruit skilled and professional workers but rarely to recruit seasonal farm workers. Instead, farmers often hire groups of workers, as when they request one or more crews of 20 to 40 workers each.

How are crews of seasonal workers who do not speak English matched with farmers who do not speak Spanish? The key is a bilingual intermediary, a crew boss employed by the farmer or an independent farm labor contractor who recruits crews, often by asking current workers to bring friends and relatives, making word-of-mouth social networks the major method of recruitment in farm labor markets. Crew supervisors sometimes visit places where workers congregate, as with day labor markets, where workers gather to seek jobs that may last only a day (Fisher 1953).

Large farms may have dozens of crew supervisors, many of whom are former harvest or hand workers who have moved up the job ladder. The supervisor's job is to keep the crew at full strength and to monitor the crew's speed and quality of work performed. Many crews include families from the supervisor's Mexican hometown, which may ensure loyalty. Dissatisfied workers usually find it easier to exit the job by switching to another crew rather than voicing complaints about a supervisor who favors or harasses particular workers.

Farm labor contractors are nonfarm businesses that bring workers to farms. As previously noted, about 40 percent of the workers on US crop farms, and 60 percent of the workers on California crop farms, are brought there by nonfarm crop support businesses, and two-thirds of crop support business employment is accounted for by FLCs. Data on FLCs are murky because federal and state laws require many of the people involved in recruiting, transporting, and supervising farm workers to obtain licenses, while unemployment insurance laws record only FLC establishments that pay UI taxes; consequently, California has 1,500 UI-registered FLC establishments but almost 10,000 licensed FLCs and FLC employees.

FLCs are a puzzle. They should benefit both employers and workers. Both a farmer who needs workers only seasonally and workers who must string together several seasonal jobs to achieve sufficient earnings can pay small fees to FLCs who match workers and jobs. However, FLCs have long been associated with labor market problems rather than efficiencies, an example of fissuring the workplace in ways that disadvantage vulnerable workers (Fisher 1953; Weil 2014).

When FLCs bring workers to farms, the FLC is normally *the* employer under immigration, labor, and employment laws. During the heyday of farm worker unionization in the 1970s, Cesar Chavez and the United Farm Workers refused to allow FLCs to be considered employers under California's Agricultural Labor Relations Act (ALRA), fearing that FLC employees could vote for union representation only to see the FLC go out of business. The farm to which FLCs bring workers, rather than the FLC, is the employer for collective bargaining purposes under the ALRA, so an FLC that brings workers to a Gallo vineyard may leave Gallo with an obligation to bargain with the union even if the FLC workers were present for only for a few weeks.

Farmers feared that the ALRA's FLCs-cannot-be-employers provision could lead to an FLC leaving a dozen farms with union contracts by moving from farm to farm, but experience quickly showed that FLCs whose employees vote for union representation soon went out of business. Instead, most California FLCs became employers under all labor laws by becoming more than labor contractors. The ALRA defines custom harvesters as businesses that bring more than workers to a farm, such as bins into which fruit is picked and forklifts to load the bins onto trucks to transport to packing houses. Custom harvesters are the sole employers of their employees under all labor laws, including the ALRA.

FLCs and custom harvesters compete with each other to win work for their employees on farms, and farm operators sometimes ask FLCs to lower their commissions in order to win their business. Commissions are a sensitive and opaque topic. There are many arrangements to get farm work done, from paying a fixed price per acre or ton to harvest a crop to paying an hourly wage to workers and an overhead or commission to the FLC. Commissions cover nonwage costs, including payroll taxes and business costs that range from recruitment to toilets and equipment as well as profits. FLC commissions vary but are typically 30 to 40 percent, with workers' compensation insurance often the largest single item.

A farm with a $10 million wage bill knows that each percentage point of FLC commission is $100,000. This means that an FLC that wants a 40 percent commission but is offered 38 percent must decide whether to accept the lower commission. On the one hand, the FLC needs jobs for employees, but on the other, the FLC needs a commission sufficient to cover costs and make a profit.

Farm operators are often in a stronger economic position than FLCs, encouraging some to accept lower commissions and compensate by cheating workers or not paying all required social security and unemployment insurance taxes or workers' compensation premiums. There are many exposés of FLCs that accept low commissions in order to win business for their employees and then cheat these employees or government agencies to keep their businesses viable.

There is no database of FLC commissions, so there is no easy way to use analysis of data to detect whether low commissions lead to labor law violations. California enacted state laws to strengthen the hand of contractors in agriculture, garments, and other low-wage industries by requiring written contracts between contractors and their clients that include commissions sufficient to conduct a lawful business. For example, a California contractor who uses ladders to pick tree fruit should charge at least a commission of at least 40 percent. If an investigation found labor law violations and a written contract with a 30 percent commission, the farm operator could be jointly liable for the violations under state laws.

There are efforts to help lawful or good FLCs to identify themselves, so that farmers seeking good FLCs can find them and know that they are using compliant contractors. Stronger Together, the Equitable Food Initiative, and other NGOs train and certify FLCs that satisfy their standards; the hope is that employers will seek out certified FLCs and begin to transform an industry that has long been associated with taking advantage of farm workers.[51]

Remuneration

Work is the exchange of effort for reward, and remuneration is the wage paid to motivate workers to perform their jobs. Most jobs pay hourly wages or monthly salaries, and managers assess the speed and quality of each employee's performance to ensure "an honest day's work for an honest wage." The labor market is unusual because of there is continuous interaction between employers and employees. Workers risk being fired for poor performance, while employers risk having workers quit to pursue other options.

The major challenge in hourly or monthly wage system is to minimize shirking by monitoring the quantity of work performed. Agriculture is different. Farmers in the past hired everyone who wanted to pick apples or peaches, including children, and they developed a wage system that made their cost of getting work done predictable even with a diverse workforce. A piece rate or incentive wage system means that the cost of getting a bin of apples picked is $30 whether workers are fast or slow. However, a fast picker may pick four bins a day and earn $120 or $15 an hour, while a slower picker picks three bins and earns $11.25 an hour. Piece rate wage systems feature predictable costs for employers and variable earnings for workers.

Hourly wage systems are common when workers are homogeneous or of similar productivity and employers can control the speed of the work. For example, employers can control the speed of a machine that travels in front of lettuce harvesters and fire those unable to keep up. Similarly, a working supervisor can set the pace of work for a crew weeding a field.

Agriculture is moving toward hourly wage systems for several reasons, including labor laws that prevent children from doing farm work, minimum wage laws that require employers to "make up" the piece rate earnings of slower piece rate pickers to the minimum wage, and machines that set the pace of work such as conveyor belts that travel in front of workers.[52]

Piece rate wage systems remain the norm when it is hard to monitor the speed of work but easy to measure the amount of work performed, such as bins of apples and oranges picked as in Photo 3.4. Employers set piece rates so that the average worker earns more than the minimum wage, which gives workers an incentive to work fast. Most tree fruits, berries, and vegetables such as tomatoes are picked under piece rate wage systems, and supervisors

Photo 3.4 Piece Rate Wages Are Paid When It Is Hard to Monitor Effort but Easy to Monitor Output
Source: Philip Martin

monitor the quality of the work, so that workers do not include branches or dirt clods in bins and buckets to fill them faster.

The combination of a government-set minimum wage and an employer-set piece rate wage creates a minimum productivity standard. If the minimum wage is $15 an hour and the piece rate for picking cherries is $0.20 a pound, workers must pick at least 75 pounds an hour to earn $15. A worker who picks only 50 pounds an hour would earn $10, and the employer would have to "make up" or add $5 to the worker's earnings or fire the worker for poor performance.

What if the minimum wage increases but piece rates remain stable? Suppose the minimum wage is $15 an hour and the piece rate for picking a bin of apples is $30, so a worker who picks six bins in an eight-hour day earns $180 or $22.50 an hour and a worker who picks four bins earns $120 or $15 an hour. If the minimum wage rises 10 percent to $16.50 or $132 in eight hours but the piece rate remains at $30, the fast picker still earns more than the minimum wage, but the slower picker earns less and could be terminated for low productivity. If minimum wages increase and piece rates remain stable, older and slower workers can be squeezed out of the workforce for failing to meet productivity standards.[53]

Most farm workers earn the minimum wage or slightly more, such as $16 an hour in California in 2022 when the minimum wage was $15. Some workers are employed long hours, especially during peak seasons. The federal Fair Labor Standards Act requires most private sector employers to pay 1.5 times the usual wage after 8 hours a day and 40 hours a week but exempts agriculture, an example of the agricultural exceptionalism in many federal labor laws.[54] California and five other states require overtime wages for farm workers, including on the same 8/40 basis as nonfarm workers in California.[55] Farm employers generally oppose overtime pay, arguing that agriculture remains different and that overtime will prompt them to cut hours and leave farm workers with lower earnings even as workers strive to maximize their seasonal earnings.

Three types of workers typically work more than 8 hours a day or 40 hours a week: livestock (dairy) workers, irrigators, and equipment operators. Requiring overtime pay means that employers must weigh the additional costs of hiring and training more workers versus paying overtime wages to current employees. In many cases, overtime pay is cheaper, especially when employers report difficulty finding workers and their employees operate expensive equipment.

Retention

Retention, the third key function of labor markets, is also different in agriculture. Some workers are employed by one employer for their entire career, as with a worker employed year-round on a dairy farm, while others may have dozens of employers a year and over their farm work career.

Agriculture offers both year-round and seasonal jobs, and farm operators hire workers both directly and indirectly via contractors. Farmers sometimes offer their year-round workers housing and other benefits. Seasonal worker policies are different, since most are on the farm only a few weeks or months, making retention a question of how to keep seasonal workers as long as desired and how to induce them to return next season.

The crew supervisors who hire and monitor seasonal workers also lay them off at the end of the season. Even though many farms have payroll systems that allow them to identify the most productive workers, few acknowledge such workers in any public way at the end of the season or promise to rehire them next season. One description of typical attitudes toward obtain seasonal farm workers uses the analogy of ensuring sufficient irrigation water, where farmers can work collectively to build more dams to maximize the supply of water available to all rather than investing individually to stretch limited water supplies on their farms. Similarly, farmers often work collectively to maximize the pool of seasonal workers available to agriculture rather than investing in their own workforces.

Selecting guest workers from lower-wage countries is the ultimate way to maximize the supply of seasonal workers. Mexican workers earn at least 10 times more in US agriculture than in Mexican agriculture, ensuing that there are more workers seeking US jobs than DOL-certified farms to fill with guest workers. Farmers have invested significant sums to persuade Congress to give them easier access to farm guest workers, just as they invest in politics to ensure that more water is available to irrigate crops.

Unions

Farm worker unions have been described as "much ado about nothing." (Jamieson 1945). Hired farm workers often receive low wages and work only seasonally, and they have been hard to organize into unions because many are employed by labor contractors and are seeking better nonfarm jobs.

The most able farm workers who could be effective union leaders are typically the first to exit for better nonfarm jobs, so farm worker unions must constantly organize and educate the new workers to maintain their ranks. Second, farm worker unions have found it hard to raise wages and benefits for the workers they represent because of the layering of the farm labor market; the crew supervisors and contractors who are employers in the eyes of workers may not set the wage. Third, farm workers are dispersed across many farms, making it costly for unions to organize and serve them (Martin 2003).

There have been many efforts to organize farm workers, but there are no links between past and present farm labor unions. The first farm worker unions, such as the Industrial Workers of the World (Wobblies) before World War I, had radical leaders who wanted to replace the employer-employee system with worker-run cooperatives. During the 1930s, the Communist-led Cannery and Agricultural Workers Industrial Union wanted to eliminate capitalist employers. The clash of extremes between radical unions and conservative growers in agricultural areas often led to violence that was suppressed by local authorities linked to farm employers opposed to "outsider" agitators (Martin 2003, ch. 3).

The United Farm Workers, founded by Cesar Chavez in 1962, was able to use sympathy from many Americans during the 1960s, when there was widespread concern for those left behind by economic growth. Instead of mounting strikes, as AFL-CIO-linked farm worker unions did in the 1950s (and which, as we have seen, were broken by labor contractors and braceros), Chavez enlisted clergy and students to boycott table grapes in order to persuade growers to recognize the UFW as representative of their employees. The grape boycott of the late 1960s is considered one of the most successful US union activities, persuading 15 percent of Americans to avoid grapes, which lowered grower prices and encouraged them to sign contracts with the UFW in 1970.

The 1970s were a roller-coaster decade for the UFW. Growers who signed UFW contracts and some workers disliked the union for many reasons, including hiring halls that allocated jobs to workers based on their seniority with the UFW rather than with a particular farm, with the result that farm worker families that carpooled were sometimes assigned to different farms. This dissatisfaction prompted some growers to switch to the Teamsters when their UFW contracts expired, preferring the union that already represented their nonfarm workers.

The UFW was saved by the election of Jerry Brown as California governor in 1974. Brown made it a top priority to enact the Agricultural Labor Relations Act, to give farm workers union organizing rights. The ALRA, modeled on the 1935 National Labor Relations Act, which governs unions in most of the US private sector, became law in June 1975 so that the first elections could be held before seasonal workers were laid off. The ALRA differs from the NLRA by offering quick elections, a make-whole remedy for workers if employers fail to bargain in good faith with a certified union, and stronger protections for unions in their internal operations.

The UFW won most of the first elections amid predictions that California agriculture would soon have a construction-style labor market, with high earnings for seasonal workers and unemployment insurance benefits during the off-season. Most union contracts in the late 1970s offered minimum or general laborer wages that were 50 percent higher than the state's minimum wage and enrolled covered workers in UFW-run health and pension plans.

At its peak in the late 1970s, the UFW reported almost 200 contracts and 70,000 members, although a careful count found only 108 contracts in effect in 1978.[56] The number of contracts and union members shrank, and today there are about 30 contracts and fewer than 7,000 union members. There are four major explanations for the demise of the UFW: internal union issues, politics, changes in farm structure, and illegal immigration (Martin 2003; Pawel 2009).

First, Cesar Chavez in the early 1980s purged dissident UFW leaders by dismantling the UFW's legal department when attorneys refused to move from Salinas to UFW headquarters in Keene, California (Pawel 2014). Second, Republicans took control of the state government, and the new governor, George Deukmejian, appointed decision makers to the Agricultural Labor Relations Board who were sympathetic to farm employers rather than farm worker unions. Third was the exit from agriculture of easy-to-boycott conglomerates with farming operations, making the UFW's boycott threat less potent.

The final factor in the UFW's demise was rising unauthorized migration. Oil was discovered in the Gulf of Mexico in the late 1970s, and the Mexican government borrowed money in anticipation of an oil-funded economic boom. However, the price of oil crashed in the early 1980s, many Mexicans lost their jobs, and the peso was devalued, making US farm wages 10 to 20 times more than Mexican wages. Hundreds of thousands of Mexicans streamed north, encouraging US workers to exit for nonfarm jobs and making it hard for the UFW to win wage increases for the farm workers it represented.

The UFW got new leadership in the 1990s, and again in the 21st century; Democrats have been in control of state government for the past decade; and there are ever more agribusiness operations with consumer labels such as Dole and Driscoll's. The UFW demonstrated its significant influence in the California state legislature by getting the ALRA amended in 2002 with provisions for mandatory mediation and conciliation seen in Photo 3.5 (Martin and Mason 2003) and again in 2022 to allow farm worker unions to be certified to represent workers without a secret-ballot election.

The amended ALRA has so far had few effects on union activities,[57] prompting the UFW to take up a new cause, federal immigration reform. The UFW argues that immigration reforms that legalized unauthorized farm workers would empower them to vote for union representation. The UFW was a major supporter of both the 1998 Agricultural Job Opportunity Benefits and Security Act and 2019/2021 Farm Workforce Modernization Act proposals, described in Chapter 6.

Photo 3.5 UFW Calls for Binding Arbitration to Obtain First Contracts in 2002
Source: Philip Martin

The other major farm worker union is the Farm Labor Organizing Committee (FLOC) in Ohio and North Carolina, which represents more active farm workers than the UFW. FLOC was founded in 1967 by Baldemar Velasquez, and in the 1980s it followed in the footsteps of the UFW by organizing boycotts of Campbell's and Vlasic to persuade these firms to require the Ohio farms from which they bought cucumbers and tomatoes to recognize FLOC as the bargaining representative of their farm workers. The FLOC negotiated agreements with Campbell's and Vlasic that laid out wages and benefits for farm workers. Farmers did not participate in the negotiations, but if they wanted to sell to Campbell's and Vlasic, they had to recognize FLOC and pay the wages and benefits specified in the agreement.

FLOC used similar top-down pressure to win a contract with the North Carolina Growers Association (NCGA) as shown in Photo 3.6, which brings up to 10,000 H-2A guest workers from Mexico to North Carolina tobacco and cucumber farms each year. FLOC boycotted the Mt. Olive Pickle Company until Mt. Olive in 1999 negotiated an agreement with FLOC that required farmers selling cucumbers to Mt. Olive to recognize FLOC as the representative of their

Photo 3.6 FLOC Celebrating Contract with NCGA
Source: Farm Labor Organizing Committee

workers, most of which were brought to farms by the NCGA. North Carolina is a right-to-work state, meaning that FLOC, Mt. Olive, and the NCGA cannot require farm workers to join the FLOC, so FLOC educates guest workers in Mexico about the importance of paying 2.5 percent of their wages in union dues to FLOC.

As with Cesar Chavez's leadership of the UFW, Baldemar Velasquez's leadership of FLOC has become controversial. Velasquez won reelection as president of FLOC at the union's convention in September 2022, but challenger Leticia Zavala, a former FLOC vice president, charged that Velasquez manipulated the vote by allowing nonfarm workers and relatives to vote in the election by paying $30 a year to be associate members of FLOC. DOL is investigating Zavala's complaint, which, if substantiated, suggests that FLOC is following the same path as the UFW by becoming an enterprise run by and for the descendants of the founder.

PART II
FARM WORKERS AND ALTERNATIVES

The first two chapters of Part II review the characteristics of the rural Mexicans who dominate North American farm workforces. Canada has more than 100,000 seasonal farm workers, including over half who are legal guest workers from Mexico and the Caribbean. Mexico has 3 million workers employed for wages in agriculture sometime during the year, including 750,000 who are employed on farms that export fresh fruits and vegetables to the United States. Some 2.5 million workers are employed on US farms each year, including 80 percent who were born in Mexico.

Hired farm workers everywhere are concentrated in three interrelated ways: by geography, by commodity, and by size of farm. Chapter 4 profiles the workers employed on Mexican farms that export fruits and vegetables to the United States. These local and internal migrant workers are an average 32 years of age, have eight to nine years of schooling, and earn two to three times Mexico's minimum wage. Almost half are women, making women a significantly higher share of workers in Mexican than in US agriculture, where 30 percent of hired workers are women.

Chapter 5 explains that the US hired farm workforce of 2.5 million includes 2 million Mexican-born workers, including 1.7 million who are settled in the United States and 300,000 who are Mexican H-2A guest workers. Most of the settled Mexican-born workers arrived illegally in the 1990s and early 2000s, when they were in their 20s and 30s. These settled workers, half unauthorized, are now in their 40s and 50s, and their US-educated children shun seasonal farm work. The other half of the Mexican-born settled workers are legal, including many legalized in the late 1980s. The 500,000 US-born farm workers include a few families based in Florida and Texas who follow the ripening crops north and a greater number of local equipment operators and skilled workers.

Chapter 6 explores the alternatives to farm workers, highlighting mechanization that replaces hand workers and mechanical aids that make hand workers more productive, guest workers, and imports of labor-intensive commodities. The mechanical tomato harvester that revolutionized the production of processing tomatoes in the 1960s demonstrates that mechanization is a process rather than an event, often requiring many changes from farm to fork. H-2A guest workers are young and productive but cost more than US workers, a trade-off that an increasingly greater number of farmers find favors H-2A workers. Imports of fruits and vegetables allow trade to substitute for migration.

4

Farm Workers in Mexico

Who works on Mexican farms? This question is difficult to answer due to incomplete data and an agricultural system that includes both modern farms that export most of what they produce and subsistence farms that barely feed farm families. Fewer than 25,000 Mexican farms employ about 750,000 workers to produce fruits and vegetables that are exported mostly to the United States. These export farms resemble modern farms in Canada and the United States, with college-educated and English-speaking managers who are attuned to food safety requirements in foreign markets. Export farms hire local residents with little education as well as internal migrants, many of whom are from Mexico's poorer southern states. As periods of employment lengthen in export agriculture, more southern Mexicans are settling near their places of employment in northern Mexico.

Competing Narratives

Are workers employed on Mexican farms that export fruits and vegetables routinely exploited, or do export farms offer good jobs to Mexicans with little education? The exploitation story was reinforced in a pair of *Los Angeles Times* articles (Marosi 2014, 2016) that suggested Americans are eating the products of child and trafficked labor when they consume Mexican avocados and tomatoes. The good-jobs story, on the other hand, emerged from scientific surveys of workers employed on export farms, which found that most workers earned two or three times more than Mexico's minimum wage and were enrolled in the Mexican social security system, IMSS, which provides work-related health and pension benefits (Escobar, Martin, and Starbridis 2019).

This chapter explains that the *Los Angeles Times* articles prompted the Mexican government to increase enforcement of labor laws to ensure that export farms were enrolling their employees in IMSS. Export growers formed or strengthened associations that encourage member farms to comply with

Bracero 2.0. Philip Martin, Oxford University Press. © Oxford University Press 2024.
DOI: 10.1093/oso/9780197699973.003.0004

Mexican labor laws, and US buyers stepped up efforts to ensure that their Mexican suppliers were in compliance. Fresh produce exports and grower prices rose after 2014, and this combination of more enforcement, peer and buyer pressure, and a favorable economic situation explain why export agriculture was associated with good jobs for workers with little education in the 2020s.

The *Los Angeles Times* articles leveled four major charges. First, the articles suggested that many farm workers on export farms were migrants from poorer areas of Mexico trapped in poor-quality housing in camps on or near the farms where they work. One complaint was that the tomatoes and strawberries grown for Americans were treated better than the internal Mexican migrant workers who harvested and packed them.

Second, migrant workers are often recruited and supervised by contractors from their area of origin, who withhold workers' wages to discourage them from moving to other farms for higher wages, better working conditions, or improved housing. Some contractors retain workers' wages until the end of their contracts, making the workers effectively indentured during their typical three-month contracts because leaving early could mean forfeiting their earnings.

Third, some contractors advance money to migrant workers, providing them with cash advances at the place of recruitment so that their families have money until remittances arrive. Workers are provided with food and housing while away from home, but many purchase alcohol, supplemental food, and other items at in-camp stores that may charge inflated prices. These camp-store debts must be paid from worker earnings, which reduces the savings that workers have at the end of the season.

Fourth, US buyers of Mexican produce often have social responsibility guidelines that require their Mexican suppliers to comply with Mexican labor laws, pay their employees regularly, and provide migrants with decent food and housing. The *Los Angeles Times* articles concluded that these guidelines are not enforced effectively, documenting cases of US supermarkets that continued to buy produce from farms where labor law authorities found violations of labor laws.

Most of the worker exploitation found by the *Los Angeles Times* involved indigenous and sometimes non-Spanish-speaking workers who are recruited in poor areas of states that do not export farm commodities and employed in the six Mexican states that account for most Mexican fruit and vegetable exports. The articles highlighted that recruiters made payments and promises to workers where they lived, and then transported the migrants on a two- or three-day journey to export farms in northern and western Mexico in buses or trucks. Recruiters often stayed with and supervised the indigenous workers they recruited, and some took advantage of workers who did not know that Mexican labor law requires them to be paid weekly or that children under 18 are generally not allowed to work on export farms.

The *Los Angeles Times* articles led to several reactions. Associations that represent farmers who export fruits and vegetables did not dispute the cases profiled in the series but emphasized that such cases were the exception rather than the rule. Mexican exporters created a new organization, Alianza Hortofrutícola Internacional para el Fomento de la Responsabilidad Social (AHIFORES, International Fresh Produce Social Responsibility Alliance), to educate farm employers about their labor obligations and to exert peer pressure on export farms to comply with Mexican labor laws.

There were other reactions as well. The Mexican government stepped up its enforcement of labor and tax laws in export agriculture, and US buyers reinforced the need for their suppliers to comply with labor laws or risk being blacklisted. Since farmers receive higher prices for the commodities they export than for the commodities they sell in the Mexican market, the threat of being unable to export fruits and vegetables helped to induce compliance with Mexican labor laws. NGOs warned that, just as buyers of Bangladeshi garments and Thai seafood threatened to stop buying clothing and shrimp produced with exploited labor, Mexican farmers risked losing their high-priced US market for their fruits and vegetables if they did not improve wages and working conditions for farm workers.

Mexico does not have reliable information on farm workers, so we interviewed over 3,000 workers employed on berry and vegetable farms that export to the United States (Escobar, Martin, and Starbridis 2019). We stratified our worker sample by size of employer, since large employers produce most fruits and vegetables and hire most workers. Five years after the *Los Angeles Times* articles, we found a different labor market on Mexican farms that export fresh produce.

First, we found that the average worker was 32 years old, had 7.2 years of schooling, and earned 200 to 300 pesos ($10 to $15) a day plus in-kind benefits, two to three times Mexico's minimum wage of 103 pesos a day in 2019. Second, we found that over 90 percent of the workers on export farms were enrolled in IMSS, far higher than the 48 percent share of all Mexican workers. However, some of the farm workers we interviewed reported that they had limited access to IMSS health and child care services, and few qualified for retirement benefits.

Third, we found that the rapid expansion of export agriculture had positive spin-off effects, increasing internal migration from poorer to richer areas of Mexico and reducing rural poverty. Moving to areas with higher wages and more opportunities, migrant workers use their higher earnings to invest more in their children's education and health. Ever-longer seasons encourage some migrants to settle near farms that sometimes employ them for more than six months, giving workers and their children more opportunities for upward mobility.

These same "good job" factors have a flip side: the labor market in Mexican export agriculture is on a knife edge, poised to either tilt further upward to improve livelihoods and reduce rural poverty or slip backward into worker exploitation. For example, indigenous migrant workers, who are a rising share of workers on export farms, earned slightly less than other workers and had more difficulty accessing IMSS services. Second, farm workers do not value the benefits financed by the taxes that their employers contribute to IMSS, which provides incentives for tax avoidance if employers do not report all of their workers or report that their employees receive only the minimum wage rather than their actual higher wages.

Third, attracting migrant workers to farms that export commodities is a double-edged sword. On the one hand, migrants from poor Mexican states earn higher wages. However, as migrants settle near their jobs, they move from on-farm housing into nearby settlements where governments may not provide expected public services such as water and sewer connections. The result can be worker frustration because they lack the services they had when they lived on farms. Farmers say they cannot provide services to workers who do not live on their farms, while local governments say they lack the funding to provide the water, sewer, education and other services for new residents that export farms brought to their cities.

We also found a gray-area farm labor market in areas with export agriculture that involves day laborers who live in informal settlements and are hired by contractors to work on farms whose produce is usually sold in domestic markets. However, some of the fruits and vegetables produced on these farms with informal workers get exported if export farms need more produce and acquire it from farms that normally produce for the Mexican market. Gray-area farms and informal workers likely account for less than 20 percent of Mexican fruit and vegetable exports, but their existence means that some of the Mexican fresh produce consumed by Americans is from Mexican farms that do not comply with labor laws.

Farm Employment

The share of a country's workers employed in agriculture falls as incomes rise, but at different rates in different countries. Mexico and Turkey had similar gross national incomes (GNIs) per capita of about $9,500 in 2019, but Figure 4.1 shows that employment in Turkish agriculture fell faster than in Mexico, in part due to faster income growth in Turkey over the past two decades. Mexico's GNI per capita rose 50 percent in the first two decades of the 20th century, while Turkey's GNI per capita more than doubled. In 2019, about 18 percent of Turkish workers and 13 percent of Mexican workers, were employed in agriculture.

The OECD reported that Mexico's labor force was 55.5 million in 2018 and was 62 percent male (Table 4.1); Mexico has one of the lowest female participation rates among OECD countries. Mexico's labor force increased by an average 850,000 a year over the last decade, and employment in agriculture rose from 6.4 million in 2010 to 6.8 million in 2018, up 6 percent. Of the 53.4 million employed persons in Mexico in 2018, two-thirds or 36.4 million

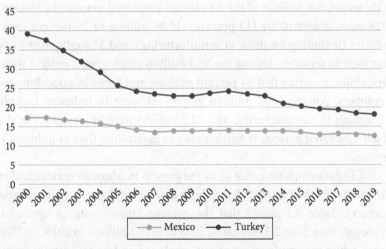

Figure 4.1 Employment in Mexican and Turkish Agriculture 2000–19 (%)
Source: World Bank

Table 4.1 Mexican Labor Force by Sector and Status, 2018

	Millions	Share
Civilian labor force	55.5	
Growth 2010–18	0.9	
Men	34.2	62%
Employed	53.4	96%
Unemployed	1.8	
Sector (all employed)		Share
Agriculture	6.8	13%
Industry	13.9	26%
Services	32.7	61%
Employment	53.6	100%
Sector (employees)		Share (employees)
Agriculture	3	44%
Industry	10.7	77%
Services	22.7	70%
Employees	36.4	68%

Source: OECD Labor Force Statistics, 2019

were employees or wage and salary workers and 17 million were either self-employed (15 million) or unpaid family workers (2 million).[1] Almost 2 million workers were unemployed.

By sector, 6.8 million of the 53 million employed persons in Mexico in 2018 were in agriculture (13 percent), 13.09 million or 26 percent were in industry (including 9 million in manufacturing), and 32.6 million or 61 percent were in services. Among the 36.4 million employees, 3 million were in agriculture, meaning that 44 percent of those employed in agriculture were employees. Another 10.7 million employees were in industry, including 7.1 million in manufacturing, and 22.7 million were in services. The share of self-employed persons is much higher in agriculture than in industry and services.

OECD data emphasize that all of the growth in Mexican agricultural employment over the past decade has been among employees (wage and salary workers). Table 4.2 shows that the average employment of agricultural employees rose from 2.3 million in 2008 to over 3 million in 2018, up 70,000 a year, while the employment of self-employed and unpaid family workers in agriculture was stable at 3.8 million. There are still more self-employed

Table 4.2 Self-Employed and Wage Workers in Mexican Agriculture, 2008–18

	Self-Employed in Agriculture (000)	Employees in Agriculture (000)	Total Agricultural Employment (000)
2008	3,800	2,260	6,059
2009	3,736	2,322	6,058
2010	3,987	2,430	6,417
2011	3,699	2,547	6,246
2012	3,910	2,664	6,573
2013	3,930	2,665	6,594
2014	3,903	2,776	6,680
2015	3,892	2,881	6,773
2016	3,604	3,011	6,615
2017	3,819	2,992	6,811
2018	3,789	3,037	6,826
Change 2008–18	0%	34%	13%

Source: OECD Labor Force Statistics

and unpaid workers in Mexican agriculture than wage and salary workers, but the gap is narrowing as hired workers replace farmers and their families on fewer and larger farms.[2] In the United States and most other industrial country agricultural systems, there are two wage and salary workers for each self-employed farmer and unpaid family worker.

Mexico's 32 states can be divided into 6 that export a high share of the farm commodities they produce, Baja California, Guanajuato, Jalisco, Michoacán, Sinaloa, and Sonora, and 26 that produce mostly for the Mexican market. Mexico's National Occupation and Employment Survey (ENOE) interviews a sample of households each quarter and collects employment and earnings data for all persons 15 and older, generating data on employed workers by occupation, industry, and area.[3] The ENOE reported 3.2 million hired farm workers in the fourth quarter of 2019, with 1.1 million of those (a third) in the six export states. Mexico's hired farm workforce has been increasing, up 40 percent between 2005 and 2019 in all of Mexico and up 50 percent in the six major farm export states.

Mexico's hired farm workers were a median 36 years old and had a median seven years of schooling in 2019, but the hired workers in export states were younger, a median 34, and better educated, a median eight years.

Table 4.3 Rural Employment in Formal and Informal Jobs, 2013

	Total Employment (000)	Informal (%)
All activities	4,734	77
Agriculture/Rural	6,615	90

Rural areas are defined as having no population center with more than 2,500 residents.
Informal is not affiliated with IMSS, that is, not having an employer who registers workers with IMSS
Source: Levy, Table 3.1

Female hired farm workers in nonexport states had a large jump in years of schooling, from less than five years in 2005 to over seven years in 2019.

A major issue in Mexico is informality, defined as employed workers who are not enrolled by their employers in the IMSS health and social security benefit programs (IMF 2018). Table 4.3 shows that most workers in rural areas of Mexico have informal jobs, and that only 10 percent of those employed in agriculture, including farm operators, unpaid family members, and hired workers, are enrolled in IMSS.

Formal sector workers have more education and higher productivity than informal workers, which helps to offset the cost of payroll taxes that formal sector employers and employees pay to government agencies such as IMSS and Infonavit. Formal workers can sue for unfair dismissal, adding a risk that may discourage some small firms from becoming formal employers. Santiago Levy (2018) argues that informality begets more informality, as young and less educated workers who have few opportunities and incentives to acquire new skills have low productivity and low wages.

Worker Surveys

Mexico lacks reliable data to distinguish workers who are employed on export farms from those working on other farms. Farms that export belong to associations that collect data on acreage, production, and employment, which allows stratified random sampling of their farm workers. If the 100 largest tomato-exporting farms employ three-fourths of all workers on farms that export tomatoes, stratified random sampling means that three-fourths of interviews are with workers employed on these 100 large tomato farms.

It is important to distinguish between workers and farms. Thousands of Mexican farms produce tomatoes, and most are not in compliance with labor laws. However, if the largest farms are in compliance with labor laws, then most *workers* can be employed on compliant farms even if most *farms* are not in compliance, a fact often overlooked in media reports.

Interviews in 2019 with 2,700 workers on export farms found that those farms employed a total of 97,000 workers, making the results applicable to the 750,000 workers employed in Mexico's export agriculture. The sample, which included 1,488 workers employed in berries, 538 in bell peppers, 522 in cucumbers, and 517 in tomatoes, found that 56 percent of the workers were born in the state in which they were employed—that is, 44 percent had migrated to an export farm from another state. Two-thirds of these migrants maintained homes outside the state in which they were working, while a third had settled in the state where they were employed.

Over half of the workers interviewed were employed in berries, an export sector that included more older workers than the vegetable sector did. Some 45 percent of male berry workers were in their early 20s, as were 35 percent of female berry workers, but a significant share of berry workers were 40 and older.

Most workers employed on export farms have little schooling, including 10 percent who did not attend any school; a typical worker is seen in Photo 4.1. Only 50 workers, less than 2 percent, were under 18, largely because most export farms refuse to hire workers under 18; the checkers seen in Photo 4.2 typically earn more than pickers. Wages vary by commodity and state and are highest for berry workers in Baja California. Monthly earnings are highest in berries and lowest in cucumbers. Four percent of all farm workers earned less than the minimum wage, compared with the 38 percent of all Mexican workers who earn less than the minimum wage.

Interviewers obtained data on farm workers as well as their families and were able to estimate household earnings by multiplying the earnings of each worker who was interviewed by the number of earners in the worker's household in order to estimate per capita income and poverty. Average farm worker household incomes were 42 percent above the urban poverty line. Nonmigrant farm workers had incomes that were 33 percent above the income needed for well-being in urban areas, while migrants had incomes that were 53 percent higher. Workers employed on export farms earn about as much as factory workers during the low season and more than many factory workers during the peak harvest season, when they are paid piece rate wages.

Photo 4.1 Picking Blackberries in Jalisco
Source: Philip Martin

Workers enrolled in IMSS by their employers are entitled to health and child care at IMSS facilities, a year-end bonus, paid vacation, and loans to buy or remodel homes. Table 4.4 shows that 94 percent of the workers on export farms reported that their employers enrolled them in IMSS. Smaller shares of workers reported being enrolled in the programs financed by IMSS payroll taxes, such as bonuses, vacations, and child care. However, enrollment does not guarantee access to IMSS services, as is especially apparent for child care and housing benefits.

Photo 4.2 Checking Raspberries in Jalisco
Source: Philip Martin

Table 4.4 Enrollment in and Access to Work-Related Benefits (%) Among Workers on Export Farms

Enrollment	IMSS	Bonus	Vacation	Child Care	Housing
Women	94	84	56	12	36
Men	93	81	61	8	33
Total	94	82	58	10	34
Access					
Local workers	80	72	49	1	15
Migrants	73	59	27	0	9
Total	77	68	42	0	13

Source: 2019 worker survey

Why do workers whose employers enroll them in IMSS have trouble accessing IMSS services? One major reason is the time needed to access IMSS services, which may require workers to take time off from work and wait at IMSS clinics for services. Many IMSS child care facilities are in cities and towns and close at 2:00 p.m., which makes them of limited use to farm workers who work until 5:00 p.m. and may face lengthy commutes to the facility. To access housing benefits through the Instituto del Fondo Nacional de Vivienda para los Trabajadores (Infonavit), workers must find a house in an Infonavit development, arrange to use their Infonavit credits for a down payment, and then obtain an Infonavit mortgage. Most farm workers with little education cannot fulfill these steps.

Recruitment, Housing, Attitudes

We found no evidence of labor trafficking. Less than 1 percent of the workers reported that they paid a fee to be hired, and a similar small percentage reported deductions from wages to reimburse transport costs. Two percent of workers reported receiving cash advances when hired, and 3 percent reported that they were in debt to their employers.

There were few differences between the housing conditions of local and migrant workers, since almost all reported that their houses had electricity, indoor plumbing, cement floors and roofs, and brick walls. Housing for solo migrant workers often involves bunk beds for six to eight workers per room and a shared bathroom and sometimes cooking facilities for small groups of workers or a kitchen that serves meals.

Focus groups explored the lives and hopes of workers on export farms for themselves and their children. Many of those interviewed had difficult lives as children or as adults, with parents or partners who encouraged them to do farm work to supplement family incomes.

Seasonal farm work played many roles in workers' lives. For some berry harvesters, farm work was a way to obtain savings for education, to buy a house, or to repay debt, while for others farm work offered an opportunity to earn money after being laid off from a nonfarm job. Picking berries for piece rate wages could generate higher daily earnings than factory work, explaining why the berry harvest workforce includes some workers with college degrees.

Migrants from Oaxaca liked their berry-picking jobs because of the high earnings but also emphasized that the job was strenuous and required careful work. Male migrants sometimes organize themselves into crews of 10 to 12 and move from farm to farm to maximize their earnings, while women are more likely to stay with one farm the entire season.

The Oaxacan migrants reported that places of recruitment are often swarming with contractors and workers, so few people try to read and understand the contracts that are offered before signing those contracts and boarding buses. Most of the Oaxacan migrants owned houses in their village of origin and produced corn and beans on subsistence farms, picking berries after planting crops on their own farms and returning home for the harvest.

Many female migrants stressed that they work only for contractors who are vetted by other women. In areas offering greenhouse and open-field jobs, migrant women reported that the greenhouse employers comply strictly with labor laws, requiring workers to present documents when hired. Open-field farmers, on the other hand, were willing to hire workers under 18, and daily wages in open-field agriculture were sometimes higher than in greenhouses if farm employers and workers did not contribute to IMSS.

Women were more sensitive to work rules than men because when someone in the family is sick, it is women who are most likely to provide care. Greenhouses with contracts and more formal work rules were less flexible about absences than open-field farmers. However, women reported that greenhouses did not tolerate the sexual harassment that often occurred in open-field agriculture, leading to a preference for such work.

Trade or Migration?

Mexico has become the world's largest exporter of fresh avocados and tomatoes by taking advantage of its proximity to the United States and developing farms capable of producing high-quality fresh produce. As with factories in Bangladesh and China that produce goods for export, the question is whether the jobs created on Mexico's export farms provide a step up the economic ladder for Mexican workers or are another way for richer countries to take advantage of workers in poorer countries.

Surveys of the workers employed on Mexican farms that export fresh fruits and vegetables paint an optimistic picture, suggesting that export agriculture creates good jobs for Mexican workers with little education. These workers would earn ten times more performing similar jobs in the United States, but working in Mexico means they do not have to cross the Mexico-US border illegally or as guest workers, and if they have formal jobs they can receive benefits from Mexican government agencies.

Mexican export agriculture is an example of an industry centered in previous emigration areas that now attracts internal migrants. The industry is a success in the sense that US growers became familiar with Mexican farming areas via labor migration and recognized opportunities to promote trade in place of migration for some commodities during some times of the year. The result was much less outmigration and a new inmigration from poorer regions of Mexico to areas with export agriculture.

There are many critics of conditions on Mexican export farms. US-based NGOs such as the Equitable Food Initiative (EFI) and Fair Trade USA that audit and certify farms as in compliance with their privately developed protocols for food safety and good treatment of workers have enrolled more farms abroad than in the United States. The core of EFI's program is the creation of worker-supervisor teams to educate workers about their rights, while Fair Trade aims to return some money to farms and workers that they can use to improve their lives.

These NGOs have convinced foundations to subsidize the development of labor standards, certify farms that are in compliance, and encourage buyers to favor purchasing from certified farms. Many researchers are skeptical, calling NGO standards and certification a form of "fairwashing" that can misleadingly suggest to consumers that workers on certified farms are protected (Kuruvilla 2021). A particular issue in Mexico is employer protection unions, which sign agreements before workers are hired, deduct union dues from worker wages, and oppose worker efforts to create independent unions (Daria 2022). One of the labor law changes required by USMCA is to allow workers to vote via secret ballot on whether they want a union to represent them and, if so, which one.

The future of Mexico's export agriculture depends on decisions made in Mexico and the United States. Mexican president Andres Manuel López Obrador (often known by the acronym AMLO) wants to return to 1970s nationalistic economic policies, when state-owned enterprises such as Pemex dominated the economy. AMLO promised a fourth revolution, after independence from Spain, the 19th-century liberal reforms, and the Mexican revolution of 1910–17, to reduce poverty by curbing the power of the elite, which AMLO believes has kept many Mexicans impoverished.

AMLO supports rapid increases in the minimum wage and introduced a higher minimum wage in Mexican states near the US border, where living costs are higher. The question is whether AMLO's populist strategy will help workers remain in the formal sector and benefit from higher minimum wages or, instead, wind up enlarging the informal sector, which already employs most Mexican workers.

In the 2020s, Mexico is at a crossroads in politics, economics, and migration. AMLO's six-year term ends in 2024, and the question is whether his Morena party can retain power and continue to implement nationalistic policies that aggravate tensions with NAFTA-USMCA partners Canada and the United States. The economic uncertainty is whether formal job growth can grow beyond the current one-third of the workforce that is enrolled in IMSS.

Mexico has changed over the past quarter century, especially in the rural areas that were the major source of migrants bound for US farm jobs. Declining fertility, rising incomes and expectations, and more integration into Mexico and North America have made many rural Mexican youth aware they cannot get ahead if they follow in the footsteps of their parents and grandparents. As these rural youth change their residence and occupation, the question is whether they will stay inside Mexico or seek upward mobility outside Mexico.

5

Farm Workers in the United States

Agriculture has unusual demographics. Most farm employers are older, white, and US citizens, while most farm workers are younger, minority, and noncitizens. The slowdown in unauthorized Mexico-US migration since 2008–9 means that there is an aging and settled Mexican-born farm workforce as well as youthful Mexican H-2A guest workers. Half of US farm workers are in the Pacific coast states, including a third in California, where state governments have enacted laws that require farm workers to be treated like nonfarm workers. This chapter opens several windows onto farm workers, explaining why and how the data sources vary in size and clarity to explain who works on US farms but converge in showing that US farm workers include a shrinking number of unauthorized and nonmigrant farm workers alongside a rising number of younger Mexican H-2A guest workers who fill seasonal farm jobs.

ACS and CPS

The American Community Survey (ACS) is a monthly survey that contacts 295,000 of the 140 million US addresses to obtain demographic and housing information as well as employment and earnings data on all persons at the sample address.[1] The employment and earnings questions ask whether each person at the address worked during the past week, the industry of their employer and each worker's occupation, and the average hours worked per week and weeks worked over the past year, as well as wages and bonuses earned over the past year.

ACS farm laborers are identified by occupation in the Standard Occupational Classification system that distinguishes between crop and livestock workers as well as graders and sorters, equipment operators, and supervisors. The ACS portrays a young, male, and Hispanic farm workforce.

Figure 5.1 shows that fewer than half of ACS farm workers in 2017 were born in the United States, compared with 82 percent of all US private sector

Bracero 2.0. Philip Martin, Oxford University Press. © Oxford University Press 2024.
DOI: 10.1093/oso/9780197699973.003.0005

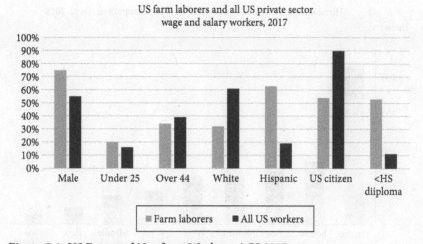

Figure 5.1 US Farm and Nonfarm Workers, ACS 2017

Source: US Department of Agriculture, Economic Research Service, "Farm Labor," last modified March 22, 2023, https://www.ers.usda.gov/topics/farm-economy/farm-labor/

wage and salary workers. Over half of ACS farm workers do not have a high school diploma, compared with 11 percent of all US workers. The ACS finds that Hispanic farm workers are concentrated in crops, while over half of livestock workers are non-Hispanic whites who were born in the United States. Almost 60 percent of crop workers did not complete high school, compared with 40 percent of livestock workers.

The Current Population Survey (CPS) is a monthly survey of 60,000 households and the basis for the monthly employment and unemployment estimates released by DOL's Bureau of Labor Statistics.[2] The CPS classifies each household member who is 16 or older as employed, unemployed, or not in the labor force. For each employed worker, the CPS collects data on wages, hours worked, and the worker's industry and occupation. A March supplement obtains data on individual and household income that was received during the previous calendar year, and these data are used to generate an annual report on US income, poverty, and health insurance.

The CPS finds mostly white hired farm workers in the Midwest and mostly Hispanic hired farm workers in the western states. Figure 5.2 shows that 60 percent of CPS farm workers are in metro counties. The United States has 3,142 counties, but only a minority are considered metro, defined as having 50,000 or more residents. Most CPS farm workers are in metro counties largely because the 24 states west of the Mississippi River have most of the

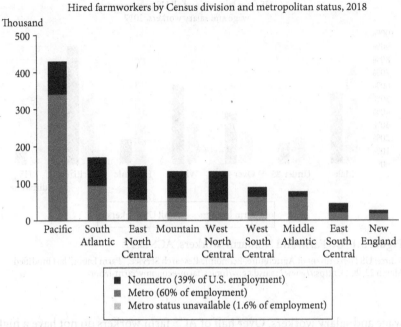

Hired farmworkers by Census division and metropolitan status, 2018

Nonmetro (39% of U.S. employment)
Metro (60% of employment)
Metro status unavailable (1.6% of employment)

Notes: Metro status is not reported for a small share of people in the CPS. The States in
each Census division are: New England (VT, NH, ME, MA, RI, CT), Middle Atlantic (NY, PA,
NJ), East North Central (WI, MI, IL, IN, OH), West North Central (ND, SD, NE, KS, MN, IA,
MO), South Atlantic (WV, VA, NC, SC, GA, FL, DE, MD, DC), East South Central (KY, TN,
MS, AL), West South Central (OK, AR, TX, LA), Mountain (MT, ID, WY, NV, UT, CO, AZ,
NM), and Pacific (WA, OR, CA, AK, HI).
Source: USDA, Economic Research Service using data from U.S. Census Bureau and
Bureau of Labor Statistics, 2018 Current Population Survey monthly files. Covers all hired
wage and salary workers in farm and support industries, regardless of occupation.

Figure 5.2 Most Farm Workers Are in Metro Counties
Source: Current Population Survey, 2018

US land area and much larger counties. The leading US counties by farm
sales, Kern, Tulare, and Fresno, all in California's Central Valley, are metro
counties.

The CPS is a household-based survey, meaning that the goal is to interview
residents in a random sample of US housing units. Between 1945 and 1990,
the USDA provided funds to add a supplement to the December CPS to obtain data on farm workers, reasoning that in December migrant farm workers
have returned to their usual homes and could be more easily interviewed
there rather than in their temporary homes where they did farm work.

The December CPS data were published by USDA in the Hired Farm Work Force (HFWF) reports through the 1980s. In 1987, one of the last years in which the report was produced, the HFWF report portrayed a mostly young and white hired farm workforce of 2.5 million, which included fewer than 10 percent migrants,[3] defined as persons who stayed away from home overnight to do farm work for wages (Olivera 1989). The average employment of US farm workers was 1 million, suggesting 2.5 workers for each year-round-equivalent job. Three-fourths of HFWF farm workers earned wages only from farm work.

HFWF farm workers were 78 percent white, 14 percent Hispanic, and 8 percent Black in 1987. A quarter were 18 to 24 years old, and over 20 percent were in each of the age cohorts 25–34 and 14–17. Among the 1.3 million hired workers who were 25 and older, three-fourths of the whites had completed high school, compared with only 30 percent of the Blacks and 20 percent of Hispanics. The midwestern and Appalachian states, stretching from Minnesota to North Carolina, had over 40 percent of hired farm workers, compared to 12 percent in the Pacific states.

The concentration of CPS hired farm workers in the Midwest explains why a quarter of HFWF farm workers had most of their days of farm work in grain production, while only 10 percent worked mostly in fruit production. Indeed, more hired farm workers were employed primarily in grains in 1987, some 558,000, than were employed in fruits, vegetables, and horticultural specialties, 517,000. Whites were concentrated in grains, Blacks in tobacco, and Hispanics in fruit production.

The HFWF report painted a picture of a young and mostly white hired farm workforce that did farm work when people otherwise would not be working for wages, so the farm labor market was a "salvage labor market" for students and homemakers to earn wages when they would otherwise not be working (Fuller and Mason 1977). Workers who did both farm and nonfarm work earned more from their nonfarm jobs than from farm jobs, suggesting that farm workers would do more nonfarm work if they could find nonfarm jobs and reinforcing the notion that farm work is a short-term job rather than a lifelong career.

The quarter of hired farm workers who were Hispanic and Black were different from the white majority of farm workers. Two-thirds did only farm work, compared with less than half of whites, explaining the lower incomes of Hispanics and Blacks and suggesting that Hispanics and Blacks were dependent on farm work for most of their incomes rather than using farm work to salvage time when they otherwise would not earn wages.

The mental picture of US farm workers was shaped by media reports and HFWF data in the 1960s and 1970s, when thousands of low-income families packed into cars or trucks to follow the sun from south Florida, Texas, or California to harvest ripening crops in northern states. The 1960 documentary *Harvest of Shame* exposed the poor working and living conditions of these migrant families, emphasizing how little had changed since the Joad family displaced during the Dust Bowl in the Midwest sought a better life in California in the 1930s, the story portrayed in John Steinbeck's novel *The Grapes of Wrath*.

Both the US House and Senate created subcommittees that held hearings and proposed legislation to improve conditions for migrant farm workers. These subcommittees, led by liberal northern Democrats such as Senator Hubert Humphrey (D-MN), wanted to extend protective labor laws and union organizing rights to farm workers, but southern Democrats and Republicans blocked labor law changes that would have strengthened farm worker labor rights. Instead, there was agreement to provide health services to migrant farm workers and their children, leading to the creation of the Migrant Health Program in 1962, which makes grants to community clinics in farm worker areas to serve migrant and seasonal farm workers.

During the War on Poverty, other federal programs were added, including Migrant Head Start to provide daycare and early childhood education to migrant parents with young children, the Migrant Education Program to help school-aged children in migrant families to keep up with their schooling as they moved with their parents, and job training for adult migrant and seasonal farm workers who wanted to learn skills that improved their earnings (Martin and Martin 1994). At a time of rapid labor-saving mechanization and expectations that farmers would hire ever fewer farm workers, the policy emphasis was on preparing migrant and seasonal farm workers for nonfarm jobs rather than on deciding exactly who was a farm worker in need of federal assistance.

As the bracero program shrank in the early 1960s, most farm workers were white US citizens. Throughout the 20th century, there were some unauthorized Mexican farm workers, but their number did not reach significant levels until the late 1970s, when a combination of UFW-called strikes for higher wages and the depreciation of the Mexican peso encouraged more unauthorized Mexico-US migration.

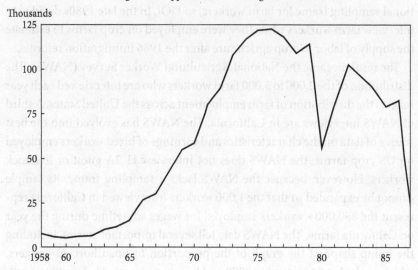

Figure 5.3 Border Patrol Apprehensions of Unauthorized Farm Workers, 1958–87

Source: Olivera 1989

The US Border Patrol enforced immigration laws at the border and in the interior of the United States, recording the industry in which unauthorized foreigners were employed when they were apprehended inside the country through the 1980s. Figure 5.3 shows that the Border Patrol apprehended fewer than 25,000 farm workers a year until the bracero program ended in 1964, after which apprehensions of unauthorized farm workers began to rise toward their peak of almost 125,000 in 1975. Apprehensions of farm workers fell to fewer than 10,000 in 1986, when the Immigration Reform and Control Act (IRCA), which included an amnesty for unauthorized foreigners who had done farm work in 1985–86, was enacted. IRCA largely ended Border Patrol activities in US agriculture.

NAWS

Reliable statistical data requires a sampling frame, such as a list of all US households or all US farms, so that analysts know they are interviewing one of each 1,000 households or farms, enabling them to expand or multiply results by 1,000 to get a picture of all households or farms. There is no national sampling frame for farm workers, so DOL in the late 1980s decided to interview farm workers while they were employed on crop farms to estimate the supply of labor to crop agriculture after the 1986 immigration reforms.

The result became the National Agricultural Worker Survey (NAWS). The distribution of the 2,000 to 3,000 farm workers who are interviewed each year reflects the distribution of farm employment across the United States. A third of NAWS interviews are in California. The NAWS has evolved into the best source of data on the characteristics and earnings of hired workers employed on US crop farms; the NAWS does not interview H-2A guest or livestock workers. However, because the NAWS lacks a sampling frame, its sample cannot be expanded so that the 1,000 workers interviewed in California represent the 850,000+ workers employed for wages sometime during the year on California farms. The NAWS data tell several important stories, including the hump shape of the graph of the proportion of unauthorized workers, which peaked at 54 percent in 2000 and has since dropped below 40 percent; the aging and settling of mostly Mexican-born crop workers; and very little follow-the-crop migration.

The NAWS finds that two-thirds of crop workers are parents. One aphorism is that farmers tend to be 40 or older because of the need to inherit or amass enough capital to operate a modern farm, while farm workers tend to be under 40 because of the physical demands of farm work. This aphorism was true in the 1990s, when 80 percent of crop workers were 18 to 44, but the near stop to the arrival of unauthorized Mexicans since the 2008–9 recession means that only half of crop workers today are 18 to 44. By contrast, the average age of farmers has been about 60 over the last three decades.

Crop worker families are best described as the working poor, with average personal incomes of $2,000 a month and average family incomes of $2,500 a month. Even though almost all farm workers are covered by work-related programs to which employers and workers contribute, such as social security, a declining share of crop workers, less than 20 percent, report that someone in their household received social security, unemployment insurance (UI), or workers' compensation benefits for work-related injuries and accidents in the past year. By contrast, over half of workers report that someone in their household received means-tested benefits such as Medicaid or Supplemental Nutrition Assistance Program (SNAP) benefits, also known as food stamps. In farm worker households, the recipients of these benefits were often US-born and US-citizen children.

US Trends

Figure 5.4 shows that the workers legalized after IRCA was enacted in 1986 soon left agriculture; IRCA-legalized farm workers fell from 30 percent of crop workers in the early 1990s to 10 percent within two decades.[4] Legal farm workers were soon replaced by unauthorized farm workers, so the share of crop workers who were unauthorized topped 50 percent by 2000 and has remained at about half.

Crop workers are aging, settled, and doing about 200 days of farm work for one farm employer a year, earning almost $20,000 at $12.30 an hour for 1,600 hours a year in 2018–19, the most recent data available. Farm work is like nonfarm work in the sense that crop workers live in rented or owned housing off the farm, commute to work in a car or truck, and at the end of the workday return to families that often include US-born children.

Almost 90 percent of crop workers interviewed in the NAWS were hired directly by the farm operator on the farm where they were interviewed, suggesting that the NAWS is missing many workers brought to farms by labor contractors. By design, the NAWS does not interview H-2A workers. The NAWS collects income data in ranges and finds family incomes similar to the ACS about $2,500 a month. Less than a fifth of farm worker families have incomes below the official poverty line.

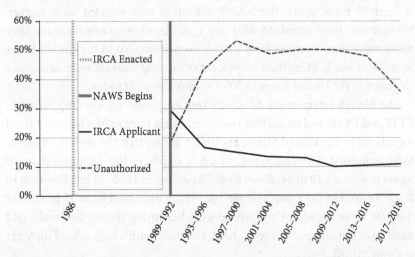

Figure 5.4 IRCA Legalized and Unauthorized Crop Workers, 1989–2018

Source: NAWS; "3 Decades of NAWS Data," *Rural Migration News* blog, September 13, 2021, https://migration.ucdavis.edu/rmn/blog/post/?id=2643

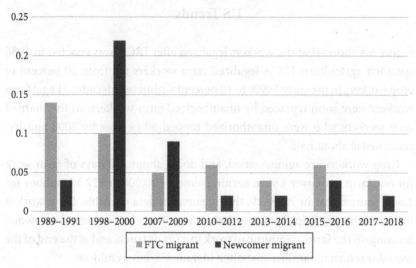

Figure 5.5 The Share of Crop Workers Who Are Migrants Has Declined
Source: NAWS

Many people believe wrongly that most crop workers are migrants with homes in south Florida or Texas who follow the sun northward to harvest crops on dozens of farms between March and October. Follow-the-crop migration was always rare and is now practically nonexistent; Figure 5.5 shows that fewer than 5 percent of crop workers have two or more farm employers at least 75 miles apart, the NAWS definition of a migrant farm worker. Newcomers from rural Mexico are considered migrants because they move more than 75 miles from their homes in Mexico to the United States to do farm work. More than 20 percent of all crop workers were newcomer migrants to the United States in 2000, versus 2 percent today.

The NAWS interviewed 2,600 workers employed on US crop farms in FY17 and FY18, and found that two-thirds were born in Mexico and a third were born in the United States. Figure 5.6 shows that the crop farm workforce is mostly male and aging, which is visible in the declining share of workers who are 18 to 44, down from 78 percent in 1989–91 to 51 percent in 2017–18, and in the rising average age, which increased from 33 to 41 over the past three decades. Crop workers are becoming slightly less male, and most have not completed high school; the share with a high school diploma is about a third.

Half of US crop workers are parents, and many of their children were born in the United States. Almost 85 percent of crop workers live away from the

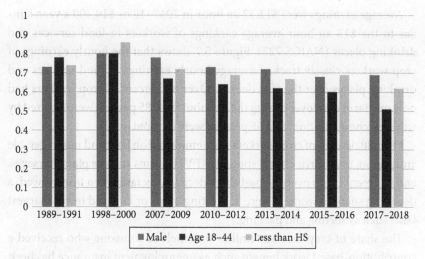

Figure 5.6 The Share of Male, 18–44, and Less Educated Crop Workers Is Declining
Source: NAWS

farm where they work and usually commute less than 25 miles to their farm job; three fourths own a vehicle. Half of crop workers rent housing and a third own US housing, while only a seventh lived in employer-provided housing. Almost 60 percent of crop workers live in single-family houses; a quarter live in crowded housing, defined as housing with more than one person per room.

Workers reported doing 35 weeks and 198 days of farm work during the year before they were interviewed in 2017–18, an average of 5.7 days or 45 hours a week and 1,575 hours of farm work a year. The average hours worked per week in the current farm job was 45, and the number of weeks worked on a US farm during the previous 12 months was 35. Two-thirds of workers who left an employer in the past year reported that they left voluntarily rather than being laid off or fired.

Workers spent an average of nine weeks in the United States not working and two weeks abroad. Nonwork weeks and weeks abroad varied widely. Younger workers had more nonwork weeks, probably because some were in school when not doing farm work, while unauthorized workers had fewer nonwork weeks. Similarly, shuttle migrants or green card commuters with US immigrant visas and homes in Mexico spent more than 10 weeks each year outside the United States.

Average earnings were $12.32 an hour in 2017–18 or $19,400 a year, similar to the $13-an-hour average earnings of workers in food services and drinking places (NAICS 722). Figure 5.7 shows that the hourly earnings of crop workers closely tracked average hourly earnings in food services and drinking places over the past decade. Over 80 percent of crop workers had only one farm employer during the previous year, 85 percent were covered by workers' compensation, and 55 percent were covered by UI.

Over 80 percent of crop workers were employed on fruit and nut, vegetable and melon, and horticultural specialty (FVH) farms such as plant nurseries and in greenhouses over the past three decades. By task when interviewed, a declining share of workers were harvesting crops or engaged in postharvest tasks such as sorting and packing.

The share of crop worker families that include someone who received a contribution-based work benefit such as unemployment insurance has been falling, while the share of families that include someone who received a means-tested benefit such as Medicaid has been rising. The falling share of families receiving contribution-based work benefits is somewhat surprising because the crop workforce is aging and become more legal. The rising share of families with a member who received means-tested benefits is more

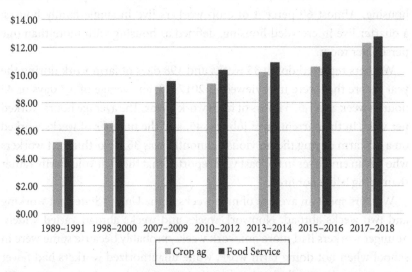

Figure 5.7 Crop and Food Service Worker (NAICS 722) Hourly Earnings, 1989–2018

Source: NAWS

understandable, as many states do outreach to enroll US-born children in Medicaid and other safety net programs.

Farm work is more often a job for newcomers to the United States rather than a career for settled US residents. However, 80 percent of the crop workers interviewed in 2017–18 said they planned to do farm work at least five more years, and almost 80 percent planned to continue to do farm work as long as possible, especially those who are less educated and unauthorized. Crop workers were asked if their parents did US farm work, and over half said never—that is, their parents were likely small farmers in Mexico who never migrated to the United States. However, 15 percent of workers said that their parents were currently doing US farm work or had done US farm work during the previous five years, while almost a third of those interviewed in 2017–18 reported that their parents did US farm work more than a decade ago.

California Trends

At least a third of US farm workers are in California, where a third of NAWS interviews are conducted. Data from 3,600 workers who were interviewed between FY15 and FY19[5] emphasize that California crop workers are more likely to be born in Mexico and more likely to be unauthorized than crop workers elsewhere in the United States.

The share of unauthorized crop workers in California has always exceeded the share of US citizens. Figure 5.8 shows that the gap between unauthorized workers and citizen workers peaked in 2007–9, when two-thirds of California crop workers were unauthorized and less than 10 percent were US citizens. The share of US citizens has been rising, matching the decline in the share of unauthorized workers.

California has always had less follow-the-crop migration than other states, and fewer than 5 percent of California crop workers reported two farm jobs at least 75 miles apart in 2017–18. The share of foreign-born newcomers in the state's crop workforce peaked at almost 30 percent in 1998–2000[6] but has fallen to less than 5 percent due to declining unauthorized migration.

As in other US states, about 70 percent of California crop workers are male and most did not complete high school. California crop workers are less well educated than crop workers in other states, largely because a higher share were born abroad. The share of California crop workers who are 18 to 44

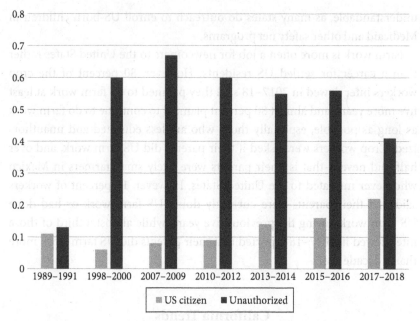

Figure 5.8 US Citizen and Unauthorized Crop Workers in California, 1989–2018
Source: NAWS

closely tracks US trends, peaking at over 80 percent in 1998–2000 and falling to half recently.

The higher share of foreign-born workers in California means that a lower share of the state's crop workers report reading and writing English well. A higher share of the California farm workers are parents, which may explain the lower frequency of follow-the-crop migration, as parents do not want to uproot their children.

California crop workers were less likely to be hired directly by the farm operator where they worked than workers in other states because of the prominence of farm labor contractors in the state. California crop workers were more likely than workers elsewhere to have more than five years of US farm work experience, reinforcing the picture that California has mostly Mexican-born workers who have been in the United States for over a decade.

The hourly earnings of farm workers have traditionally been higher in California than in other states due to the profitability of fruit and vegetable crops and the state's high cost of living. When unauthorized Mexico-US migration was peaking before the 2008–9 recession, and during the recovery from the 2008–9 recession, the hourly earnings of California crop workers were slightly lower than hourly earnings in other states.

Since California began to raise its minimum wage in 2016, the hourly earnings of California farm workers have been higher than in other states. There are no hourly earnings data available for California food service workers, but Figure 5.9 shows that California farm worker hourly earnings rose faster than hourly earnings in the state's leisure and hospitality sector (NAICS 70) over the past five years.

The NAWS finds that the aging and settled California crop workforce, generally employed by one farm employer during the year, is working more hours per week and more weeks per year. Both hours per week and weeks per year rose about 15 percent over the past three decades.

Almost all of California's NAWS crop workers are employed in FVH commodities, but most are not harvesting or packing fruits, vegetables, and horticultural specialties. Instead, most are semiskilled workers such as equipment operators (almost 40 percent) or engaged in preharvest tasks such as planting and irrigating (20 percent), which may help to explain why so many are employed directly by the farm on which they work. Preharvest and semiskilled workers are usually hired directly, while harvest and postharvest

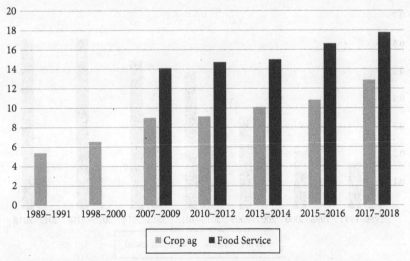

Figure 5.9 US Citizen and Unauthorized Crop Workers in California, 1989–2018

Source: NAWS

workers are often brought to farms by labor contractors and other support service firms.

Figure 5.10 shows that California has a declining share of crop worker families who are receiving benefits from contribution-based programs such as unemployment insurance, and a rising share who receive benefits from need-based programs such as MediCal (California's version of Medicaid). The share of families receiving benefits from contribution-based programs may rise as the crop workforce includes a higher share of US citizens and other authorized workers, and the share of families receiving benefits from need-based programs may rise as California and other states make unauthorized residents and their families eligible for means-tested benefits.

The NAWS portrays an aging, settled, and largely unauthorized Mexican-born crop workforce in California whose hourly earnings are keeping pace with nonfarm sectors that employ workers with similar characteristics. California's crop workers differ from crop workers in other states because a higher share were born abroad and are unauthorized. The hourly earnings of California crop workers began to rise faster after the state increased its minimum wage to $10 an hour in 2016 and to $15 in 2022, with future increases linked to the cost of living.

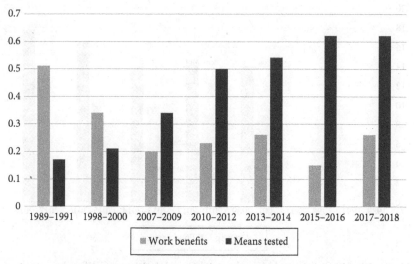

Figure 5.10 Families Receiving Contribution-Based and Means-Tested Benefits, California, 1989–2018
Source: NAWS

Thinking About Farm Workers

All surveys and studies of farm workers reach similar conclusions: most hired farm workers are people for whom farm jobs are their best option because they lack the language, skills, contacts, legal status, and other characteristics needed to find nonfarm jobs. A few mothers may dream of their children growing up to be cowboys, but most farm worker parents hope that their children will acquire the education and skills needed to avoid following them into the fields.

Many eminent thinkers have grappled with how to think about farm labor and farm workers. On the one hand, food is essential to life, and farm workers are essential to the production of especially labor-intensive FVH commodities. However, the number and characteristics of farm workers also reflect policy choices that influence farm worker wages and working conditions.

Agricultural economist Varden Fuller spent a lifetime studying California agriculture and farm workers. Fuller concluded that the leitmotif of farm labor policy was to ensure an ample or excess supply of people willing to fill seasonal farm jobs. Lack of education and few nonfarm job opportunities encouraged these "residual workers" to accept seasonal farm jobs in order to have some earnings.

Fuller concluded that the general excess supply of farm workers had several effects. First, with farm wages about half of nonfarm levels, farm workers and their children learned that climbing the economic ladder generally required occupational and geographic mobility, moving to cities and finding nonfarm jobs. Farmers accepted such worker exits as inevitable, turning the farm labor market into a revolving door that recruited newcomers to replace exiting workers and making it unnecessary to change the structure of agriculture or the farm labor market.

Second, Fuller found that the low farm wages made possible by the continued influx of newcomers were capitalized into higher land prices, benefitting landowners and their allies in banking and packing, who opposed policies that could lead to higher wages, such as including farm workers under nonfarm labor laws. Farmland remains attractive to pension funds and other investors in the 21st century who are looking for long-term investments that generate income while increasing in value over time.

Third, an ample supply of seasonal farm workers that holds down farm wages discourages family farmers who rely on their own labor, since the value of the time they spend doing their farm work is the same as the low wages paid to hired workers. Agriculture in the western states began with large acreages due to land grants made for preirrigation grain farming and livestock grazing. These large farms did not have to be broken into family-sized parcels to obtain a seasonal hired farm workforce because land owners were able to find workers willing to accept seasonal jobs at low wages.

Farmers in the 21st century continue to assume that seasonal workers will be available when needed to harvest their crops, either from within the United States or as guest workers from abroad. If consumer demand for labor-intensive fresh berries or cherries is rising, farmers plant crops and expect harvest workers to be available. Land prices continue to increase, augmenting the wealth of landowners and making it harder for small farmers without land to get into farming.

There are 21st-century technologies to monitor water pesticide residues, and other factors to keep fresh produce safe, so that any suspect produce can be traced to the field and to the crew of workers who harvested particular heads of lettuce or bags of apples. There are fewer efforts to monitor employer compliance with farm labor laws. One 21st century truth is that Mexican-born workers with little education pick most of the fresh produce in Canada, Mexico, and the United States for affluent consumers in Montreal, Mexico City, and Manhattan.

6

Alternatives to US Workers

Are US workers necessary to produce fresh fruits and vegetables for Americans? There are three major alternatives to US workers: labor-saving mechanization, migrant guest workers, and imported fruits and vegetables. Mechanization is being spurred by rapidly rising farm wages and by rapid progress in robotics and artificial intelligence that produces machines to detect and harvest fruits and vegetables with minimal damage. The H-2A program tripled in size over the past decade. A sixth of jobs on US crop farms are filled by guest workers, raising the question of how to give farmers access to migrant workers while preventing abuse and exploitation. The United States imports 60 percent of its fresh fruit and 35 percent of its fresh vegetables. Mexico provides half of fresh fruit imports and three-fourths of fresh vegetable imports, so most of the avocados and tomatoes consumed by Americans are products of Mexico. The choices are machines, migrants, and imports.

Mechanization

Human history is the story of productivity improvements in agriculture that allowed fewer farmers to feed more people, setting the stage for the emergence of cities and ruling elites. In modern times, labor-saving mechanization in agriculture is a response to economic and risk factors (Taylor and Charlton 2019). Farmers mechanize when the cost of hand labor exceeds the cost of machine services, and when there is a risk that farm workers may not be available. Rising nonfarm wages draw workers out of agriculture, while biological and engineering innovations make it possible to replace workers with machines.

US agriculture has experienced several waves of mechanization. Tractors replaced horses in the 1920s, cotton harvesters replaced sharecropper families and Mexican braceros who hand-picked cotton in the 1940s and 1950s, and machines replaced workers in sugar beet fields in the 1950s. Precision planting reduced the need to thin plants, herbicides reduced the

Bracero 2.0. Philip Martin, Oxford University Press. © Oxford University Press 2024.
DOI: 10.1093/oso/9780197699973.003.0006

need for hand weeding, and bulk bins holding 800 to 1,000 pounds of apples and oranges and moved by forklifts eliminated jobs lifting and stacking smaller lugs, baskets, and other containers.

Most remaining hand-harvested commodities are fresh fruits, vegetables, and nursery plants and flowers (Calvin and Martin 2010; Mohan 2017). Farms producing fruits and nuts, vegetables and melons, and horticultural specialties (FVH) are a sixth of US farm employers, but they accounted for half of farm labor expenditures in 2017. Within this FVH sector, a handful of commodities account for most hand work, including apples, oranges, strawberries, lettuce, and tomatoes.

Mechanizing the remaining tasks done by hand workers in fresh fruits and vegetables is hard because the work is outdoors in unpredictable settings (Charlton et al. 2019). By contrast, jobs in packing houses are easier to mechanize; packing house jobs are similar to manufacturing jobs because tasks are more predictable and done in controlled environments. Figure 6.1 from McKinsey (2015) predicted that, by restructuring farming systems to make it easier for machines to identify and harvest fresh produce, almost 60 percent of farm jobs could be mechanized.

There are two general harvest mechanization rules: once-over harvests and crops destined for processing are easiest to mechanize (Sarig, Thompson, and Brown 2000; Schmitz and Moss 2015; Charlton et al. 2019). Harvesting all of a commodity during one pass through the field allows the machine to destroy the plant, which is why most root vegetables such as potatoes are harvested by machines that dig the crop from the soil, remove the dirt, and convey the harvested crop to a truck or wagon.

Harvesting fruit and nuts from perennial trees poses more challenges. Catch-and-shake harvesters are nonselective in the sense that they remove all of the fruit and nuts in one pass through an orchard. Catch-and-shake machines aim to minimize damage to trees by using a rubber-coated head to grasp the trunk or limb and deliver a jolt that dislodges the crop. Vine crops such as grapes can be harvested by machines with rotating fingers that dislodge the fruit and allow it to fall onto conveyor belts for transport to bins or gondolas traveling on or alongside the machine.

Crops that do not ripen uniformly must be picked several times. Humans can distinguish mature and immature fruits and vegetables much more efficiently than machines, which must locate an apple, determine its maturity,

Exhibit 9
Technical potential for automation across sectors varies depending on mix of activity types

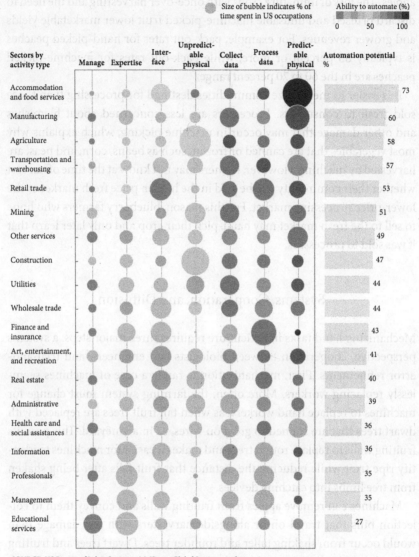

SOURCE: US Bureau of Labor Statistics; McKinsey Global Institute analysis

Figure 6.1 McKinsey Predicts That 60 Percent of Farm Jobs Could Be Mechanized

Source: US Bureau of Labor Statistics; McKinsey Global Institute Analysis

and harvest it without damage to the picked apple and nearby immature apples. The loss of immature crops with once-over harvesting and the need to discard bruised and unusable machine-picked fruit lower marketable yields and grower revenues. For example, pack-out rates for hand-picked peaches is typically 85 percent or more, while pack-out rates for machine-picked peaches are in the 60 to 70 percent range.

It is easier to mechanize commodities destined for processing than those sold fresh to consumers. Processors are less concerned about blemishes and other damage that may occur in machine picking, which explains why most vegetables that are canned or frozen, such as beans, corn, and peas, are harvested by machine. However, farmers may not know at the time of harvest whether their commodity will be sold in the higher-price fresh market or the lower-price processing market. For this reason, blueberry farmers who hope to sell to the fresh market may hand-pick their crop and only later learn that it was sold to processors.

Systems, Cooperation, and Diffusion

Mechanizing hand tasks in agriculture requires three major steps: a systems perspective, cooperation between biologists and engineers, and trial-and-error refinements. First, mechanization is rarely a case of machines seamlessly replacing workers. More often, the farming system must change for machines to replace hand workers, as when tall fruit trees are replaced with dwarf trees that are trained to grow on wires, as in a vineyard. This permits fruiting walls to replace round trees and makes it easier for machines to identify ripe fruit while reducing the distance that fruit falls after being shaken from tree limbs into catching devices.

Machines can remove apples from fruiting walls and convey them to collection bins that travel on or alongside harvesters with less damage than would occur from shaking taller and rounder trees. Dwarf trees and fruiting walls also make it easier to hand-harvest fruit because they eliminate the need for workers to climb ladders and facilitate the use of hydraulic platforms that carry harvest workers and bins.

The second key to labor-saving mechanization is cooperation between biologists and engineers. Scientists must often modify plant behavior so that engineers can develop cost-effective harvesting systems. For annual crops such as leafy vegetables, one key to mechanization is uniform ripening, so that 90 percent or more of the crop can be harvested in one pass through the field.[1]

Plant breeders traditionally focus on maximizing crop yields and resistance to disease, but more recently they have tried to improve flavor and to make fruits and vegetables more amenable to machine harvesting, such as developing varieties that ripen uniformly or have thicker skins. Developing new plant varieties often takes a decade or more and involves trade-offs. Do plant breeders aim for maximum flavor, which may make the commodity more fragile and less amenable to machine harvesting, or breed fruits and vegetables with thicker skins and changed shapes to facilitate machine harvesting, as was done when oblong processing tomatoes with thicker skins were developed? Rising farm labor costs are changing the priorities of plant breeders, but incorporating machine-friendly traits into new plant varieties takes time.

Many fruits are picked multiple times, from apples and blueberries to oranges and peaches, and the first pick often yields 50 to 75 percent of the total harvest. However, the remaining fruit may make the difference between profit and loss, so there are incentives to pick all marketable fruit. Raising the share of the total crop that can be picked during the first harvest makes machine harvesting more cost-effective.

Crops such as strawberries are often picked twice a week and 40 to 50 times during the season. Workers pick strawberries directly into the clamshells in which they are sold, pushing a light wheeled cart ahead of them that holds a tray with eight 1-pound clamshells. Putting slow-moving conveyor belts in front of pickers increases hand worker productivity by eliminating the need to carry full trays to collection stations. In European countries with higher labor costs, strawberries are sometimes grown on tabletops or trained to grow on vertical walls, which reduces the need for workers to stoop to pick ripe berries. Mechanizing the harvest of fragile berries requires sophisticated and expensive machines that to date are too slow to compete with hand workers.

The third mechanization challenge is to refine labor-saving machines in a trial-and-error process to develop commercially viable systems. The first machines are rarely those that dominate a decade later because of the refinements made in response to experience. Dust, uneven ground, and moisture can damage sensitive equipment, which is why experimentation often leads to more durable machines that adapt to ever-changing field conditions.

Prototype harvesting machines litter agricultural areas, making farmers cautious about buying expensive machines if farm workers are available. Many machines developed in labs do not work as well as anticipated in the field, so early adopters may buy a machine and also pay hand workers to pick the crop, raising costs. Harvesting aids that make hand workers more productive may reduce incentives to develop fully mechanized systems. For example, the conveyor belts that travel in front of workers who are harvesting heads of lettuce raise the bar for a lettuce harvesting machine.

There is a final economic difference between hand and machine work that influences decision-making. Hand workers are variable costs, meaning that farmers do not pay wages if weather or disease ruin the crop or if prices are so low that the crop is not harvested. A purchased machine, on the other hand, becomes a fixed cost that must be paid for whether there is a crop to be harvested or not. Some firms provide machine harvesting as a service, but they must set prices that reflect the possibility of having nothing to harvest.

Processing Tomatoes

The mechanical tomato harvester developed by University of California at Davis scientists and engineers in the 1960s illustrates the systems, cooperation, and trial-and-error process of harvest mechanization. During the 1950s, most farms had a few acres of processing tomatoes as well as other commodities, and relied on braceros to move from one harvest to the next on their farms. Mechanization required tomato farmers to invest in harvesters and trucks to convey harvested tomatoes to processing plants, which led to fewer and larger farms that specialized in growing tomatoes.

UC Davis plant scientist Jack Hanna developed uniformly ripening and thicker-skinned pear-shaped tomatoes in the 1950s,[2] and UC Davis agricultural engineer Coby Lorenzen designed a machine to cut tomato plants and shake tomatoes from the vines in the early 1960s; the machine was licensed to Blackwelder Manufacturing. Growers changed their farming systems, planting the new tomatoes in large and flat fields that had sufficient room for the machines to turn around at the end of rows. The first harvesting machines did not remove all of the material other than tomatoes, and ride-along sorters eliminated dirt, stems, and leaves until cutting and shaking systems were improved and electronic eyes were able to isolate the desired tomatoes.

Federal and state governments played key roles to accelerate tomato mechanization. Governments subsidized research at UC Davis, eliminated the supply of bracero workers (making mechanization necessary), and created testing stations that sampled machine-harvested tomatoes to determine their quality (and thus the price paid by the processor to the grower). These testing stations, since privatized, were critical to the diffusion of the tomato harvester because of the economic stakes involved. California processing tomatoes are worth about $80 a ton or $0.04 a pound.[3] Farmers are paid by weight, and processors can reject or reduce the price of substandard tomatoes. Having a 50-pound lug of hand-picked tomatoes rejected would cost a farmer $2, but rejecting a 25-ton load involves $2,000. Testing stations operated by a neutral party resolved what could have been a contentious debate between growers and processors.[4]

Table 6.1 shows that braceros were almost three-fourths of the workers who harvested processing tomatoes in the early 1960s. Farmers who wanted the bracero program to continue argued that they would have to follow their workers to Mexico in order to grow processing tomatoes. Congressional testimony asserted that the 3-million-ton processing tomato crop of the early 1960s would drop by half or more without braceros, and that catsup would become a luxury.[5]

What actually happened? The tomato harvest was mechanized quickly. In 1962, less than 1 percent of California's processing tomatoes were harvested by machine; by 1969, almost 100 percent of the state's processing tomatoes were machine-harvested. Machines improved, so the 1,500 in use in 1969 were very different from the 25 in use in the early 1960s (Rasmussen 1968).

The cost of processing tomatoes fell during the 1960s and 1970s just as the fast-food revolution was increasing the demand for processed tomato products. Figure 6.2 shows that processing tomato production doubled from 3 million tons a year in the early 1960s to 6 million tons a year in the mid-1970s and 12 million tons today.[6] Necessity is the mother of invention, and ending the bracero program led to the rapid mechanization of tomato harvesting.

The mechanization of processing tomatoes highlights factors involved in combining changes in farming systems with research cooperation to spur the

Table 6.1 Braceros Harvested 72 Percent of California's Processing Tomatoes in 1962

Product	California acreage	California as percent of U.S. production	California farm value	Mexican labor in major seasonal tasks		Status of laborsaving equipment, especially for harvesting
				Man-weeks	Percent of total	
Tomatoes	200,900	54	$130,114,000	449,990	72	Feasible but 8 to 10 years away.
Lettuce	106,400	59	87,510,000	185,590	68	Some mechanization now. Reduce labor by 50 percent by 1968.
Strawberries	10,500	40	36,500,000	177,820	61	Little mechanized equipment; none in sight.
Lemons	50,000	94	33,440,000	149,120	76	Little mechanization; none in sight.
Oranges	59,544	13	87,398,000	78,300	42	Do.
Sugarbeets	241,000	26	54,890,000	65,600	38	Substantially mechanized now.
Melons	85,550	25	37,787,000	63,880	45	Some mechanization for loading, one for picking.
Asparagus	66,600	54	27,531,000	57,360	48	Experimental machine developed but has not proved practical because of wastage.
Celery	13,500	52	31,703,000	42,950	55	Some equipment used in past; too expensive for small growers.
Snap beans	8,500	7	8,182,000	33,890	54	Not feasible for pole beans.
Total, 10 crops above.	842,494	32	534,965,000	1,304,500	61	
All crops (not including dairy, livestock, and poultry).			1,967,877,000	1,643,400	26	

Source: US House of Representatives 1963

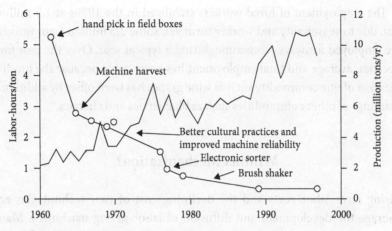

Figure 6.2 Processing Tomato Production Rose as the Harvester Spread
Source: Thompson and Blank 2000.

diffusion of machines. The systems approach reexamined the entire field-to-factory supply chain of growing, harvesting, and processing tomatoes into paste and other products. Second, cooperation between scientists and engineers was essential to develop uniform ripening varieties and a machine to harvest them. Third, early adopters of new tomato varieties and harvesting machines learned through trial and error how to refine planting systems and machines to harvest tomatoes with a tenth of the pre-mechanization harvest workforce.

There were fears in the 1960s that automation would displace low-skilled workers in agriculture and nonfarm industries. Agricultural engineers and social scientists used the processing tomato story to predict the rapid mechanization of remaining hand-harvested fruits and vegetables and urged federal and state governments to retrain farm workers and their children for nonfarm jobs (Cargill and Rossmiller 1970).

There was labor-saving mechanization in the 1970s, but not the predicted harvest mechanization of asparagus, lettuce, and other commodities. Instead of mechanization, Mexican workers arrived, making it unnecessary to develop harvesting systems and machines. For example, there were over 80 projects aimed at mechanizing the harvest of fresh oranges in the late 1960s, and none in the late 1970s after a decade of rising Mexico-US migration.

The employment of hired workers stabilized in the 1980s at 1.5 million but, due to seasonality and worker turnover, some 2.5 million farm workers are employed for wages sometime during a typical year. Over the past four decades, average and total employment has been stable because the mechanization of one commodity such as wine grapes has been offset by additional plantings of other commodities such as blueberries and cherries.

Whither Mechanization?

Rising farm labor costs and the declining cost of new technologies encourage the development and diffusion of labor-saving machinery. Many commodities that were hand-harvested in the past are now mostly machine-harvested, such as wine grapes, or are amenable to machine harvesting, including blueberries and raisin grapes.

The pace of mechanization is influenced by how fast technologies evolve to replace ever more expensive labor. Figure 6.3 shows that the average annual

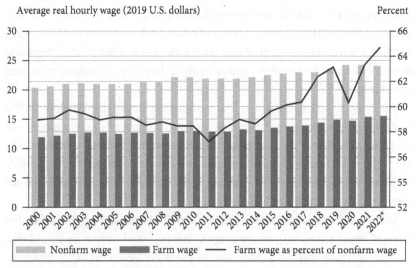

Note: * = Annual values for 2022 were predicted using incomplete data and year-to-date comparisons with 2021. **Real wages** are adjusted for inflation and pegged to 2019 values.

Figure 6.3 Farm and Nonfarm Wages 2000–2019

Source: US Department of Agriculture, Economic Research Service, "Rising Farm Worker Wages Suggest Tightening Farm Labor Markets," last modified January 5, 2023, https://www.ers.usda.gov/data-products/chart-gallery/gallery/chart-detail/?chartId=105546

hourly earnings of hired farm workers rose 28 percent between 2000 and 2022, adjusted for inflation, higher than the 17 percent real increase in the hourly earnings of nonfarm workers, so the gap between farm and nonfarm earnings is narrowing. With farm wages rising faster than nonfarm wages, farmers have more incentives to mechanize.

Government policies affect both the development of labor-saving technologies and farm labor costs and thus the speed of mechanization. During the 1960s, most farm labor-saving biological and engineering research was funded by federal and state governments and conducted at land-grant universities, while today venture capital supports the development of many new farm technologies. The federal minimum wage has been $7.25 an hour since 2009, but the Adverse Effect Wage Rate that must be paid to H-2A guest workers is rising steadily, to between $13 and $18 an hour in 2023. Many states have raised farm labor costs by raising their own minimum wages and requiring farm employers to pay overtime wages.

Public support for labor-saving research was controversial. The research in the spotlight during the 1970s was the mechanization of the processing tomato harvest as a result of the cooperation between biological and engineering researchers at UC Davis. Journalist and later Texas agriculture commissioner Jim Hightower, in a 1972 book entitled *Hard Tomatoes, Hard Times*, argued against the use of tax dollars to modify tomatoes and to develop harvesting machines, and showed that this research by land-grant universities benefitted large farms and accelerated the demise of small farms.

Hightower's work became the basis of a suit filed in 1977 by the California Rural Legal Assistance program on behalf of the United Farm Workers union against the University of California. The suit argued that UC used taxpayer monies meant to benefit all rural Americans to benefit only large farmers capable of adopting the mechanized tomato harvesting system (Martin and Olmstead 1985). The suit did not focus on the displacement of bracero farm workers, and it did not note that mechanization created more jobs for local Mexican American women, who removed debris on harvesting machines and worked in tomato processing plants.

The suit was settled in the early 1980s by adding farm worker advocates to UC advisory boards that review agricultural research proposals. This was a hollow victory for worker advocates because the upsurge in unauthorized Mexico-US migration reduced grower, government, and research interest in labor-saving mechanization.[7] In retrospect, the years between the end of the bracero program in 1964 and the devaluations of the Mexican peso in the early 1980s were a golden era for US farm workers. Farm wages rose rapidly, farm workers were covered by minimum wage regulations, unemployment insurance, and union organizing laws, and many farmers hired personnel managers and took steps to improve the treatment of farm workers. However, these changes eroded in the 1980s as illegal immigration surged, conglomerates that owned farms exited production agriculture, and unions faltered (Martin 2003).

There has been renewed interest in labor-saving farm mechanization since the 2008–9 recession, which slowed unauthorized Mexico-US migration and put upward pressure on farm wages. Low interest rates combined with technological advances to spur a new round of research into labor-saving mechanization that is now often funded by private capital rather than governments.

Private developers seek to maximize return on investment, so they seek the easiest problems and the largest markets. Most firms that offer technology to farmers provide devices that generate information to help farmers determine how much to irrigate or fertilize. The next-most-common devices are those that automate pre-harvest tasks such as planting, thinning, and weeding. Machines that know where seeds or plants are or should be located can remove other plants, and can do so for multiple crops.

Mechanizing the harvest of a particular commodity is less attractive for two major reasons. First, developing a machine to harvest apples or oranges as efficiently as human hands is hard and may require many changes in farming, packing, and marketing that are difficult for a machine developer to coordinate. Second, the market for a commodity-specific harvesting machine is smaller than the market for a device that can be used in multiple crops, such as a tractor or a precision planter or weeder. The largest-acreage US tree fruit is oranges, almost 500,000 bearing acres, followed by apples, with almost 300,000 bearing acres. The bearing acreage of most other tree fruits, including cherries, peaches, pears, and tangerines, is less than 100,000 acres and for many commodities is falling.

The example of cantaloupes is instructive. Acreage has declined by almost two-thirds in the 21st century, and new varieties that do not have to be grown in dry environments have led to more production closer to East Coast consumers and more imports. A prototype machine has been developed to harvest western cantaloupes, but even if it can be refined to compete with hand harvesters, the likely maximum market would be about 50 machines, so even a very high profit margin per machine is unlikely to generate big payoffs.[8]

Guest Workers

The second way to produce fresh fruits and vegetables in the United States is to recruit guest workers from lower-wage countries. Most countries that are richer than their neighbors have guest or temporary foreign worker programs that allow labor-short employers to recruit migrant workers to fill vacant jobs, and most have special programs for farm workers. During COVID-19 lockdowns that included closing borders to nonessential travel, Canada and the United States made exceptions to permit the entry of farm guest workers.

Guest worker programs can be compared along two major axes: what employers must do to obtain permission to hire guest workers, and what guest workers may do in host country labor markets. Most governments have hire-local-workers-first policies, meaning that employers must try and fail to recruit local workers before recruiting and employing guest workers. Employers who are seeking to fill jobs in labor-short sectors are sometimes exempt from local recruitment requirements.

The first column of Table 6.2 highlights the requirements that employers must satisfy to recruit and employ guest workers. One option is attestation, meaning that employers assert that they need foreign workers and satisfy other conditions, opening the door to foreign workers. The other end of the spectrum is certification, which involves employers trying to recruit local workers under government supervision before receiving certification to employ guest workers.

In the United States, attestation programs such as the H-1B program aim to protect US workers with a cap or quota on the number of visas available. Certification programs such as H-2A for farm workers are not capped but require employers to prove on a job-by-job basis that US workers are not available. Employers may sometimes hire foreign workers who are already in the country for other reasons without attestation or certification, as with foreign students and some other temporary visitors.

The second major axis of guest worker programs deals with worker rights. Are guest workers nonimmigrants (temporary visitors) or are they probationary immigrants who can earn immigrant visas? H-2A workers are nonimmigrants, meaning that an H-2A visa can be denied to a foreigner who wants to immigrate to the United States, and working in the United States year after year does not lead to immigrant status. The H-1B visa, by contrast, allows foreigners to arrive as probationary immigrants

Table 6.2 Guest Worker Programs

	Employer	Worker	Example	Note
Attestation	Assert compliance to agency	Tied by contract to employer; can be sponsored by employer for immigrant visa	H-1B visas for college-educated foreigners who fill US jobs requiring degrees	Quota of 85,000 H-1B visas a year for for-profit employers
Certification	Government agency certifies	Tied by contract to employer; must leave United States when contract ends	H-2A visas for foreigners to fill seasonal farm jobs up to 10 months	No cap; 372,000 farm jobs certified in FY22; about 300,000 H-2A visas issued (80% of certified jobs)
Other	No government involvement in hiring F-1 students	Can change US employers and stay in United States as long as visa allows	Major reason for being in United States is non-work-related, such as education	F-1, J-1, OPT, and other visas

Source: Author's elaboration

who can be sponsored by their employers for immigrant visas after several years. H-1B and H-2A guest workers are tied to their employers by contracts, but H-1B workers gain freedom in the labor market after receiving immigrant visas.

There are variations on these certification-versus-attestation cornerstones and nonimmigrant-versus-probationary-immigrant statuses. Foreigners in a country primarily for a non-work-related purpose, such as foreign students or working holidaymakers,[9] may normally work for any employer, and that employer is not required to try to find local workers before hiring foreign students or working holidaymakers. Foreign students and working holidaymakers are free agents in host country labor markets who are free to employers, and their employers are obliged to abide by local labor laws rather than paying special wages and providing their foreign worker employees with housing.

There are also free-movement areas including the European Union, which allows EU citizens to be employed in other member states on an equal basis with local workers. NAFTA (now USMCA) allows college-educated Americans, Canadians, and Mexicans to work indefinitely in a partner country with TN visas if they have a local job offer, creating a more limited free-movement area.

Most guest worker policies aim to welcome skilled workers and to rotate low-skilled workers in and out of the country. College-educated guest workers and foreign students are often treated as probationary immigrants who can bring their families, and many governments allow the spouses of high-skilled migrants to work and their children to attend local schools. Low-skilled guest workers usually arrive without their families, often live in employer-provided communal housing, and are expected to depart when their contracts end. Welcome-the-skilled and rotate-the-unskilled is the (unspoken) goal of most guest worker programs.

From H-2 to H-2A

The H-2A program has since 1952 allowed US farmers who anticipate too few US workers to be certified by the US Department of Labor to recruit and employ guest workers to fill seasonal farm jobs. In order to receive DOL certification, farm employers must satisfy three major criteria. First, DOL must certify that the employer tried and failed to recruit enough US workers. Second, after being certified, employers must recruit workers abroad, pay worker travel expenses to and from their home countries, and offer free and approved housing to H-2A workers while they are employed in the United States and daily transportation between this housing and the workplace.[10]

Third, the employer must offer and pay the higher of the federal or state minimum wage, the prevailing wage rate, or the Adverse Effect Wage Rate to H-2A and US workers in similar employment. The AEWR is normally the highest of these wages, and ranged from almost $14 to over $18 an hour across states in 2023. Adding at least $5 an hour for transportation, housing, and other expenses makes the total cost of H-2A workers at least $19 to $23 an hour, which is more than the cost of US workers who are not provided with transportation and housing. H-2A guest workers provide labor insurance because they are tied to their US employer by contracts and are in the United States an average of six months (Martin and Rutledge 2021).

The H-2 program was relatively small between 1952 and 1986. During the 1950s, the separate bracero program was much larger, peaking at over 445,000 admissions in 1956, when DOL certified fewer than 10,000 jobs to be filled by H-2 workers (Martin 2008). US farm workers were not covered by federal minimum wage laws until 1967, so US farm workers were sometimes paid less than braceros and H-2 workers, who had contracts that specified a minimum wage (Hawley 1966).

DOL studied the effects of the bracero program in the late 1950s and concluded that the presence of braceros reduced wages for US farm workers. As a result, it implemented AEWRs that must be paid to braceros to prevent their employment from adversely affecting US farm workers (US Department of Labor 1959; Martin 2008). After the bracero program ended in 1964, DOL required farmers who hired H-2 guest workers to pay US workers in similar jobs the AEWR (Mize 2019). Since the US farm workers who were 95 percent of all farm workers were not covered by minimum wages (Kim 2004), few farmers switched from braceros to H-2 workers in the 1960s because they did not want to pay US workers the minimum wage specified for braceros and H-2 workers.[11]

The Immigration Reform and Control Act of 1986 legalized unauthorized farm workers and divided the H-2 program into H-2A for farm workers and H-2B for nonfarm workers. With unauthorized workers accounting for up to a quarter of US farm workers, IRCA's introduction of sanctions on employers who knowingly hired unauthorized workers was expected to increase the size of the H-2A program as newly legalized farm workers demanded higher wages or sought nonfarm jobs; it was assumed that there would be no unauthorized workers to replace them.

IRCA failed on many dimensions, from legalizing far too many farm workers to spurring the creation of a false-documents industry that allowed newly arrived unauthorized workers and their employers to satisfy I-9 procedures (Rural Migration News Blog 2020; Martin 1994).[12] Falsely documented unauthorized workers spread throughout the United States, and the H-2A program remained relatively small in the early 1990s, certifying fewer than 20,000 jobs a year, including half to cut sugarcane in Florida (GAO 1988).

The H-2A program expanded after 2000 for several reasons. First, the Immigration and Customs Enforcement (ICE) agency began to audit the I-9 forms completed by newly hired workers and their employers; it discovered that many employees presented false documents when they were hired, and instructed their employers to inform the employees that they should contact government agencies to fix their records. Instead, most suspect workers quit, prompting employers to form the North Carolina Growers Association and the Snake River Farmers' Association in Idaho to recruit and transport H-2A workers to member farms that wanted to employ legal workers.

A second reason for more H-2A workers in the 21st century was the 2008–9 recession, which marked a turning point in unauthorized Mexico-US migration. Mexicans stopped coming to the United States for fear that, after paying thousands of dollars in smuggling fees, they would be unable to find jobs. In 2000, over half of US crop workers were unauthorized, including a quarter who were newcomers, meaning that they were in the United States less than a year before being interviewed. After 2010, the unauthorized share of crop workers fell to 40 percent and the share of newcomers dropped to 2 percent.[13]

Reduced Mexico-US migration was mirrored in the rising number of H-2A guest workers. The number of farm jobs certified to be filled by H-2A workers increased from less than 100,000 in FY13 to 372,000 in FY22 and is on track to top peak bracero admissions of 450,000 by 2025. Not all of the jobs certified to be filled by H-2A workers are in fact filled by such workers, and some H-2A visa holders are able to fill two or more certified jobs. The number of H-2A visas issued is typically 80 percent of the number of jobs certified, about 300,000 in FY22.

Third, farm employers realized that they could profitably employ H-2A workers despite their higher costs because H-2A workers are younger and more productive than US workers. Most settled and unauthorized Mexican-born farm workers arrived in the United States in the 1990s and early 2000s when they were in their 20s, which means they are now in their 40s and 50s and unable to work as fast as they did when they were younger. Most H-2A workers, by contrast, are in their 20s and 30s and, because education levels have been rising in Mexico, are better educated than the older unauthorized Mexican-born workers who have settled in the United States.

There are about 1.5 million full-time-equivalent (FTE) jobs in US agriculture, including 1.1 million in crops and 400,000 in animal agriculture.[14] H-2A workers are in the United States an average six months, so 300,000 H-2A workers filled about 15 percent of the FTE jobs in US crop agriculture in 2022.

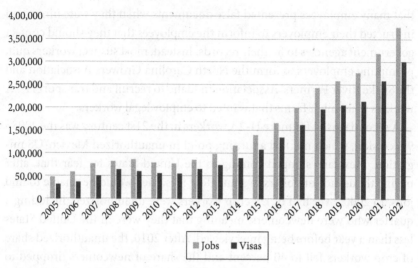

Figure 6.4 H-2A Jobs Certified and Visas Issued, FY05–22
Source: US Department of Labor, US Department of State

Should the rapid expansion of the H-2A program seen in Figure 6.4 be welcomed or feared? Answering this question requires an understanding of how the program works and the options to change it, including proposals to end the requirement that employers try to recruit US workers, to allow farmers to provide H-2A workers with a housing allowance of $1 to $2 per hour worked rather than providing them with free housing, and freezing or eliminating the AEWR.

Second, is DOL certification effective to prevent H-2A workers from adversely affecting US farm workers? H-2A workers are generally younger than US workers and selected for their ability to do the job, and they are 15 to 30 percent more productive than US workers in terms of bins of apples or oranges picked per hour or day. How can US workers be protected if H-2A workers are more productive, willing to work long hours if needed, and loyal to their employer because they cannot leave for another job?

Third, how does the availability of H-2A workers affect grower interest in mechanization? Does the availability of H-2A workers slow labor-saving mechanization (Martin 2009)? Can H-2A workers act as a bridge to mechanization, as when their availability facilitates the planting of new apple varieties in orchards that are designed to permit the eventual use of machines rather than hand pickers? Do US growers have any obligation to guest and US workers who may be displaced after mechanization or imports substituting for US production?

H-2A Program

Three federal agencies have a role in the H-2A program. The Department of Labor determines whether employers need H-2A workers and enforces H-2A regulations. The Department of Homeland Security (DHS) determines whether the employer petition for H-2As is accurate and then checks incoming workers with H-2A visas. The Department of State (DOS) issues H-2A visas to foreign workers abroad. DOL certification of an employer's need for H-2A workers means that DOL agrees with the employer (1) that US workers are not available to fill seasonal farm jobs and (2) that the presence of H-2A workers will not adversely affect similar US workers. DHS ensures that the employer is legitimate and that H-2A workers did not pay for their jobs. And DOS determines whether the workers recruited by the employer are eligible for visas (GAO 2017).

Figure 6.5 shows that employers begin the H-2A process at least 60 days before their need date by filing a job offer with their local state workforce agency (SWA). Employers assert in their Form ETA 790A job orders that they are (1) offering full-time temporary or seasonal jobs, (2) require a specific number of H-2A workers to fill them, and (3) have accurately described the job and its location, the anticipated hours of work per day and days per week, and the start and stop dates (Martin 2008).[15] Employers also provide information on the housing available to H-2A workers, whether they will provide meals or cooking facilities, and spell out hourly and piece rate wages and any experience requirements or productivity standards.

State SWAs review employer job offers before uploading them into a database available to US job seekers,[16] while DOL's National Processing Center

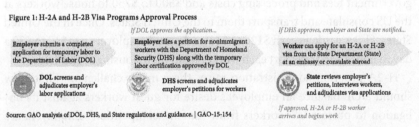

Figure 1: H-2A and H-2B Visa Programs Approval Process

If DOL approves the application...   *If DHS approves, employer and State are notified...*

Employer submits a completed application for temporary labor to the Department of Labor (DOL)

Employer files a petition for nonimmigrant workers with the Department of Homeland Security (DHS) along with the temporary labor certification approved by DOL

Worker can apply for an H-2A or H-2B visa from the State Department (State) at an embassy or consulate abroad

DOL screens and adjudicates employer's labor applications

DHS screens and adjudicates employer's petitions for workers

State reviews employer's petitions, interviews workers, and adjudicates visa applications

Source: GAO analysis of DOL, DHS, and State regulations and guidance. | GAO-15-154

If approved, H-2A or H-2B worker arrives and begins work

Figure 6.5 H-2A Approval Process

Source: US Government Accountability Office, "H-2A and H-2B Visa Programs: Increased Protections Needed for Foreign Workers," GAO-15-154, March 2015, https://www.gao.gov/assets/gao-15-154.pdf

(NPC) reviews employer-submitted forms and makes a decision on the employer's application at least 30 days before the need date.[17]

The result is a 15-day window to recruit US workers before the NPC certifies or denies the employer's need for H-2A workers.[18] Both SWAs and employers try to recruit US workers, and employers must submit a recruitment report to the NPC at least 30 days before the start date that identifies any US workers who responded to the job ads and postings and provides "lawful job-related reason(s)" for not hiring them. The NPC subtracts any US workers who were hired and certifies an employer's need for sufficient H-2A workers to fill the remaining jobs.[19] There is no fee to apply for DOL certification, although employers pay $100 plus $10 per job for certification, far less than what DOL and SWAs spend on the program.

Employers attach DOL's certification to the I-129 petition for nonimmigrant workers that is submitted with a $460 fee to the Department of Homeland Security's US Citizenship and Immigration Service (USCIS) agency, which checks that the employer is legitimate and ensures that neither the employer nor the agent charged recruitment fees to H-2A workers. Most petitions for nonimmigrant workers do not name the foreign workers requested, so USCIS forwards approved petitions to the Department of State consulate abroad that is specified by the employer.

The foreign workers recruited by the employer travel to a US consulate, where they are fingerprinted and may be interviewed by US consular officers before receiving H-2A visas, which cost $190 plus an additional $100 for biometrics processing (Hernández-León 2020). Most Mexican H-2A workers are bused by their US employers from consulates in Mexico to the US border, are inspected by DHS's Customs and Border Protection (CBP) officers as they enter the United States, and then continue to their US workplace.

The total cost to employers of each Mexican H-2A worker is about $750 in government fees and processing costs and $500 to $750 to house workers at the US consulate and transport them to the United States. Once in the United States, H-2A workers earn $120 to $150 a day and employers pay $10 to $30 a day to house and transport each worker from their housing to the fields.

H-2A program administration raises three major challenges. First, how should DOL balance an employer's desire for guest workers against its obligation to protect US workers from "unfair" competition? Employers are encouraged to hire US workers by the extra steps and costs imposed by H-2A regulations, but they are rewarded with productive workers whose presence can ensure that work is done in a timely and efficient way. What is the optimal balance between giving employers access to the guest workers they prefer versus protecting US farm workers?

The second challenge involves the funding for and the incentives of the agencies that administer the H-2A program. SWAs are perennially underfunded, helping to explain why they do little to recruit US workers and conduct few prevailing wage-and-practice surveys that could require employers to pay higher-than-AEWR wages.[20] Underfunded SWAs are generally more responsive to employers and their agents who complain if their job offers and housing inspections are not handled in a timely way than to US workers who may be seeking seasonal farm jobs.

The third challenge involves the expansion of the H-2A program to new commodities, areas, and types of employers. Understaffed SWAs and the NPC may accept misleading or false employer job offers, as when employers call workers who construct buildings on farms "crop workers" and pay them a crop worker wage rather than a construction worker wage. Some trucking firms call their drivers "agricultural equipment operators," which allows them to pay lower farm wages rather than higher truck driver wages and avoid overtime pay, since the federal Fair Labor Standards Act exempts employers of farm workers from paying premium wages for work after 8 hours a day or 40 hours a week.[21] The growing importance of labor contractors, who employ almost half of H-2A workers, poses special concerns, since they have a history of violations of labor laws and exploitation of farm workers.

H-2A Recruitment

Issues arise in each step of the H-2A process. The recruitment issue arises first in the United States, when employers try and fail to find US workers, and then in Mexico and other countries where foreign workers are recruited.

Employers set recruitment in motion by preparing a job offer and requesting certification to hire foreign workers,[22] which also obliges them to try to recruit US workers. Why is it so hard to find US workers to fill jobs that pay more than the minimum wage? Employers say that US workers do not want the seasonal jobs they offer, or that US workers want a job right now rather than 30 days in the future, when the crop will be ready to be harvested.[23] The number of H-2A workers is reduced for each US worker who is hired, which means that if the employer hires US workers who do not report or quit, they may be shorthanded at critical times.

Worker advocates tell a different story. They cite examples of farm employers who segregate US workers from H-2A workers or assign them more difficult tasks to encourage them to quit (Tofani 1987). A farm labor contractor who was eventually debarred from the H-2A program, Global Horizons, told US workers who were hired to report to worksites where there was no work to be done, leaving some with travel expenses and no work because Global Horizons filled the jobs with Thai H-2A workers who had unlawfully paid for their jobs.[24] Almost all employers have already identified their desired foreign workers before seeking DOL certification, and less than 5 percent of the jobs advertised by employers seeking H-2A certification are filled by US workers (GAO 1988).

Recruitment issues in Mexico and other migrant-sending countries often involve workers who pay intermediaries for US jobs (Centro de los Derechos del Migrante 2020). Recruiters travel to the rural villages where potential H-2A workers live and promise high US wages and employer-paid transportation and housing. Some recruiters are legitimate agents of US farm employers who screen workers and do not charge for jobs, while others charge workers for nonexistent jobs. Both Mexican and US laws require employers to pay all of the costs associated with hiring migrant workers for jobs away from their homes in Mexico or the United States, but these laws are hard to enforce, especially in rural Mexico.

One survey found that 44 percent of US farm employers listed recruitment agents on their petitions to USCIS for H-2A workers (GAO 2017). Since US employers are required to pay all recruitment costs, recruiters in Mexico, who typically receive $200 to $300 per worker from US employers,[25] should not receive any payments from workers, but interviews with H-2A workers after they return to Mexico find that most paid recruitment fees (Centro de los Derechos del Migrante 2020).[26] When H-2A workers enter the United States, they are asked by CBP officers if they paid recruitment fees, but they are coached to say no to avoid being refused entry. Once in the United States, H-2A workers may tell their US employers that they paid no fees to avoid being blacklisted by the Mexican recruiters who offered them jobs, or say that they paid recruitment fees in the hopes that the employer will reimburse them (Hernández-León 2020).[27]

Recruitment costs should fall with experience, as returning workers learn that they do not have to pay recruitment fees and inform friends and relatives of the no-fee rule. Most employers eventually turn to network hiring, which means asking current workers to refer qualified friends and relatives.

Experienced H-2A workers are often the best recruiters, since they know what is required to perform the job and the capabilities of their friends and relatives.

H-2A and US Workers

As mentioned previously, H-2A workers are generally more productive than US workers who are performing the same job. There are many reasons, including the fact that most H-2As are younger than workers settled in the United States (in their early 30s rather than early 40s), are in the United States without their families, and often want to maximize their US earnings and remittances to families at home.

The higher productivity of H-2A workers raises a question: should employers be required to hire US workers if H-2A workers are more productive? When Elton Orchards in 1974 sought certification to hire Jamaican apple pickers, the Louisiana SWA found US workers who were willing to travel to New Hampshire and pick Elton's apples. Elton refused to hire them, arguing that experienced Jamaican guest workers would be more productive than the Louisiana workers who would be picking apples for the first time. Elton's job order did not require apple-picking experience.

The orchard won a district court injunction that allowed it to employ the experienced Jamaican guest workers in 1974. However, a court of appeals later invalidated the injunction and asserted that US workers must be hired first, concluding that "there may be good reason for appellee's [Elton Orchard's] wish to be able to rely on the experienced crews of British West Indians who have performed well in the past . . . [but such a] business justification would be to negate the policy which permeates the immigration statutes, that domestic workers rather than aliens be employed wherever possible."[28]

The Elton ruling means that if US workers can work fast enough to earn the AEWR, they must be hired even if the H-2A workers are more productive, which may mean that an employer must hire more workers to accomplish the work. However, enforcing that ruling is very difficult, since there are many factors that contribute to whether an employer considers a worker to be satisfactory.

Many commentators note that judges sometimes issue injunctions that overrule DOL denials of certification because of potential losses if farm work is not completed in a timely way. However, some of these injunctions are later overturned by appeals courts, which argue that protecting US workers is the primary goal of US immigration policy (de Lone 1992). Appeals courts have ruled that if growers are inconvenienced one year when they hire US workers, this inconvenience will encourage them to be more diligent about recruiting and training US workers for the following year, adopting labor-saving machines, or changing to crops that do not require migrant workers to fill seasonal jobs.

AEWR Minimum Wages

The H-2A program allows US employers to hire foreign workers to fill seasonal farm jobs if US workers are not available *and* if the employment of guest workers will not adversely affect US workers. Economic theory suggests that adding to the supply of labor can depress wages, so how does DOL prevent adverse effects on US farm workers?

DOL's answers are the AEWR minimum wage and prevailing wage rate systems. Prevailing wage standards to protect US farm workers were introduced in 1958, and DOL established the first AEWRs in 1962, requiring that braceros and any US farm workers employed alongside them receive at least $0.50 an hour at a time when US farm workers were not covered by federal minimum wage laws (Rural Migration News Blog 2020c). Since 1987, the AEWR minimum wage that must be paid to H-2A workers, and any similar US workers employed by the same employer, has almost always been the average hourly earnings of nonsupervisory crop and livestock workers reported by employers to USDA's Farm Labor Survey (FLS) for the prior year.[29] Figure 6.6 shows that AEWRs ranged from less than $14 to over $18 an hour in 2023.

The AEWR is controversial. Employers complain that the AEWR is too high and ratchets upward each year because it is the mean rather than the median hourly earnings of all types of field and livestock workers, including skilled equipment operators. When designing its wage survey a century ago, USDA recognized that there were many farm wage systems and developed a methodology that involves collecting data on total wages paid and hours worked for all types of workers on a farm, so USDA divides total wages by hours worked during the week that includes the 12th of the month to calculate average hourly earnings.[30]

Figure 6.7 shows that the hourly earnings of nonsupervisory farm workers have been rising faster than the earnings of nonsupervisory nonfarm workers

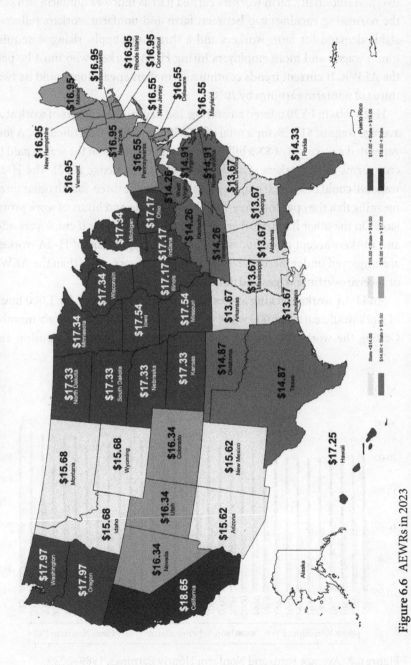

FY 2023 Adverse Effect Wage Rates

$16.95 Maine
$16.95 New Hampshire
$16.95 Vermont
$16.95 Massachusetts
$16.95 Rhode Island
$16.95 Connecticut
$16.55 New York
$16.55 New Jersey
$16.55 Pennsylvania
$16.55 Delaware
$16.55 Maryland
$14.91 West Virginia
$14.91 Virginia
$14.91 North Carolina
$13.67 South Carolina
$13.67 Georgia
$13.67 Alabama
$13.67 Mississippi
$13.67 Louisiana
$13.67 Arkansas
$14.26 Tennessee
$14.26 Kentucky
$14.26 Indiana
$14.26 Ohio
$17.17 Ohio
$17.34 Michigan
$17.34 Wisconsin
$17.17 Illinois
$17.17 Indiana
$17.54 Iowa
$17.54 Missouri
$17.33 Kansas
$14.87 Oklahoma
$14.87 Texas
$14.33 Florida
$17.17 Minnesota
$17.34 Minnesota
$17.33 North Dakota
$17.33 South Dakota
$17.33 Nebraska
$15.68 Montana
$15.68 Wyoming
$16.34 Colorado
$15.62 New Mexico
$15.68 Idaho
$16.34 Utah
$15.62 Arizona
$15.68 Washington
$17.97 Oregon
$16.34 Nevada
$18.65 California
$17.25 Hawaii

Alaska

Puerto Rico

Legend

	State <$14.00
	$14.00 < State > $15.00
	$15.00 < State > $16.00
	$16.00 < State > $17.00
	$17.00 < State > $18.00
	$18.00 < State

Figure 6.6 AEWRs in 2023

Source: US Department of Labor, "FY 2023 Adverse Effect Wage Rates," https://www.dol.gov/sites/dolgov/files/ETA/oflc/pdfs/AEWR-Map-2023.pdf

since 1989, to an average of almost $15 and $26 an hour in 2020, respectively. Traditionally, farm workers earned half as much as nonfarm workers; the narrowing earnings gap between farm and nonfarm workers reflects a stable demand for farm workers and a shrinking supply, rising state minimum wages, and more employers hiring H-2A workers who must be paid the AEWR. If current trends continue, farm worker earnings could be two-thirds of nonfarm earnings by 2030.

H-2A jobs in FY20 offered an average 168 days and 943 hours of work at an average wage of $13.29, for a total of $12,500, so 275,430 certified H-2A jobs generated a wage bill of $3.5 billion or about 10 percent of the wages paid by crop farms to all workers (Castillo, Martin, and Rutledge 2022). The H-2A wage bill could be lower if employers satisfy only the three-fourths guarantee, meaning that they pay for three-fourths of the days and hours of work promised. On the other hand, worker earnings could be higher if employers offer and workers accept more hours of work or if a high share of H-2A workers are employed under piece rate wage systems and earn more than the AEWR or receive overtime wages and bonuses.

An H-2A worker picking apples and earning $16 an hour for 1,000 hours of work would earn $16,000 while in the United States for five to six months. Getting the worker to the US farm may cost $600, and US housing and

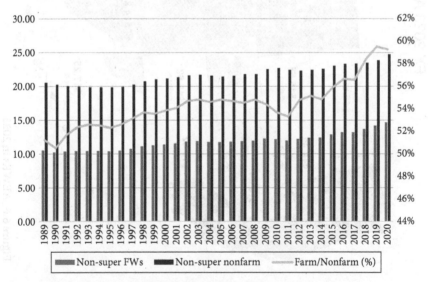

Figure 6.7 Average Farm and Nonfarm Hourly Earnings, 1989–2020
Source: US Department of Agriculture, US Department of Labor

transport costs of $13 a day for 150 days add $1,950, to make nonwage costs $2,550, equivalent to $2.55 an hour. Employers do not pay social security or federal unemployment insurance taxes on the wages of H-2A workers, saving them about 8 percent on payroll taxes, or $1,280 for a worker with $16,000 in earnings.[31] US workers paid the same $16 an hour but not provided with housing and other benefits cost $17.92 an hour when adding employer-paid social security and unemployment insurance taxes.

Employers assert that they would hire US workers if they were available, to save money. Worker advocates, on the other hand, point to the labor insurance provided by H-2A workers, who must leave the United States if they lose their jobs. Advocates note that instead of protecting US workers, AEWRs can put a ceiling on farm wages. A US worker who may be willing to work in a high-cost-of-living area such as Napa for $25 an hour, but not for the $18 AEWR, can be rejected as unavailable, since US employers must hire only US workers willing to accept the AEWR.

There is now one AEWR per state or multistate region that covers all farm workers, from apple pickers to truck drivers. DOL in 2023 issued regulations to "establish separate AEWRs by agricultural occupation to better protect against adverse effect on the wages of similarly employed workers in the US." Instead of the current system of one AEWR for all farm jobs in a state, there will be 5 to 10 AEWRs per state, each reflecting the wage for a particular job title (Rural Migration News Blog 2023).

Determining the AEWR for a particular job title or occupation begins with the employer's job offer that specifies the work to be done, including any experience requirements. SWAs review these employer job descriptions and assign a job title or Standard Occupation Classification (SOC) such as 45-2092, which covers farmworkers and crop, nursery, and greenhouse workers. Once the SOC of the job is determined, DOL looks first to the USDA Farm Labor Survey for an AEWR, and if the FLS has an hourly wage for that occupation, the FLS average becomes the AEWR.

If the FLS does not have an hourly wage for a particular SOC occupation, DOL will use the Occupational Employment and Wage Statistics database to find the appropriate AEWR.[32] The OEWS surveys almost 200,000 nonfarm firms twice a year to obtain employment and wage data, and uses three years or six surveys with data from 1.2 million establishments to generate wage and employment estimates for 800 occupations. The data are published for all states and for metro and nonmetro areas, making the OEWS one of the most comprehensive US wage surveys.

The OEWS generates mean and median wages as well as wages at the 25th and 75th percentiles of the wage distribution to distinguish the wages of entry-level from experienced workers. For the estimated 43,000 California crop workers (SOC 45-2092) in May 2021, the hourly mean OEWS wage ranged from less than $15 in the San Joaquin Valley to $18 or more in Napa and Sonoma. Median wages were lower, since the state's minimum wage of $14 in 2021 puts a floor under wages, while higher wages for supervisors and equipment operators pull up mean wages. The 25th-percentile wage for entry-level California crop workers ranged from $14 to $17 an hour, while the 75th-percentile wage for experienced workers ranged from $14 to $19. The OEWS does not collect data from farms, only from firms that provide services to farms, such as farm labor contractors.

AEWRs have long been a political football because they transfer money between farm employers and workers.[33] USDA cancelled the FLS in fall 2020, prompting DOL to respond with a regulation to freeze AEWRs for most field and livestock occupations at their 2020 levels until 2023, after which AEWRs were to be adjusted according to changes in DOL's Employment Cost Index (ECI) for private wage and salary nonfarm workers. AEWRs for other agricultural occupations, such as supervisor and equipment operator, would be set using the mean statewide OEWS wage.

Worker advocates sued, and a federal judge ordered USDA to resume the farm labor survey and DOL to use the FLS to set AEWRs. After DOL implemented the AEWR-by-job-title system, farm employers sued, arguing that the AEWRs for some job titles such as construction workers who build farm buildings or truck drivers who transport produce over public roads to processing facilities could double. Farm employers also tried to block DOL's specification that a worker who performs two or more jobs in one day, such as driving a crew of workers to the fields and then working alongside the crew, should be paid the highest AEWR for all hours worked that day (so, for example, the van driver would be paid a higher wage than the other farm workers).

As we have seen, AEWRs were developed in the late 1950s amid concern about the wage-depressing effects of braceros. Since 1987, AEWRs have almost always been set on the basis of USDA's FLS of farm employers and resulted in one AEWR per state. The changes made in 2023 to set AEWRs by job title or occupation mean more AEWRs and more databases used to set them. Farm employers want to eliminate AEWRs, arguing that DOL must first prove that the presence of H-2A workers adversely affects US workers, while worker advocates counter that the AEWR fails to protect US farm workers. Despite over a half century of efforts to protect US farm workers from any adverse effects of guest workers, controversy over AEWRs appears destined to continue.

PWRs and Productivity Standards

Employers must offer and pay the higher of the AEWR or the prevailing wage for the job in the commodity and area of employment. This means that if the statewide AEWR is $18 an hour, an employer may have to pay the prevailing wage of $20 an hour in a high-cost area such as Napa or guarantee the hourly AEWR *and* offer the prevailing piece rate of at least $30 a bin to pick Gala apples.

Prevailing wages raise the iron-triangle issue: the relationship between the AEWR, the employer-set piece rate, and the resulting productivity standard.[34] Many commodities are harvested for piece rate wages, meaning that workers are guaranteed an AEWR of $15 an hour but have an incentive to work fast without close supervision because a piece rate of $30 per bin of apples picked can enable them to earn more than $15 an hour. Piece rates are set by employers to enable the average worker to earn more than the minimum wage, and that the average hourly earnings of piece rate workers usually exceed the minimum wage. For example, a worker who picks six bins of apples in an eight-hour day at $30 a bin would earn $180 or $22.50 an hour.

Suppose the minimum wage increases by 10 percent to $16.50. If the piece rate remains $30 a bin, a worker who picks six bins would still earn $180 or $22.50 an hour, but the worker would have less incentive to work fast because his piece rate earnings now generate a smaller premium above the AEWR. If the AEWR continues to rise and the piece rate is unchanged, workers must work harder to earn more than the AEWR.

Employers do not have to retain workers who are unable to earn the AEWR at the employer-specified piece rate, so rising AEWRs and stable piece rates can raise productivity standards[35] and change the composition of the workforce by eliminating slower workers, who may be disproportionately US workers. This is what occurred in the Florida sugarcane industry, where employers did not raise what they called the task rate as the AEWR rose, instead requiring workers to work faster to accomplish the task they were assigned (Martin 2009, ch. 5).

Sugarcane is a perennial grass native to Asia that can grow to a height of 8 to 12 feet in tropical and semitropical environments. Almost half of US sugar is from cane and more than half is from sugar beets,[36] whose harvest was mechanized in the 1960s. Sugar beet production is concentrated in northern states such as the Red River Valley in North Dakota, while sugarcane production is in southern states. Florida produces over half of the US sugar from cane (over 2 million tons a year), Louisiana over 40 percent, and Texas the rest.

Green cane is cut into short segments and planted in the fall. The first harvest a year later is the plant-cane crop, the second-year harvest is called the first ratoon or first stubble, and the third-year harvest is the second ratoon or second stubble. The sugar is in the cane's stalk, which is 80 percent water, and the percentage of sugar is greatest at the bottom of the stalk, so cane is cut close to ("three fingers" from) the ground. Cane deteriorates rapidly after harvest, so mills must be close to the fields so that they can grind the stalks and extract the juice.[37]

Florida's sugarcane was cut by hand by Jamaican H-2A workers under a task or piece rate system. The mills estimated the tonnage of cane in each field and set a task rate that required a worker to cut 100 to 200 feet of cane in two adjoining rows (a cut row) in one hour. The minimum feet-per-hour requirement or productivity standard reflected the field's yield and other factors such as how much of the cane was bent rather than straight. Workers had to "make the task" by cutting at least the specified number of feet in an hour or they could be "checked out" for being too slow.

Beginning between 6:00 and 7:00 in the morning, workers cut cane from two adjoining rows and threw the cut cane stalks left or right into a "pile row" that was shared with the worker in the next cut row, making it easier for machines to pick up the harvested cane. Ticket writers, who were former cane cutters, recorded each worker's start and stop times and the number of feet cut on tickets that were distributed at the end of each day to workers as in Figure 6.8. Workers typically cut 1.3 to 1.5 tons an hour or up to 9 tons in a six-hour workday.

Lead men (supervisors) monitored the quality of the cutting and enforced the task rate system by checking out slower cutters, who had to sit on the bus until the rest of the crew stopped cutting cane; Figure 6.9 shows a checkout ticket. After three checkouts, workers could be fired and returned to Jamaica. Most checkouts occurred at the beginning of the season, and many involved cutters who cut more than 1 ton of cane an hour but less than the 1.3 to 1.5 tons per hour expected by the mills.

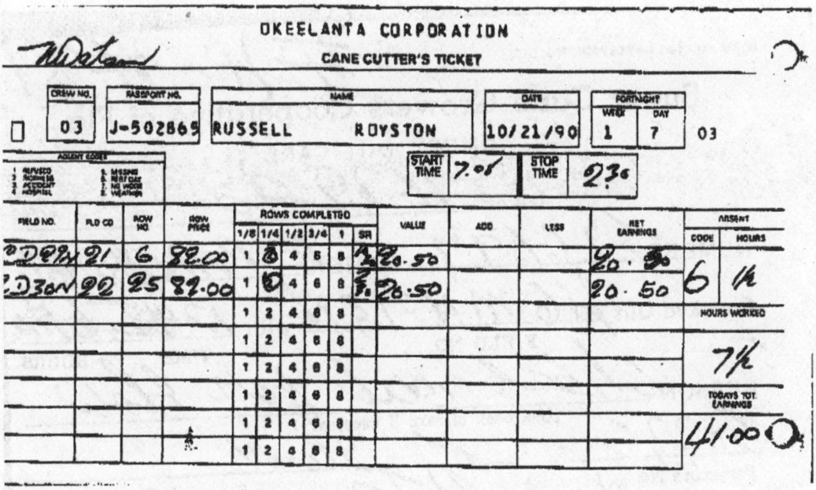

OKEELANTA CORPORATION

CANE CUTTER'S TICKET

CREW NO.	PASSPORT NO.	NAME	DATE	FORTNIGHT WEEK	FORTNIGHT DAY	
03	J-502865	RUSSELL ROYSTON	10/21/90	1	7	03

START TIME 7.05 STOP TIME 2.30

FIELD NO.	FLD CD	ROW NO.	ROW PRICE	ROWS COMPLETED 1/8	1/4	1/2	3/4	1	SR	VALUE	ADD	LESS	NET EARNINGS
	21	6	82.00	1	2	4	6	8		20.50			20.50
	22	25	82.00	1	2	4	6	8		20.50			20.50
				1	2	4	6	8					
				1	2	4	6	8					
				1	2	4	6	8					
				1	2	4	6	8					
				1	2	4	6	8					
				1	2	4	6	8					

ABSENT CODE 6 HOURS 1/2

HOURS WORKED 7 1/2

TODAYS TOT. EARNINGS 41.00

Figure 6.8 Cane Cutters Received Tickets with Their Daily Earnings
Source: Okeelanta Corp.

An acre yielding 40 tons of sugar cane has about 40,000 stalks that weigh two pounds each. The mills estimated cane yields accurately and set task rates that required workers to cut up to 1.5 tons an hour, three times the typical 0.5-tons-an-hour cutting rate in Jamaica.[38] There are 43,560 square feet in an acre,[39] and since the cane was planted in rows five feet apart, a field yielding 43.56 tons an acre has 1 ton of cane in every 100 feet of two adjacent rows (the cut row), which covers 1,000 square feet. Setting a task rate of 150 feet an hour is equivalent to setting a productivity standard of 1.5 tons an hour, since cutting 150 feet of cane in two adjoining rows means cutting 1 ton of cane. Most sugar cane fields were about 25 acres and were harvested by crews of 50 to 100 workers. Mills typically ground 20,000 to 30,000 tons of cane a day, so 1,700 workers who each cut 1.5 tons an hour or 12 tons an eight-hour day could supply a 20,000-ton mill.

The cane cut by each worker was not weighed, so the mills argued that the task rate system did not satisfy DOL's definition of a piece rate wage, which defines piece rate wage systems as those that measure or weigh the work done by each worker. This means that DOL did not require the mills to reduce the task rate or productivity standard as the AEWR rose; as a result, the productivity standard or the average tons of cane that workers had to cut could increase over time. The AEWR was $5.30 an hour in the late 1980s, meaning

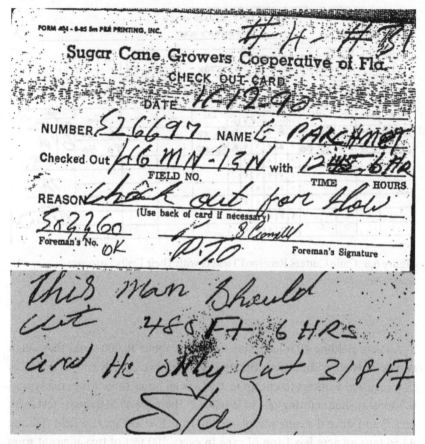

Figure 6.9 Slower Cane Cutters Could Be "Checked Out" and Fired
Source: Okeelanta Corp.

that all cane cutters earned at least $5.30 an hour and faster cutters earned between $5.50 and $6 an hour.

The sugar mills were required to advertise for US workers, and their job orders included the statement that "a worker would be expected to cut an average of eight (8) tons of harvest cane per day throughout the season." Workers who failed on three days to cut fast enough to "make the task" were checked out each day and could be terminated.

Class-action suits were filed on behalf of cane cutters that combined two statements to conclude that cane cutters should be paid $5.30 per ton of cane cut. The AEWR was $5.30 an hour, and if a satisfactory worker cut 8 tons in an eight-hour day or 1 ton an hour, then the productivity standard was 1 ton an hour. The mills budgeted $3.75 a ton for hand harvesting because they expected cutters to average 1.5 tons an hour, saving $1.55 a ton at the expense of worker wages, according to worker advocates. A Florida state judge agreed with the workers and in August 1992 ordered the sugar mills to pay each cutter $1,000 to $1,500 in back wages for at least three years, for a total of $100 million in back wages and interest.

The largest mill, US Sugar, responded with a "Labor Peace" program that acknowledged that the task rate was a piece rate wage system, paid $5.6 million to workers and their lawyers, and promised to pay cutters a piece rate of $5.10 per net ton, similar to the $5.30 per gross ton demanded by advocates. US Sugar set a minimum productivity standard that required cutters to average at least 1 ton of cane an hour.

The other sugar mills appealed the judge's ruling. During jury trials in the mid-1990s, worker attorneys argued that the combination of the $5.30 AEWR and the 1-ton-per-hour productivity standard created a piece rate of $5.30 a ton. Attorneys for the remaining sugar mills made three major counterarguments. First, they cited DOL to emphasize that task rates are not piece rates because the output of each worker was not measured or weighed. Second, Jamaican cutters testified that their work assignments were made in feet, not tons, so they worked for task rate wages, not piece rate wages. Third, the mills did not pay always pay $3.75 a ton. They adjusted the task rate from field to field, paying slightly more in fields with recumbent or flattened cane and slightly less when the cane was straight and easier to cut.

Juries in cases involving the Atlantic, Okeelanta, and Sugar Cane Growers Cooperative mills agreed with the mills, and their former cutters did not collect any back wages.[40] The juries were persuaded that H-2A workers were guaranteed only the AEWR of $5.30 an hour, and since they received at least $5.30 an hour, no back wages were owed. The major effect of the litigation was harvest mechanization: all of Florida's sugarcane was hand-harvested in 1990, and all was harvested by machine after the mid-1990s.

This sugarcane experience holds three major lessons for managing migrant farm worker programs.[41] First, the task rate system gave employers extreme control over workers, some of whom had gone into debt to obtain H-2A visas. Workers did not know exactly how many tons per hour they had to cut to keep their jobs, but checking out slower workers mean that remaining cutters were motivated to work hard as soon as they arrived in Florida. By checking out or sending home 50 to 75 of the 10,000 workers early in the season, the number of cutters required was reduced, saving the mills more than the cost of returning slower workers to Jamaica.

Second, the mills argued that they needed hand cutters because the harvesting machines used in other US states and industrial countries would bog down in Florida's muck soils. After the 1992 ruling, Florida mills discovered that balloon tires and adjustments to the machines so they did not pull plants out of the ground made harvesting on muck soils feasible. As with processing tomatoes near the end of the bracero program in the early 1960s, arguments that hand harvesting with migrant workers was necessary proved to be wrong.

Third, decades of reliance on guest workers resulted in poor "sugar cities" such as Belle Glade and Pahokee on the southern shores of Lake Okeechobee. Most residents of the sugar cities are US citizens, some of whom cut sugar cane in the past but were pushed out of cane cutting as they aged by the task rate system. The *Palm Beach Post* on December 11, 2005, demanded that the Fanjul family, immigrants from Cuba and major beneficiaries of US sugar and labor migration policies, contribute to improving life in these sugar cities.[42]

Was there an alternative to worker suits alleging that task rates were piece rates? H-2A regulations allow SWAs to conduct prevailing wage rate surveys (PWRs). If such surveys had been conducted, DOL would have had to decide whether the piece rate was $3.75 or $5.30 a ton and whether the productivity standard to be an acceptable worker was 1 ton an hour or more. The PWR system aims to provide prevailing wage and practice labor market data so that US workers within a diverse state are not adversely affected by a single statewide AEWR.

Most SWAs do not receive enough funding from DOL to accomplish their primary tasks under the H-2A system—that is, review employer job offers and inspect farm worker housing. This means that few PWR surveys are conducted and posted on DOL's Agricultural Online Wage Library,[43] leaving the AEWR as the major protection for US workers. The absence of PWRs can allow a recurrence of what happened in Florida sugarcane, when rising productivity standards squeeze out US workers.

The methodology for conducting PWRs is laid out in DOL's Handbook 385, which requires SWAs to survey the employers of at least 15 percent of total employment in a particular commodity, task, and area. There are no reliable data on the number of employers or average or peak employment to pick Gala apples in Yakima, Washington, and SWAs used a variety of mail, telephone, and internet strategies to collect data from employers. Many employers do not respond, and it is often hard for an SWA to determine the reliability of the employer-reported data, especially as employers realize that reporting higher piece rates may mean being required to pay them, which prompted some associations to recommend that employers report only the AEWR guaranteed hourly wage, not a piece rate.[44]

DOL revised its PWR methodology in 2022, abandoning the Handbook 385 methodology to allow SWAs to use any methodology that can be explained to determine the prevailing wage of the "largest number of US workers" who perform a particular task in a particular crop and area, such as harvesting summer strawberries in Monterey County. DOL expects SWAs to include data from at least five employers (or all employers if fewer than five), with no single employer accounting for more than 25 percent of sample employment. These sample employers must employ at least 30 US workers, defined as employees who satisfied I-9 requirements when hired.[45] DOL reviews the SWA submissions, and if they are accepted and published they remain valid for one year, after which the AEWR becomes the wage that prevents adverse effects on US workers.

The new DOL regulations are unlikely to lead to more prevailing wage surveys. Instead of providing more monies to states to conduct surveys, DOL announced that non-SWA state agencies and universities may conduct wage and employment surveys in particular commodities and areas with their own funds and submit them to SWAs for review before the SWAs submit the results to DOL. After another review, DOL will publish acceptable surveys in its online wage library and expect employers seeking certification to offer at least the published prevailing wage.

DOL downplayed the importance of PWRs in its 2022 regulations by asserting that US workers can be protected against any adverse effects of H-2A workers if DOL requires employers to pay the AEWR, which DOL says is the highest wage on 95 percent of H-2A applications. DOL asserted that it "is not obligated to establish a prevailing wage separate from the AEWR for every occupation and agricultural activity in every state," which is a goal of some worker advocates in order to prevent rising productivity standards from squeezing US workers out of the farm workforce. DOL ignored what could happen if AEWRs rise, piece rates remain stable, and productivity standards rise—workers must work harder and faster to earn the higher AEWR, making it harder for older US workers and women to be considered acceptable workers.

The likely outcome of the new DOL regulations is a variety of surveys and disputes over their validity. Some SWAs may submit prevailing wages for very narrowly defined tasks and areas, such as the first harvest of a small-acreage fruit or vegetable in a particular county, while others may add questions to existing statewide surveys and generate statewide PWRs, prompting disputes over wage differences within a state that reflect the relative supply and demand of US workers and cost-of-living differences. Grower or worker groups could sponsor surveys conducted by universities, raising questions about whether the source of funding influenced the survey results. In sum, the prevailing wage issue is likely to become more rather than less contentious as the H-2A program expands.

Immigration Reform and Agriculture

The United States has struggled to determine the appropriate roles of foreign workers in US agriculture. The bracero programs of 1917 to 1921 and 1942 to 1964 are more often seen as examples of government failure to protect foreign and US workers than successes. Many books and articles emphasize that many braceros worked in crops that were in surplus such as cotton, that Mexican workers were taken advantage of in both Mexico and the United States, and that Mexican Americans who had to compete with braceros in the fields but not in cities moved to Los Angeles and San Jose in the 1950s.

IRCA fundamentally changed the US farm labor market (Martin 1994). The Special Agricultural Worker (SAW) program allowed 1.1 million mostly Mexican men to become legal immigrants after documenting at least 90 days of farm work in 1985–86. Most of the unauthorized foreigners who were legalized under the SAW program did not do the requisite farm work, resulting in "one of the most extensive immigration frauds ever perpetrated against the United States government."[46] This fraud was made possible by SAW regulations that required the Immigration and Naturalization Service (INS), once an applicant submitted documentation of farm work (including a one-sentence letter from a labor contractor that said something like "Juan Martinez picked tomatoes for 92 days in the Stockton area in summer 1985"), to prove that the worker-provided documentation was false. INS was unable to root out fraud among SAW applicants, leading to one INS estimate that 70 percent of SAW applications were fraudulent.[47]

Most newly legalized SAWs, including those who had not done farm work, soon found nonfarm jobs away from California and the Southwest, where unauthorized foreigners were concentrated before IRCA. The SAW program legalized only workers, not family members who remained in Mexico, so unauthorized Mexicans continued to arrive in the 1990s to join now-legal relatives in the Midwest and Southeast. IRCA diffused legal and unauthorized Mexicans from California and the Southwest throughout the United States and from agriculture to construction, meatpacking, and many service jobs (CAW 1992).

The H-2A program did not expand as expected because unauthorized workers were readily available. Instead of arranging housing for H-2A workers and paying an AEWR, farm employers could hire unauthorized workers who paid their own way to the United States and found their own housing. According to National Agricultural Worker Survey data, over the past three decades the unauthorized share of US crop workers doubled from less than 25 percent in California to 50 percent throughout the United States by the mid-1990s and has remained at this level since (Martin, Mines, and Diaz 1985).

Farmers acknowledged that half of their workers were unauthorized and encouraged Congress to approve an alternative to the H-2A program to provide guest workers in a more flexible and less costly manner. For example, the House Agriculture Committee in March 1996 approved a bill by Representative Richard Pombo (R-CA) that would have granted temporary work visas to 250,000 foreign farm workers at a time when DOL certified 17,000 jobs to be filled by H-2A workers, "to provide a less bureaucratic alternative for the admission of temporary agricultural workers."[48] Under Pombo's proposed legislation, guest workers would have been expected to find their own housing and "float" from farm to farm as needed. To encourage them to leave the United States when they could not find farm jobs, the US employers of these guest workers were to withhold 25 percent of worker wages and forward them to a US government agency, which would return the withheld wages to the guest workers in their home countries.

Congress did not approve the Pombo bill and other alternative H-2A guest worker programs for several reasons, including opposition from Republicans such as Senator Alan Simpson (R-WY), the guiding force in the Senate behind IRCA, and Democrats such as Representative Romano Mazzoli (D-KY), IRCA's advocate in the House. The bipartisan Commission on Immigration Reform, chaired by former representative Barbara Jordan

(D-TX), issued a statement in June 1995 concluding that "a large scale agricultural guest worker program . . . is not in the national interest" and that "such a program would be a grievous mistake." President Bill Clinton added: "I oppose efforts in the Congress to institute a new guestworker or 'bracero' program that seeks to bring thousands of foreign workers into the United States to provide temporary farm labor" and threatened to veto any such bill approved by Congress.

Despite Clinton's opposition, the Senate approved the Agricultural Job Opportunity Benefits and Security Act, or AgJOBS (S 2337), by a 68–31 vote in July 1998.[49] This first version of AgJOBS would have required DOL to maintain registries of legal US workers seeking farm jobs in farming areas, with DOL and INS cooperating to ensure that the workers seeking to be registered were authorized to work in the United States. Farmers would request workers from the registry, and if too few were available to fill all of their jobs, they would be certified by DOL to recruit guest workers to fill the remaining jobs. AgJOBS guest workers would have received renewable 10-month visas from INS to enter the United States, and employers would have paid federal social security taxes on AgJOBS worker wages into a separate fund to cover costs incurred by DOL and INS to administer the program.

There was no cap on the number of AgJOBS workers, but if the attorney general found that a significant number of AgJOBS workers stayed in the United States, 20 percent of guest worker wages could have been retained and repaid at a US consulate in the country of origin when the worker surrendered a visa/ID that included a photo and biometric information. In a bid to win support from worker advocates, AgJOBS workers who did at least six months of farm work in each of four consecutive calendar years could apply for immigrant visas. The major proponent of AgJOBS, Senator Larry Craig (R-ID), said that it would provide farmers with a "stable, predictable, legal work force that would receive good, fair, market-based compensation."[50]

Worker advocates opposed this first version of AgJOBS, arguing that it did not require farmers to truly search for US workers before being certified to employ guest workers, that it eliminated the AEWR that protected US and foreign workers, and that farmers no longer had to provide free housing to low-skilled guest workers. AgJOBS introduced the concept of a housing allowance. If a state's governor certified that there was sufficient farm worker housing in an area, AgJOBS would have allowed farmers to offer each guest worker a housing allowance equivalent to "the statewide average fair market rental for existing housing for nonmetropolitan counties for the State . . . based on a two-bedroom dwelling unit and an assumption of two persons per bedroom," that is, one-fourth of the rent of a two-bedroom apartment or perhaps $150 to $300 a month.[51]

AgJOBS was not enacted while Clinton was president, but the election of Mexican president Vincente Fox and US president George W. Bush in 2000 prompted worker advocates to negotiate a revised version AgJOBS with growers. This revised AgJOBS repeated the agricultural grand bargain at the heart of IRCA, which was to legalize unauthorized farm workers and make it easier for farmers to employ guest workers.

The advocate-grower AgJOBS compromise, introduced in 2003 by Senators Larry Craig (R-ID) and Edward Kennedy (D-MA), would have allowed unauthorized farm workers who did at least 100 days of farm work during a 12-month period in 2002–3 to become provisional legal farm workers. If these provisional workers did at least 360 days of farm work during the next six years, they could become immigrants. Spouses and minor children of provisional farm workers in the United States would not be deportable, but they could not get work visas or social safety net benefits. However, spouses and children could become immigrants when their farm worker spouse qualified for an immigrant visa by continuing to do farm work.[52]

The Craig-Kennedy AgJOBS bill would have made the H-2A program more employer friendly by ending the DOL-supervised recruitment of US workers; instead, farm employers would attest that they needed guest workers to fill farm jobs. If no local workers responded to their attestations, the employer would be certified to recruit and employ the number of H-2A workers requested in the attestation, and provided these workers with free housing or a housing allowance. The AEWR would have been frozen and studied.

The AgJOBS bill went through several more revisions but always maintained the compromise of legalization for unauthorized farm workers and easier access to legal guest workers for employers. AgJOBS was included in the comprehensive immigration reform bill approved by the Senate in 2006. Senator Dianne Feinstein (D-CA) became the AgJOBS champion in 2009, changing provisional legal status to blue card status and arguing that there was an "emergency . . . caused by the absence of farm labor" after farmers "have tried and tried and tried" to recruit US workers but found few "who are willing to take the job in a hot field, doing backbreaking labor, in temperatures that often exceed 100 degrees."[53]

The UFW and most farm organizations supported AgJOBS, but immigration reformers who feared that enacting only AgJOBS would foreclose the possibility of comprehensive immigration reforms blocked incremental or piecemeal immigration reforms. Immigration advocates argued that comprehensive immigration reforms were the only way to legalize most of the unauthorized foreigners in the United States, and they persuaded the House Hispanic Caucus to block incremental changes to immigration law such as AgJOBS.

The failure of comprehensive immigration reforms in 2006 and 2013 injected a new realism into proponents of immigration reform. Advocates who had previously held out for the "whole enchilada" of legalization for all unauthorized foreigners, expanded guest worker programs, funding for more border and interior enforcement, and development to tackle the root causes of unwanted migration reluctantly accepted incremental or piecemeal reforms.

Admissionists who want to legalize unauthorized foreigners in the United States and increase legal immigration into the United States now see the most realistic path to congressional action as incremental legislation to legalize unauthorized foreigners who were brought to the United States as children (so-called DACA recipients or Dreamers) and some version of AgJOBS to legalize unauthorized farm workers and make it easier to admit farm guest workers. Restrictionists who want to reduce legal immigration and reduce and prevent unauthorized migration want more funding for border and interior enforcement, a requirement that all employers use E-Verify to check the legal status of newly hired workers, and reduced access to asylum for foreigners who cross the Mexico-US border illegally.

The current farm labor admissionist-restrictionist compromise is the Farm Workforce Modernization Act (FWMA), which was approved by the House in December 2019 and again in March 2021 with support from most Democrats and some Republicans. The FWMA, which was re-introduced in the House in June 2023, would legalize unauthorized farm workers, make it easier to employ H-2A workers, and require farm employers to use E-Verify.[54]

FWMA's legalization program would allow unauthorized foreigners who did at least 180 days of farm work over two years to become certified agricultural workers (CAWs), who must continue to do at least 100 days of US farm work a year to maintain their status. The spouses and minor children of CAWs could receive work and residence visas and work in any industry or attend US schools. After a CAW completed four to eight more years of farm work, the CAW and his or her family members could receive immigrant visas,[55] leading to the legalization of perhaps 800,000 unauthorized farm workers and 1.5 million to 2 million family members.

FWMA's easing of access to guest workers would begin with three-year H-2A visas, rather than the current typical maximum 10-month visa, and allow up to 20,000 H-2A workers a year to be employed in year-round jobs on dairies and other livestock farms, so that there could be 60,000 H-2A workers in year-round farm jobs within three years. AEWRs would be set by job title, rather than having one AEWR per state, and then would be frozen for a year, after which any AEWR increases would be limited while DOL and USDA studied the need for and effects of AEWRs.

With H-2A workers allowed to remain in the United States up to three years and allowed to fill both seasonal and year-round farm jobs, farm employers could recruit guest workers further afield, such as in Central or South America or in Asia, where wages are lower than in Mexico. Switching from Mexico to other countries for farm guest workers from farther away could mark a return to the past, when Chinese and Japanese immigrants dominated the seasonal farm workforce in the western states.

Reforming the H-2A Program

The United States has about 100,000 farm employers who employ 2.5 million workers sometime during a typical year. About 2 million or 80 percent of these hired crop workers were born in Mexico, including 1.7 million who have settled in the United States and 300,000 who have H-2A visas (Rural Migration News 2020b). The settled Mexican-born farm workforce is shrinking as the number of H-2A workers rises, putting the United States on track for perhaps 1.5 million settled workers and 500,000 H-2A workers by 2025. Some 10,000 or 10 percent of US farm employers have H-2A guest workers, and the H-2A share of the seasonal crop workforce is likely to rise from 15 percent to 25 percent of average employment on US crop farms.

Three H-2A changes could benefit employers and workers in the absence of immigration reforms: ABC ratings, the return of experienced crews, and fewer and larger H-2A recruiters. First, DOL could create an ABC rating system (something like the Transportation Security Administration's

PreCheck system) that allows A-rated employers to self-certify their need for H-2A workers and the adequacy of their housing. H-2A workers returning to A-rated employers could receive multiyear visas that allow them to skip the US consulate and travel directly to their US employer. When these H-2A workers arrive in the United States, CBP agents can confirm with their US employer the validity of the contract sent by the employer to the worker, to reduce the likelihood that smugglers would try to send workers with fake contracts to the United States.

Second, many H-2A workers are employed in crews that work separately from US crews on the same farms, making H-2A crews analogous to miners and oil field workers who live in one place and travel to remote areas to perform their jobs, such as those employed in oil fields of Alaska's North Slope. H-2A crews can be considered part of the FIFO (fly in, fly out) labor system, arriving with the requisite skills and supervisors and ready to work with little or no on-site training, which minimizes the number of workers required to perform the work. FIFO mining and oil workers often work three-weeks-on followed by three-weeks off. Crews of experienced seasonal H-2A workers could similarly be permitted to work long hours during several months of US employment.

Third, DOL should consider requiring small employers who seek only a few H-2A workers to use approved entities such as associations or large FLCs to obtain H-2A workers. DOL cannot monitor the 10,000-plus unique farm employers who file 18,000 applications for H-2A workers each year, most seeking fewer than 20 workers. None of the agencies that monitor the H-2A program can extirpate the fraud that occurs when small employers describe farm jobs but employ H-2A workers in nonfarm jobs, fail to pay H-2A workers the AEWR, house workers under poor conditions, or make unlawful deductions from worker wages.

If DOL required employers seeking fewer than 10 or 20 H-2A workers to apply via larger entities that have reputations to protect and staff to ensure that regulations are followed, the number of employers whose business model depends on violating labor laws could be reduced. Australia, New Zealand, and the United Kingdom are among the countries that vet and approve firms to recruit seasonal workers abroad and transport them to farmers. These countries have limited the number of recruitment firms to less than a dozen, which encourages approved recruiters to invest in compliance and achieve economies of scale in the recruitment and transport of migrant workers.

Trade

The Food and Agriculture Organization of the United Nations estimated that the value of the world's farm output was $5 trillion or 6 percent of the world's $80 trillion GDP in 2019. Most food and fiber is consumed within the country where it is produced, but 20 percent or $1 trillion worth of farm goods is traded between countries, making the value of farm trade about 6 percent of the $20 trillion of global trade in all goods. Russia's invasion of Ukraine in February 2022 reduced exports of sunflower oil, wheat, and other commodities, accelerating food price inflation around the world and especially in North African countries that import much of their food.

The value of the world's trade in farm goods tripled between 1995 and 2014 in nominal terms and doubled in real or inflation-adjusted terms, a period during which the world's population rose by 25 percent and world GDP rose by 75 percent (Beckman 2017). Most trade in farm goods is between industrial or developed countries, and this accounted for an average 54 percent of global farm exports between 2010 and 2014, led by Europe's 24 percent of farm exports and North America's 22 percent. Industrial countries received 58 percent of global farm imports, led by Europe's 26 percent share of farm imports.

US Fruits and Vegetables

The United States has an agricultural trade surplus, exporting farm commodities worth $143 billion in 2019 while importing farm commodities worth $131 billion, but a trade deficit in fresh fruits and vegetables. The $7 billion of fresh fruit and vegetables exported by the United States in 2019 was only a third of the $21 billion of fruit and vegetable imports. The US fruit and vegetable trade deficit is expected to increase, as exports remain stable while imports increase to $35 billion by 2029.

The United States imported 57 percent of its fresh fruit in 2019 and 32 percent of its fresh vegetables. Three-fourths of the 115 pounds of fresh fruit available to Americans each year involve seven items: 28 pounds of bananas, 17 pounds of fresh apples, and 8 pounds each of fresh avocados, grapes, oranges, pineapples, and strawberries.

Imports account for 100 percent of the bananas and pineapples available to Americans and 87 percent of the avocados. Imports are almost half of the fresh grapes available, 20 percent of the oranges, 15 percent of the strawberries, and 6 percent of fresh apples. Americans consume 25 pounds of melons a year, including 16 pounds of watermelon and 7 pounds of cantaloupe, and a third of the melons available to Americans are imported.

The Role of Mexico

As noted at the beginning of this chapter, half of US fresh fruit imports, and three-fourths of US fresh vegetable imports, are from Mexico. Mexico-US trade totaled $671 billion in 2019, when the United States exported goods and services worth $299 billion to Mexico and imported goods and services worth $372 billion from Mexico—that is, the US trade deficit with Mexico was $73 billion.

The United States has a widening farm trade deficit with Mexico because US imports from Mexico of fruits and vegetables are rising faster than US exports of grain and meat to Mexico. The US agricultural trade deficit increased in 2020 and 2021 during the COVID pandemic.

Figure 6.10 shows that the United States exported agricultural commodities to Mexico worth an average $18.5 billion between 2016 and 2018, and imported agricultural commodities from Mexico worth $24.5 billion for an agricultural trade deficit of $6 billion. The major US agricultural exports to Mexico include pork and other animal products, corn and grains, and soybeans and other oilseeds. Table 6.3 shows that agricultural imports from Mexico were dominated by fruits (led by avocados, worth $6.5 billion), vegetables (led by tomatoes, worth $6.7 billion), and beverages (led by beer, worth $3.7 billion).[56] Over the past decade, the value of US horticultural imports from Mexico tripled, from $5 billion a year to $15 billion a year, including a fivefold increase in the value of avocado imports.

Mexican and foreign investors have created modern export-oriented farms in northern and western Mexico that produce high-quality fresh produce for Americans. Table 6.4 shows that most Mexican production of cucumbers, asparagus, and broccoli is exported. Most of the avocados and tomatoes produced in Mexico are consumed in Mexico, but a rising share of Mexican production of these commodities is exported because Americans are willing to pay higher prices than Mexicans.

One reason for rising Mexican exports is the expansion of controlled environment agriculture (CEA)—greenhouses and other structures that protect

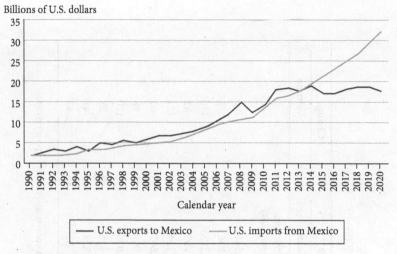

Figure 6.10 US-Mexico Agricultural Trade, 1990–2020
Source: Zahniser 2022

plants from weather and pests. Many of the tomatoes and other vegetables exported from Mexico are grown in or under CEA structures seen in Photo 6.1, which increases yields, reduces insect and weed pressures, facilitating organic production.

Table 6.5 shows that Michoacán produces three-fourths of Mexico's average 2 million metric tons of avocados each year, obtaining an average yield of 11 tons a hectare. Avocado production is expanding fastest in Jalisco, which produces a fifth of Mexico's avocados, obtains higher yields, and joined Michoacán in 2022 as a state allowed to export fresh Hass avocados to the United States.

Production of labor-intensive commodities in Mexico for local consumption and exports should continue to increase as the infrastructure improves and plants are developed for Mexican conditions. Higher Mexican interest rates and the need to import many farm inputs from the United States makes some Mexican production costs higher than in the United States, but labor costs that are a tenth of US levels enable Mexican growers to ship fresh produce to the United States at prices that are competitive with US-produced fruits and vegetables.

Mexico's major comparative advantage is climate, the ability to produce fresh fruits and vegetables when most US farmers except those in Florida are not producing. Mexico produces avocados year-round, and CEA allows

Table 6.3 The Value and Volume of Mexican Farm Exports to the United States, 2006–19

Product	2006–08		2017–19		Change	
	Value	Volume	Value	Volume	Value	Volume
	U.S. dollars (millions)	Metric tons (thousands)	U.S. dollars (millions)	Metric tons (thousands)	Percent	
Total, horticultural products	5,275	5,591	14,772	11,541	180	106
Avocados	374	188	2,287	885	512	372
Other fruit, fresh or frozen	1,214	1,564	4,357	3,283	259	110
Fruit juice	173	436	449	793	159	82
Nuts and nut preparations	177	56	734	124	314	121
Tomatoes, fresh	1,007	927	1,962	1,667	95	80
Peppers, fresh	553	493	1,089	969	97	96
Other vegetables, fresh	1,217	1,409	2,840	3,096	133	120
Vegetables, prepared or preserved	281	230	477	316	70	38
Vegetables, frozen	254	267	542	378	113	41
Pulses	23	21	33	31	45	45

Source: "Mexico-US Agricultural Trade," Rural Migration News blog, June 24, 2020, https://migration.ucdavis.edu/rmn/blog/post/?id=2436.

Table 6.4 Share of Mexican Fruits and Vegetables Destined for the United States, 2006–18

Product	2006–08	2016–18	Change	Product	2006–08	2016–18	Change
	Percent		Percentage points		Percent		Percentage points
Cucumbers	77.9	74.0	−3.9	Onions	14.5	21.9	7.3
Asparagus	95.3	60.7	−34.6	Mangoes	12.4	20.9	8.5
Broccoli	88.5	69.3	−19.1	Oranges	8.2	17.7	9.4
Strawberries	62.1	42.9	−19.2	Bananas & plantains	2.2	16.5	14.3
Tomatoes	42.4	46.9	4.5	Papayas	11.6	16.1	4.5
Lettuce	25.5	46.3	20.8	Pineapples	5.5	8.9	3.4
Watermelons	34.4	46.2	11.8	Sweet corn	4.5	5.6	1.1
Avocados	19.9	44.4	24.5	Lemons	2.7	3.1	0.4
Peppers	28.7	36.0	7.3	Apples	2.6	0.4	−2.2
Blackberries	27.7	29.6	2.0	Nopalitos	0.2	0.3	0.1

Source: "Mexico-US Agricultural Trade," *Rural Migration News* blog, June 24, 2020, https://migration.ucdavis.edu/rmn/blog/post/?id=2436.

Photo 6.1 Micro and High Tunnels Protect Tomatoes and Other Growing Plants

Source: University of California, Davis; "Mexico-US Agricultural Trade," *Rural Migration News* blog, June 24, 2020, https://migration.ucdavis.edu/rmn/blog/post/?id=2436

Table 6.5 Mexican Avocado Production by State, 2006–19

State	Annual average production		Change		Yield		Change	
	2006–08	2016–18			2006–08	2016–18		
	MT		Percent	MT	MT/HA		Percent	MT/HA
Michoacan	1,011,364	1,572,671	56	561,308	10.9	10.9	0.2	0.0
Jalisco	9,241	171,666	1,758	162,425	9.2	11.1	20.6	1.9
México	19,704	105,261	434	85,557	10.5	12.1	15.0	1.6
Nayarit	24,126	46,683	93	22,557	8.9	8.8	–0.9	–0.1
Guerrero	11,260	23,338	107	12,078	6.5	6.9	6.2	0.4
Other States	70,829	115,015	62	44,187	7.5	7.6	1.0	0.1
TOTAL	1,146,524	2,034,634	77	888,111	10.5	10.6	1.2	0.1

Source: "Mexico-US Agricultural Trade," *Rural Migration News* blog, June 24, 2020, https://migration.ucdavis.edu/rmn/blog/post/?id=2436.

Mexican farmers to extend their export seasons so that they increasingly compete with US-produced fruits and vegetables, especially in the south-eastern states.

Whither Trade?

More trade in fresh fruits and vegetables raises challenges and opportunities. The challenge for US producers is to compete with fresh produce from countries with lower labor, land, and other costs. Most US farmers produce corn and soybeans, meat, and dairy products, and they welcome the opportunity to export more of their commodities to countries such as Mexico, raising incomes there and increasing the demand for US farm commodities.

If Mexican fruit and vegetable production expands and the United States imports Mexican horticultural commodities almost year-round, will Mexico displace California as the garden state of the United States, much as California displaced New Jersey in the 1960s? Since NAFTA took effect in 1994 (and its successor, USMCA, in 2020), US imports of fresh fruits and vegetables from Mexico tripled, as did US exports of meat, corn, and soybeans to Mexico, reflecting comparative advantage at work. Mexican farmers can produce many fresh fruits and vegetables cheaper than US farmers, who can produce grains and meat cheaper than farmers in Mexico.

However, Mexican export agriculture has critics in both Mexico and the United States. Critics in Mexico emphasize that most fresh fruits and vegetables are over 90 percent water, so Mexico is exporting scarce water in the form of fresh produce. Export farms often hire migrants from poorer southern Mexican states, spurring internal migration. If water dries up or soil fertility declines, who is responsible for the migrant workers who settled in areas with export agriculture and the environmental problems they leave behind (González 2020; Gonzalez and Macias 2017)?

Proponents of export agriculture emphasize that Sinaloa vegetable farms have been exporting tomatoes and other commodities for decades, showing they are sustainable. CEA requires less water, fertilizer, and pesticides than open-field production while creating good jobs for young Mexicans with little education in areas that promise more upward mobility (Escobar, Martin, and Starbridis 2019).

US farmers have traditionally been free traders, seeing more opportunities to export farm commodities in a world of free trade rather than fearing competition from farmers abroad. The major exception is Florida's winter vegetable industry, which expanded after the United States blocked most imports from Cuba in 1962. Florida growers have been complaining about Mexican tomatoes for decades, and they periodically accuse Mexican growers of dumping fresh tomatoes in the United States at less than their cost of production, a violation of trade laws.

Florida is a political swing state, and tomato dumping charges get high-level attention, prompting investigations to determine Mexican production costs and prices. Before a final resolution, the Florida growers usually agree to suspend their dumping case if Mexican producers agree to sell tomatoes in the United States for at least a minimum or reference price. The first Mexico-US tomato suspension agreement was negotiated in 1996, and it was renegotiated in 2002, 2008, 2013, and 2018.[57] The result is that tomatoes cannot be imported from Mexico when their US price falls below the reference price, which creates a price floor for US-grown tomatoes.

Mexican President Salinas in 1990, in urging the United States to embrace what became NAFTA, asked whether the United States prefers to import Mexican tomatoes or Mexican tomato pickers.[58] Tomatoes are picked by Mexican-born workers in Canada, Mexico, and the United States, and tomatoes from each country are consumed in all three countries. Does it matter whether the tomatoes consumed in New York City are from a nearby farm or greenhouse, from California or Florida, or from Canada or Mexico? What if Mexican-born workers pick tomatoes in all three countries?

There are several new twists in Mexico-US fresh produce trade disputes. Almost all Mexican tomatoes exported to the United States are allowed to ripen on the vine before being picked, while most US tomatoes grown in open fields are picked while they are green (mature greens) and ripened with ethylene gas. Consumers prefer vine-ripened tomatoes, including cherry and other tomatoes that are packaged and sold as salad ingredients and snacks. Should trade policies treat commodities grown in open fields and in CEA structures as different items?

In some cases, biological innovations fuel trade conflicts. Blueberry plants in the past required cold-weather chilling hours to produce berries. The development of warm-weather or rabbiteye varieties allows growers in the southeastern states and Mexico to produce fresh blueberries, including during the winter months, when blueberries cannot be produced in the northern United States. The new varieties allowed the blueberry industry to expand to Florida and Georgia, prompting complaints from southeastern growers that Mexico and Peru were dumping fresh blueberries in the US market at below their production costs. Following in the footsteps of the to-mato growers, they asked the US International Trade Commission (USITC) to find that the warm-weather US blueberry industry was suffering "serious injury" due to blueberry imports.

The USITC expects an entire US commodity to support a dumping in-vestigation and remedies such as tariffs. However, the Florida and Georgia growers asked for an investigation of blueberry imports only between March and May, when their production peaks. Blueberry producers in other states opposed the Florida-Georgia request, fearing retaliation when they want to export blueberries to Mexico and other countries during the summer months. The USITC concluded that imports were not adversely affecting the US blueberry industry.

US producers of other commodities, from bell peppers to raspberries, have complained that imports from Mexico and other countries elimi-nate the high prices they expect early and late in the season. Most USITC investigations focus on costs of production in the United States and abroad and ask whether foreign producers are dumping or selling their produce in the United States at less than their cost of production. The USMCA, which replaced NAFTA in 2020, includes new chapters that require governments to enforce their labor laws and permits imports that are produced in violation of labor laws to be blocked at the border, as was done for some Mexican tomatoes in 2022.[59]

Where to Invest?

Producing fruits and vegetables requires significant investments in CEA or in multiple locations with different seasons in order to supply buyers with fresh produce year-round. Where should farmers invest to produce fresh vegetables? There are three major options: invest in machines to replace workers and in mechanical aids to raise worker productivity, invest in housing for H-2A guest workers, or produce in lower-wage areas abroad. Each option poses trade-offs. As discussed earlier in this chapter, labor-saving machines often require investments in machines that may not pay off for decades, such as planting dwarf apple trees and training the limbs to grow in vertical walls so that harvesting machines can find and pick the apples. Mechanical aids that make hand workers more productive are useful to both US and H-2A hand workers. Hydraulic platforms that can be raised and lowered by pickers eliminate the need for ladders, making fruit picking easier for women and older workers. Similarly, robots that convey harvested table grapes or strawberries to collection points allow workers to harvest faster.

The H-2A program requires employers to provide housing for H-2A and out-of-area US workers. Low-cost housing for seasonal workers is often in short supply in the areas with labor-intensive commodities, prompting many employers to rent low-end motels and replace the furniture with bunk beds to house four H-2A workers per room. Should employers who plan to rely on H-2A workers for a decade or more invest $20,000 to $30,000 a bed to build new housing?

Finally, more US farmers or buyers of fresh produce could invest in or partner with producers in lower-wage countries to produce fresh produce for Americans. Should US producers unable to mechanize and struggling to find US workers move to Mexico?

Answering these questions is most useful in the context of specific commodities in Chapter 7, but each question highlights the need to invest more. The cost of planting and harvesting the largest-acreage US crops, corn and soybeans, is less than $1,000 an acre, while the cost of planting and harvesting an acre of strawberries is $90,000 or more. Investing more in machines, aids, and housing for workers favors the few large US farm operators with access to capital, accelerating the shift toward fewer and larger growers who account for ever-larger shares of the production of particular commodities.

PART III

ALTERNATIVES TO AND PROTECTIONS FOR FARM WORKERS

Agriculture offers easy-entry seasonal jobs to low-skilled workers. It is relatively easy to learn how to pick apples or strawberries, but often hard to convince workers who have better job options to continue to harvest fruits and vegetables when year-round nonfarm jobs are available. Mechanization has been the usual response to rising farm wages and more opportunities in the nonfarm sector.

Part Three explores two issues, alternatives to US farm workers and protections for farm workers. Chapter 7 explains how farm workers help to produce the four major US-grown fresh fruits, apples, blueberries, grapes, and strawberries, and lays out the mechanization, guest worker, and import alternatives to current arrangements. Chapter 8 explains how farm workers help to produce the major hand-harvested fresh vegetables, lettuce, melons, and tomatoes, and lays out the mechanization, guest worker, and import alternatives for these commodities.

Chapter 9 reviews efforts to improve protections for farm workers. The food safety model of continuous monitoring, analysis of water purity and pesticide residues, and incremental improvement offers the most promising mechanism to ensure labor law compliance. Audits that lead to certification with a particular set of standards are akin to snapshots that can be manipulated, which argues for embracing what could be called the motion-picture model of food safety.

7

Fruit

Alternatives to US Farm Workers

American households or consumer units spend an average $12 a week on fresh fruits and vegetables.[1] Farmers receive a third of the retail price of apples and lettuce, and farm labor costs are a third of farm revenue, so a $2 pound of apples or a $2 head of lettuce generates $0.66 for farmers and $0.22 for farm workers. The choice between machines, migrants, and imports varies by commodity. Blueberry and raisin grape farms are likely to mechanize because machines are available and imports limit price increases, while apple, table grape, and strawberry farms are likely to employ more migrant guest workers until a combination of biological and engineering advances leads to mechanization in these commodities.

Machines have disadvantages compared to hand harvesters. Machines that harvest blueberries damage more of the fruit than hand harvesters, so growers must weigh lower machine harvesting costs against lower marketable yields. Many raisin grape vineyards are small and have elderly owners who do not want to invest in the new trellising systems required to harvest their grapes by machine, so they continue to rely on hand workers until they switch to almonds or an alternative mechanically harvested commodity. The premium wine grapes grown on hills in the Napa and Sonoma valleys are often hand-picked for winemakers who emphasize terroir, the idea that the wine reflects the soil and other characteristics of the place where the grapes were grown. The high prices of such wines, often more than $50 a bottle, support high wages for hand workers.

Commodities at the continued hand labor end of the spectrum include table grapes and strawberries, where there are no viable harvest machines but there are mechanical aids that increase the productivity of hand workers. Growers of table grapes and strawberries are likely to adopt harvesting aids and to employ more H-2A guest workers over the next decade.

Bracero 2.0. Philip Martin, Oxford University Press. © Oxford University Press 2024.
DOI: 10.1093/oso/9780197699973.003.0007

Apples are between the mechanization and hand labor extremes. New varieties such as Honeycrisp and Cosmic Crisp are planted on dwarf rootstocks in trellis systems, which produce apples that are easier for workers or machines to pick. The new varieties are also more valuable and bruise easily, encouraging growers to hand-harvest them to maximize pack-outs of salable fruit. Instead of workers filling bags with 50 to 60 pounds of apples from ladders that lean into tall trees, teams of six to eight workers can pick apples that grow on dwarf trees from the ground, using hydraulic platforms that can be raised and lowered and which carry bins for the apples.

Apples are the largest-acreage hand-harvested fresh fruit grown in the United States.[2] The 291,000 acres of apples require about 290 hours of hand labor per acre for pruning, thinning, netting, and harvesting, for a total of 84 million hours or the equivalent of 40,400 year-round-equivalent workers.[3] The total number of workers required to pick apples is much larger, probably 80,000 or more, because of the peak need for workers during the fall harvest. Apple harvesting machines are being developed and reliance on H-2A apple workers is increasing, but there are relatively few imports of fresh apples.

The most labor-intensive major commodity in hours per acre required is strawberries: the 50,000 US acres require 1,200 hours an acre, for a total of 49 million hours or 23,600 year-round equivalent workers. Once again, perhaps twice as many workers are employed on strawberry farms sometime during the year because of peak seasonal labor needs and worker turnover. There are several strawberry harvesting machines in development, reliance on H-2A workers is increasing, and imports of fresh strawberries from Mexico are rising.

Other fresh fruits that are hand-picked include table grapes (111,000 acres), sweet cherries (85,000 bearing acres), peaches (74,000 bearing acres), and tangerines (71,000 bearing acres). Several other fresh fruits each have about 50,000 bearing acres, including pears, grapefruit, lemons, and avocados.

Adjustments to rising labor costs vary across commodities. Citrus fruits are less perishable than many other fruits, permitting them to be harvested over weeks rather than days. The acreage of peaches and pears is shrinking as consumers switch to other tree fruits, which reduces incentives to develop harvesting machines and encourages more reliance on H-2A workers.

Several differences between commodities affect adjustments to rising costs. Apples are dispersed across many farms; the largest single apple grower accounts for less than 5 percent of US acreage. Many apple growers belong to cooperatives that fund private firms and university researchers who develop new varieties, farming practices, and machines that reduce the need for hand labor. Strawberries are similar in the sense that no single producer accounts for more than 5 percent of US acreage, but the marketing of strawberries is dominated by firms that provide growers with patented plant varieties and market the fruit. Berry marketers seek to ensure that they have berries to sell by supporting private firms and university researchers who develop new varieties of strawberries and harvesters to pick them.

Table grapes are likely to continue to be hand-picked and field-packed, but harvesting-aid robots that move lugs of harvested grape bunches from pickers to packers or packing sheds increase worker productivity. Imports of table grapes are almost half of US consumption,[4] which encourages efforts to reduce labor costs. Table 7.1 summarizes these mechanical aid and mechanization options as well as H-2A worker and import alternatives to US hand workers.

During the 2020s there are likely to be more labor-saving machines, more guest workers, and more imports of fresh fruits and vegetables. The exact mix of machines, migrant guest workers, and imports in each commodity is influenced by factors that include migration and trade policies, biological and engineering breakthroughs, marketing strategies, and consumer attitudes toward machine-harvested commodities.

Apples

Apples are the most valuable US-grown fruit, worth $3.6 billion a year. Americans had an average 45 pounds of apples available per capita in 2018, including 17 pounds available to eat fresh and 22 pounds available as apple juice and other products. By comparison, Americans consume 28 pounds of fresh bananas a year and 8 pounds each of fresh grapes, oranges, and avocados.

China produces half of the world's apples, followed by the United States, Poland, Italy, and France. US apple acreage is shrinking and yields are rising as new varieties planted in high-density orchards replace traditional Red and Golden Delicious. Modern apple orchards look like vineyards, with branches trained to grow horizontally along wires.

Table 7.1 Fruit: Mechanization, Migrants, and Imports

Commodity	Trends	Machines	H-2A Labor	Imports
Apples: *short term*, harvest aid platforms and H-2As; *long-term*, better harvest aids and mechanization, with machine pickers	Dwarf trees and fruiting walls require more investment but make harvesting easier; higher-value varieties need careful picking	Harvest aid platforms make hand pickers more productive; use of scout-and-pick machines rather than shake-and-catch for high-value apples	Rapid growth in Washington state; East Coast states have depended on H-2As for apple harvesting since the 1950s	6% of fresh apples and 85% of apple juice are imported; United States is a net exporter of fresh apples
Blueberries: *short term*, more shake-and-catch machines, H-2A workers for first fresh harvest; *long-term*, machines and imports	Acreage expanding in the United States and abroad, especially of low- or no-chill varieties; US consumption is over 2 pounds per person per year	Once-over shake-and-catch machines require careful planting and cane management; $0.30/pound cost does not rise with yield	Growing use of H-2As in CA, FL, GA, MI, NJ, NC, OR, and WA; cost of $0.50+ a pound for hand picking; processing berries are often machine-picked	60% of fresh blueberries are imported, most during winter months; 20% of US fresh blueberries are exported
Raisin grapes: *short term*, early-maturing DOV varieties are machine-harvested; *long term*, mechanization and imports	30% of raisin grapes were harvested using some mechanization in 2019, with continuous tray most common; some older vineyards replaced by tree nuts	Machines cut canes so grapes begin to dry into raisins on the vine; new vineyards are machine-ready	Relatively little H-2A labor in the Fresno area	US raisin consumption is falling; a third of US-produced raisins are exported, and a sixth are imported, with exports falling and imports rising
Table grapes: *short term*, harvesting aids to carry harvested grapes from picker to packer; *long term*, trade uncertainties	US table grape acreage and grower prices have been rising with new, sweeter varieties	Harvesting aids improve worker productivity; could a harvesting machine cut bunches that are packed in a packing house?	Relatively little H-2A labor in Coachella and southern San Joaquin Valleys	Half of fresh table grapes are imported and a third of US table grapes are exported, with imports rising and exports falling

Table 7.1 Continued

Commodity	Trends	Machines	H-2A Labor	Imports
Wine grapes: *short term*, harvest mostly mechanized, mechanization of pruning and other preharvest tasks; *long term*, further mechanization	Few barriers to more machine harvesting; machines being developed for pruning, thinning, and leaf pulling	Harvest machines are available, but harder to use on hills; more preharvest tasks are being mechanized	H-2A workers increasing in North Coast for hand-picked premium grapes that sell for two to four times the average California grower price of $800 a ton	One-third of US wine imported; United States is a net importer of wine
Strawberries: *short-term*, harvesting aids and H-2A workers; *long term*, more imports and mechanization	Acreage down but production stable with higher yields	Conveyor belts reduce walking and raise productivity; tabletop and vertical planting systems ease hand or machine picking; Agrobot, Harvest CROO, and other machines in development	More H-2As workers in Oxnard, Santa Maria, and Salinas-Watsonville	15% of fresh and half of frozen strawberries are imported; 14 percent of US production is exported

Source: Author's elaboration

Rising US apple production and stable per capita consumption means that the US apple industry relies increasingly on exports; a quarter of US fresh apples are exported. Canada and Mexico are the largest markets for US fresh apple exports, with India and China targets for the US industry. Fresh apples can be stored under controlled-atmosphere conditions that use high concentrations of carbon dioxide and air filtration to delay ethylene-induced ripening, making harvested apples less perishable than many other fresh fruits and vegetables. US growers have a comparative advantage in selling fresh apples because of their investments in controlled-atmosphere storage facilities and their access to the proprietary varieties that are favored by consumers.

Production and Trade

Most US apples are from fewer than 1,000 farms. The Census of Agriculture found 26,408 farms with 381,781 acres of apples in 2017, including 527 that each had 100 or more acres and collectively accounted for 70 percent of US apple acreage. These large US apple farms included 33 that each had 1,000 or more acres and a total of 20 percent of US apple acreage. The 1,014 US apple farms that each had sales of $1 million included two-thirds of total US apple acreage.

Washington had 2,522 apple farms with 180,000 acres in 2017, almost half of US apple acreage, including 342 farms that each had 100 or more acres and a total of 152,000 acres or 84 percent of the state's apple acreage. There were 74 Washington farms with at least 500 acres of apples; they had a total of 99,000 acres or 55 percent of the state's acreage.

Over the past four decades, US apple acreage shrank by almost 30 percent, from 412,000 acres in 1980 to 291,000 acres in 2018, while apple tonnage rose 16 percent, from 4.4 million tons in 1980 to 5.1 million tons in 2018. Production increased as acreage shrank because yields rose by 65 percent to almost 18 tons an acre as growers replaced older orchards and tall trees with dwarf trees planted close together in vineyard-style orchards.

Washington has almost half of US apple acreage, followed by New York with 13 percent and Michigan with 10 percent. Washington's eight major varieties are Honeycrisp, Granny Smith, Cosmic Crisp, Red Delicious, Cripps Pink (Pink Lady), Gala, Fuji, and Golden Delicious. The top five varieties accounted for 80 percent of Washington apple acreage in both 2001 and 2017, but Gala and Honeycrisp acreage rose while Red Delicious acreage fell by over half. Honeycrisp was not measured in 2001 but accounted for 13 percent of acreage in 2017.

New varieties are worth more: the grower price of Honeycrisp was three times the price of Red Delicious apples in 2018–19.[5] Retailers increasingly advertise and sell apples by variety, and consumers have been willing to pay more for sweeter apples such as Cosmic Crisp and Honeycrisp.

The United States is a net exporter of fresh apples and a net importer of processed apple products such as apple juice, much of which is imported from China. Washington exports a third of its annual crop, including 29 million boxes of Red Delicious, the top variety exported. Some 13 million boxes of Washington apples went to Mexico in 2019 and 5 million boxes went to Canada.

Table 7.2 Washington Apple Acreage by Variety, 2001 and 2017

	Acres in 2001	Acres in 2017	2001 Share	2017 Share	Change	Price 2018–19, 40-lb carton
Gala	25,500	41,036	13%	23%	61%	$25.60
Red Delicious	82,000	39,207	43%	22%	−52%	$17.40
Fuji	24,400	28,718	13%	16%	18%	$25.70
Honeycrisp	—	22,616	—	13%	NA	$53.40
Granny Smith	17,600	16,267	9%	9%	−8%	$28.80
Top five	149,500	147,844				
Top five share	78%	83%				
Total	192,000	179,146	100%	100%	−7%	

Source: USDA

Labor

Hand workers prune and train tree limbs and thin and harvest apples. There were 740 apple orchard establishments (NAICS 111331) in Washington in 2019 with an average 22,200 employees and a total $638 million in wages paid, down from 1,000 apple establishments and 24,100 average apple employment in 2010.[6] The state's apple industry estimates that 35,000 to 40,000 workers harvest apples each year, including 20,000 H-2A workers.[7]

Apples are hand-harvested by workers who climb ladders that lean into trees; they pick from top to bottom, putting apples into bags that hang over their shoulders. Full bags of most varieties are dumped into 925-pound bins, although Honeycrisp apples, which bruise easily, are dumped into 690-pound bins, as seen in Photo 7.2. Working from ladders in orchards on uneven ground can be dangerous, and most apple pickers who use ladders are young men who spend up to a third of their time moving and positioning ladders.[8]

A 2019 Washington State University (WSU) study of production costs for Gala apples estimated that growers invested $43,563 on each acre with 1,100 trees.[9] An acre yields sixty-eight 925-pound bins and, with an 80 percent pack-out rate, there are 740 pounds of marketable apples per bin, which means that one field bin of apples yields 18.5 salable 40-pound cartons of apples at the packing house. If each carton of Gala apples is worth $34.63, the gross revenue per acre is $43,563, the break-even figure.

Photo 7.1 Picking Apples in Traditional Orchards
Source: US Department of Agriculture

There are four major hand labor tasks: (1) pruning and training trees, at a cost of $940 or 50 hours an acre, (2) thinning fruit at a cost of $1,033, or 54 hours an acre, so that the remaining apples are larger,[10] (3) protecting apples from sunburn with netting, at a labor cost of $1,200 or 63 hours per acre, and (4) harvesting apples, at a cost of $2,390 or 126 hours an acre, plus an additional $680 for 36 hours of labor to supervise harvest workers, check the picked apples, and transport bins of apples to packing sheds. The WSU study assumed a piece rate of $28 a bin or $0.03 a pound to harvest apples.

The costs to produce Honeycrisp apples were similar. The estimated yield was 56 bins (690-pound bins) an acre and a grower price of $741 a bin or $57 per 40-pound carton with a 75 percent pack-out rate.[11] Costs of production were $41,000 per acre, meaning that yields above 56 bins an acre and prices above $731 a bin are profitable. The same four major hand labor tasks are required: (1) pruning and training trees, at a cost of $940 or 50 hours an acre, (2) thinning fruit, at a cost of $1,127 or 60 hours an acre, (3) protecting apples from sunburn with netting, at a labor cost of $1,200 or 63 hours per acre, and (4) harvesting apples, at a cost of $2,984 or 159 hours an acre, plus an additional $750 or 40 hours an acre for supervising, checking picked apples, and transporting bins.

Honeycrisp apples mature unevenly and bruise easily, so workers may pick a Honeycrisp orchard four or five times, clipping the stems each time and handling the apples gently to avoid bruising. Smaller yields during multiple harvests and more careful picking mean a higher piece rate, $28 for picking each smaller 675-pound bin or $0.04 a pound. Cosmic Crisp apples, another high-value variety, are picked only once, as are lower-value Red Delicious apple orchards.

Alternatives and Outlook

Washington agriculture employed a peak 142,000 workers in July 2019 and a low of 74,500 workers in February, for a peak-trough ratio of 1.9. Apple orchards (NAICS 111331) are the state's largest agricultural employer, reporting over 30,000 workers in July and less than 15,000 in February, for a peak-trough ratio of 2.1. Other noncitrus fruit farming (NAICS 111339) such as cherries and pears is more seasonal, with a peak-trough ratio of 3.7 that reflects the employment of 22,000 workers in July and 6,000 in February.[12]

There are three major options to reduce the cost of harvesting apples: pick by hand and improve worker productivity with mechanical aids, adapt shake-and-catch machines to harvest apples in once-over fashion, or develop machines with cameras and robotic arms to harvest individual apples. Each harvesting system functions best with dwarf trees whose limbs grow on trellis wires so that the apple trees put their energy into producing apples rather than trunks and root systems.

Mechanical aids carry workers and the bins for picked apples. Platform crews of eight workers often include four workers on the platform and four who pick the lower branches from the ground. Platform workers spend more of their time picking rather than moving ladders and report fewer injuries.

Platform crews share the piece rate wage, while ladder pickers earn individual piece rates. Workers may not be able to choose their picking partners, which can lead to tensions between faster and slower pickers on platforms and may encourage a shift from US workers who prefer individual piece rates to H-2A workers who will accept picking for an hourly wage.

Two firms produce most of the $65,000 harvesting platforms used in Washington apple orchards, which can also be used for non-harvest-related tasks such as pruning and thinning.[13] Platforms with lights can be used for night picking, which is preferred by some workers for cooler temperatures and because the lights make it easier to detect defective apples.

There are three types of apple workers: settled local workers who often do farm work more than six months a year, migrants from states such as California who move to Washington during peak apple and cherry harvesting periods, and H-2A guest workers, almost all from Mexico. The number of local seasonal farm workers is stable, the number of US migrants is falling, and the number of H-2A guest workers is rising.

The number of jobs certified to be filled with H-2A workers in Washington rose from less than 3,000 in FY10 to over 12,000 in FY15 and topped 26,000 in FY19, with WAFLA the largest H-2A employer.[14] WAFLA recruits workers for its apple farm clients in Mexico and arranges for their visas and travel to the United States at a cost of $1,200 per H-2A worker. Most employers house H-2A workers at a cost of $12 to $15 a day; housing and the cost of transporting workers to and from the work site add $2 an hour. H-2A workers are "loyal" to the employer with whom they have a contract, they often volunteer to work long hours if necessary, and they have a reputation for more careful work, so farm employers may be able to get their work done with fewer H-2A than US workers.

DOL provides Washington's Employment Security Department (ESD) $400,000 a year to administer the H-2A program. ESD's duties include checking and posting employer job offers, inspecting worker housing, and conducting prevailing wage rate studies. ESD spends far more than $400,000 on those tasks, and it proposed charging employers who apply for H-2A workers a state fee, drawing opposition from employers.

ESD's prevailing wage rate studies are controversial. Washington is one of the few states that generates a significant number of PWR studies,[15] prompting suits against ESD from both employers and worker advocates. Employers must pay H-2A and similar US workers the higher of the federal or state minimum wage, the AEWR, or the prevailing wage for the industry and occupation.

Most of Washington's apples and cherries are picked for piece rate wages, which means that workers are guaranteed the AEWR of $17.97 in 2023. However, picking apples for $28 to $32 a bin, or cherries for $0.20 to $0.22 a pound, can generate piece rate earnings of $25 to $30 an hour for fast pickers. In order to provide their employees with an incentive to work fast without close supervision, employers set piece rates so that most pickers earn 15 to 25 percent more than the AEWR.

The ESD asks apple growers to report the wage they paid for their peak week by variety, so growers may report $30 a bin to pick Gala apples and $25 a bin to pick Red Delicious apples. Alternatively, employers may report that they pay only the state's minimum wage or AEWR. If ESD does not obtain enough responses to determine a PWR piece rate, then the hourly minimum wage becomes the wage that employers must pay to H-2A and similar US workers.

After DOL certified H-2A job offers that guaranteed the AEWR but did not specify piece rates, US workers sued, asserting that instead of earning $25 to $30 an hour for picking apples and cherries for piece rate wages, they may earn only the $18 AEWR. A federal judge agreed with the workers and prohibited DOL from certifying job offers that promise only the AEWR in crops that traditionally have piece rate wage systems.[16] Litigation over the interaction of hourly wage guarantees and piece rates continues, highlighting the difficulties of finding the optimal balance between protecting US workers and facilitating employer access to guest workers.

Apple pickers are likely to be replaced by harvesting machines by 2030. Shake-and-catch machines are easiest to develop and are the fastest at picking fruit, since they make one pass through the orchard, harvest all of the fruit, and rely on electronics in packing houses to select the marketable fruit. Shake-and-catch machines are used to harvest blueberries, wine grapes, and tree nuts, so the technologies involved are mature, and they are often used to harvest apples that are processed into juice and sauce.

The machines that harvest fresh apples use cameras and robotic arms to imitate humans by picking individual apples. Selective picking machines are more expensive and complex, and must find the optimal combination of accurate recognition of ripe fruit, fast picking, and low cost (Jia et al. 2020). Growing apples on trellis systems makes it easier to use artificial intelligence and lidar (light detection and ranging radar) to find and pick ripe apples.

Several firms are developing machines with cameras that guide arms to pick individual apples and place them into bins carried by the machine. These selective harvesting machines are becoming faster and more reliable as cameras and recognition software improve, but they are not yet cost-competitive with hand pickers. The venture capital that is funding many of the efforts to develop mechanical apple harvesters is impatient for a return, and several firms have gone bankrupt before perfecting their machines. The expectation is that improved machines could pick a third or more of US apples by 2030.

This means that picking fresh apples is likely to involve both more H-2A workers and more selective harvesting machines over the next decade. H-2A workers using platforms can pick high-value varieties quickly and carefully, which raises the bar for selective machines to become cost-effective. There is little immediate threat from imports of fresh apples due to the spread of proprietary varieties such as Cosmic Crisp and Honeycrisp.

Blueberries

Blueberries are the berries of perennial flowering plants. Lowbush or wild blueberries are native to North America, while highbush or cultivated blueberries were introduced from Europe to New Jersey in the 1930s. Canada is the leading producer of lowbush blueberries, and the United States is the leading producer of highbush blueberries, which are sometimes subdivided into northern (cold-weather) and southern (warm-weather or rabbiteye) varieties.

Global blueberry production was 823,000 tons in 2019, including 309,000 tons produced in the United States, 176,000 tons in Canada, 142,000 tons in Peru, 53,000 tons in Spain, and 49,000 tons in Mexico. Blueberry production is expanding in Mexico, which had 11,000 acres yielding almost 10,000 pounds per acre in 2019, and Peru, which had 27,000 acres in 2019 yielding an average 12,000 pounds an acre. Peru is the leading blueberry exporter, sending half of its exports to the United States, where fresh blueberry consumption averaged 2.5 pounds per person in 2020.[17]

Three states, Oregon, Georgia, and California, each produced a sixth of US fresh blueberries in 2019. However, when production for both fresh and processing markets is combined, Washington and Oregon are the leading blueberry-producing states. Farmers receive about $2 a pound for fresh blueberries but less than $1 a pound for blueberries that are frozen or processed.

Production and Trade

The United States produced 670 million pounds of blueberries in 2019, including 56 percent that were sold fresh and 44 percent that were frozen or used as food ingredients. The United States imported 470 million pounds of fresh blueberries in 2019 and exported 80 million pounds, giving Americans a total of 1 billion pounds of blueberries and making the United States a net importer of blueberries.

Americans are consuming more blueberries due to their perceived health benefits and year-round availability. Almost all of the fresh blueberries available between October and February are imported, as are a third of those available in the other months. Winter blueberry imports are mostly from Peru, Chile, and Mexico, and summer imports are mostly from Canada. As we saw in Chapter 6, rising blueberry imports prompted an effort by southeastern growers to block imports that was opposed by other US blueberry growers.

Almost 16,000 farms reported 153,300 acres of blueberries in the most recent census (Census of Agriculture 2017, table 38). Only 77 percent of these acres were bearing fruit, indicating significant new plantings. Almost all blueberry farms, 15,000 farms, grew cultivated blueberries, a total of 113,200 acres, most in Michigan,[18] Georgia, Washington, and Oregon. Some were large growers: 246 farms each had 100 or more acres and a total of 64,400 acres or 42 percent of total cultivated blueberry acreage. Another 1,100 farms reported 40,000 acres of wild blueberries, mostly in Maine, and the 43 farms that each had 100 or more acres had a total of 30,000 acres or three-fourths of all wild blueberry acreage.

Labor

Blueberries can be harvested by hand or machine. Highbush cultivated blueberry plants are 5 to 10 feet tall, while lowbush or wild blueberry plants are a foot tall and raked by hand or machine. Hand workers pick ripe blueberries from highbush plants into buckets for piece rate wages of about $0.50 a pound. Farmers receive about $2 a pound for fresh blueberries, making harvest wages a quarter of grower revenues (higher when payroll taxes and supervision costs are included). High grower prices early and late in the season encourage some growers to pick by hand to maximize the pack-out rate and lead to higher piece rates of up to $0.75 a pound.

A survey of growers estimated that 15,000 production workers were employed for an average 560 hours to produce US blueberries. Table 7.3 shows that average hourly earnings were $19 an hour in 2019 for farm and nonfarm processing workers combined. Harvest workers picked an average 36 pounds of blueberries an hour at a piece rate of $0.52 a pound to earn $18.72 per hour.

Direct labor costs were about 30 percent of the average grower revenue of $1.70 a pound for fresh and frozen blueberries combined (USITC 2021, table III-18). Total hand labor costs, including payroll taxes and supervision, were higher at $0.75 to $1 a pound, compared with machine harvesting costs of $0.20 a pound.

Growers in California and Florida obtain some of the highest prices for early-season fresh blueberries, and are more likely to hand-harvest than growers in Michigan, New Jersey, and the Pacific Northwest who harvest during the summer months and send more of their blueberries to processors. The US International Trade Commission (USITC 2021, I-14) reported that 80 percent of California's blueberries are hand-harvested and that pack-out rates are up to 86 percent. Most Florida blueberries are hand-picked, but half of the Georgia crop is machine-picked.

Some growers employ H-2A guest workers to hand-pick blueberries. Washington's Zirkle Fruit was certified to employ 2,750 H-2A workers in 2019 to pick blueberries at a piece rate of $0.50 a pound, although the workers were guaranteed at least the AEWR of $15.03 per hour. During the season, the ESD found that the prevailing wage was $0.75 a pound, and DOL required Zirkle to pay this higher piece rate. Zirkle sued, and a federal judge eventually ordered Zirkle to pay the extra $0.25 a pound after concluding that ESD's prevailing wage rate survey methodology was sound. Zirkle said that it would machine-pick its blueberries if it had to pay $0.75 a pound for hand picking.

The Zirkle case illustrates the trade-offs in harvesting blueberries. Harvesting machines are available, but many growers who can pay $0.50 a pound to hand pickers and sell their berries fresh for $2 a pound prefer to hand-harvest. Some growers-hand harvest during the first pass through the field, when 50 to 60 percent of the crop is mature and grower prices are highest, and use machines for a second and final harvest (Gallardo et al. 2018).

Other labor issues in blueberry farming involve child labor and ghost workers (two workers employed under one social security number). Pan-American Berry Growers of Salem, Oregon, had 280 pickers to harvest 165 acres of blueberries in 2012, and B&G Ditchen Farms of Silverton, Oregon, had 310 workers for 150 acres, an average of almost two workers per acre. FLCs supplied workers to both farms, and the workers were paid piece-rate wages to hand-pick blueberries.[19]

DOL investigators found that some workers had very high piece rate earnings, and they assumed that the berries were picked by several workers but

Table 7.3 Blueberry Harvesters Earned an Average $19 an Hour in 2019

Item	Calendar year					January to September	
	2015	2016	2017	2018	2019	2019	2020
Reported production and related workers (PRWs) (number).— Growing operations	14,185	14,804	15,265	14,643	14,826	15,435	15,106
Freezing operations	1,289	1,240	1,118	1,063	1,167	1,111	980
Total reported PRWs	15,474	16,044	16,383	15,706	15,993	16,546	16,086
Total hours worked (1,000 hours)	8,424	8,987	9,832	8,358	8,967	8,094	7,504
Hours worked per PRW (hours)	544	560	600	532	561	489	466
Wages paid ($1,000)	138,241	148,363	156,283	156,085	168,440	154,652	153,888
Hourly wages (dollars per hour)	$16.41	$16.51	$15.89	$18.67	$18.78	$19.11	$20.51
Productivity (pounds per hour)	29.8	32.2	28.3	33.1	25.8	34.3	33.3
Unit labor costs (dollars per pound)	$0.55	$0.51	$0.56	$0.56	$0.52	$0.56	$0.62

Source: USITC 2021, table III-15.

credited to one worker. DOL found it implausible that workers would pick more than 68 pounds of blueberries an hour; at a piece rate of $0.50 a pound, earnings would be $34 an hour. DOL threatened to place a hot-goods hold on both farms' berries, preventing them from being shipped across state lines, unless the growers agreed to pay $200,000 in back wages and $30,000 in civil money penalties (CMPs) for having child and ghost employees.

The growers disputed the presence of child and ghost employees, and wanted to put the $230,000 into an escrow account, ship their berries, and appeal DOL's findings. DOL refused, so the farms paid, shipped their berries, and sued DOL, arguing that they were forced to agree with the DOL findings in order to ship their perishable fruit. A federal magistrate agreed with the berry growers and invalidated the grower-DOL settlements in April 2014.[20]

Maine developed a lowbush wild blueberry industry during the 1860s in response to a demand for fruit to feed soldiers during the Civil War. By the 1960s, Canadian Micmacs (Mi'kmaqs) provided most of the labor to harvest or rake the berries during the August harvest in Maine.[21] Canadian Micmacs were half of the 8,000 seasonal harvesters in the early 2000s, when the other half were Mexican-born farm workers.[22] Since then, hand rakers have been displaced by machines in many of the berry barrens near the coast.

Alternatives and Outlook

At least six firms manufacture blueberry harvesters, which cost $200,000 to $300,000 each. Most use rotary picking mechanisms, which beat bushes so that blueberries fall onto a conveyor belt for transport to bins or lugs. Padding the catching area reduces damage to machine-harvested berries, and new blueberry varieties have fruit that does not bruise as easily when harvested by machine.

Berries damaged by machines can be sorted efficiently in packing sheds, so growers who must decide between hand harvesting and machine harvesting compare the lower harvesting costs with machines against their lower pack-out rates. The cost of machine harvesting does not vary with yield, while the cost of hand harvesting rises with higher yields, since workers are paid per pound. Most blueberries in New Jersey, Michigan, Oregon, and Washington are harvested by machine.

Over the next decade, all three of the major options, machines, migrants, and imports, are likely to increase. Researchers and machinery manufacturers are developing new varieties and improving harvesting machines, more growers are turning to H-2A workers, and imports are likely to rise from new plantings in Mexico, Peru, and other countries.

Grapes

Grapes, most of which are the *Vitis vinifera* cultivar native to the Mediterranean, produce clusters of individual berries. Over 70 percent of the world's grapes are used to make wine, a quarter are eaten as fresh fruit, and the rest are dried into raisins.

Production and Trade

The United States had 937,000 bearing acres of grapes in 2018, up from almost 700,000 acres in 1980 but down from a peak 1,042,000 acres in 2013. US grape production rose in lockstep with acreage, up 36 percent in tonnage to an average eight tons an acre in 2018.

There are three major types of grapes: raisin, table, and wine. The 1.5 million short tons (a short ton is 2,000 pounds) of raisin grapes had an average grower value of $425 per green ton or $0.21 a pound in 2018, the 1.3 million short tons of table grapes had an average value of $980 or $0.75 a pound, and the 4.3 million short tons of wine grapes had an average value of $1,000 a ton or $0.50 a pound. California had 158,000 acres of raisin grapes in 2018, 111,000 acres of table grapes, and 560,000 acres of wine grapes.

Wine grapes were the first type cultivated in California, introduced by Spanish priests around the 21 missions established along the Camino Real (today Highway 101) in the late 1700s. The state's wine industry, which remained small due to disease and Prohibition (1920–33), relied on Thompson Seedless (sultana) grapes, which could be eaten fresh, dried into raisins, or crushed to make wine or grape juice.

The wine industry began to change in the mid-1960s when Napa's Robert Mondavi led an effort to label wines by the variety of grape used to make them. In 1966 Mondavi opened the first major new winery in Napa since Prohibition, and Napa Valley Chardonnay and Cabernet Sauvignon wines were considered the best at a 1976 judging in Paris, where French wine experts in a blind tasting rated Napa wines better than French wines. California today produces 85 percent of US wine, most from wine grapes grown in the San Joaquin Valley.

Raisin and table grape vineyards are concentrated in the southern San Joaquin Valley. Americans had 6 pounds of raisins and 8.1 pounds of fresh table grapes available per person in 2018, when table grapes sold for an average retail price of $2.35 a pound and growers received an average $0.71 a pound or 30 percent of the retail price of table grapes. Almost half (48 percent) of fresh table grapes available in the United States are imported.

Raisin Grape Labor

Almost all US raisins are from California, where production has been declining. A record crop of 400,000 tons of raisins in 2000 caused grower prices to drop to $400 a ton, well below the average $600 a ton cost of production. Turkey surpassed the United States as the world's leading producer of raisins in 2016–17, and US demand for raisins continues to decline as more consumers buy fresh fruit.

The Raisin Administrative Committee (RAC) is a federal marketing order established in 1949 that for many years attempted to keep retail raisin prices high by withholding some of the raisin crop in a reserve that was sold as food ingredients at low prices; in many years over half of raisins were sold as food ingredients.[23] Consumer demand for raisins is relatively fixed or inelastic, so the RAC's reserve created two markets for raisins, a high-priced retail raisin market and a low-priced food ingredient market. Farmers received a high price for their "free tonnage" sold to consumers and a lower price for reserve raisins. This market segmentation increased the total revenue of raisin growers and kept some growers producing raisins until the US Supreme Court declared the raisin reserve system unconstitutional in 2015.

Over 85 percent of raisin grapes are the Thompson Seedless variety. Farmers in the past waited until a month before the harvest to decide whether to harvest their grapes for wine or raisins. If harvested for raisins, workers wielding knives cut bunches of green grapes into plastic tubs and dumped full tubs of about 25 pounds onto two-by-three-foot paper trays that are laid between vineyard rows, where the green grapes dry into raisins in about a week (Fidelibus et al. 2016).

The labor issue for grape growers is finding enough harvest workers when the sugar levels in their grapes top 20 percent,[24] which makes raisin harvest a race between sugar and rain. The longer growers wait for sugar levels to rise, the more danger that the harvested grapes lying on paper trays in vineyards to dry into raisins are damaged by early rains. However, harvesting grapes too soon means raisins that are less sweet.

Industry leaders in the 1990s told Congress they needed 60,000 workers for the six-week raisin grape harvest. Most growers rely on labor contractors to obtain seasonal workers,[25] most of whom are Mexican-born immigrants.[26] Most raisin harvesters fill 40 to 45 trays an hour, and at current piece rate wages of $0.35 to $0.40 a tray, workers earn $16 to $17 an hour, slightly more than California's minimum wage.

Raisins are sold to packers, who clean and package them. The Sun-Maid cooperative, founded in 1912, packs 40 percent of US raisins and launched the dancing raisins "Heard It Through the Grapevine" commercial in the 1980s.[27]

Raisin Grape Alternatives and Outlook

Grapes can be harvested mechanically after they dry into raisins while still on the vine. The canes holding bunches of green grapes are cut in early August, and once the grapes have dried into raisins, a machine with rotating fingers can dislodge the raisins into bins. However, the dried-on-the-vine (DOV) method of producing raisins requires growers to replant their vineyards with grape varieties that reach optimal sugar levels earlier. A third of California's raisin grapes were harvested mechanically in 2021.[28]

The next frontier is a new Sunpreme grape variety that dries into raisins without the need to cut canes holding bunches of grapes.[29] However, new plantings of self-drying raisin varieties are limited by rising imports from Turkey, which can produce raisins cheaper than California, and fears that Sunpreme raisins may fall to the ground before being harvested and that consumers may shun them due to their slightly different taste.[30]

There is likely to be more mechanical harvesting of raisin grapes, but the major reason for less hand labor in raisin grapes is less US production. Instead of replanting grape vineyards with new varieties amenable to machine harvesting, many raisin growers become almond farmers. California's almond acreage rose from less than 500,000 in 1990 to almost 1.5 million in 2020, making almonds California's most valuable crop.

An intermediate labor-saving technique used on 20 percent of raisin acreage is continuous tray harvesting. Canes with bunches of grapes are cut to stimulate fruit abscission, the loosening of the berries from the stem. Once the berries are partially dried, a wine grape harvester with rotating fingers shakes them onto a conveyer belt that transports them onto a continuous paper tray as individual berries.[31] Cutting the canes allows the berries to be dislodged more easily and enables berries to retain their cap stems, which reduces juice leakage and stickiness in the raisins.[32] Partially dried grapes become raisins in a few days, after which the paper tray is picked up by a machine that puts them into bins. Continuous tray harvesting requires less retrofitting and investment in vineyards.

Several factors work against raisin mechanization, including demographics and imports. Most raisin growers are older, often in their 60s and 70s, and most have less than 50 acres of vineyards that they own with no debt.[33] With children not interested in raisin farming, many are unwilling to make the investment required to retrofit their vineyards for machine harvesting.

There are few H-2A workers in raisins because most are produced near Fresno, California, a region with many farm workers and relatively low-cost housing. Instead, the US raisin grape industry is likely to include more machines as younger growers with capital and long time horizons invest in mechanized systems, and as older growers wait to switch to crops that do not require hand labor. Meanwhile, raisin imports are likely to continue to increase.

Table Grape Labor

About 400 California grower-shippers produce almost all US table grapes in the Coachella and southern San Joaquin Valleys, harvesting them between May and October. Some 105 million 19-pound boxes of table grapes worth $2.1 billion or $20 a box were harvested in 2019, and two-thirds were shipped between September and December, including a third that were exported.[34]

The production and value of table grapes rose over the past two decades as growers planted new varieties with higher yields. Seedless grapes, better color and flavor, and other changes doubled per capita consumption of fresh grapes from 3.5 to over 7 pounds per person between the 1970s and 2000s, and consumption is now 8 pounds per person.

Grapes in the past were sold by color and seeded versus seedless, but today they are often sold by variety, as with apples. Three traditional varieties accounted for 34 percent of the 83,000 bearing acres in 2019: Flame Seedless (18 percent) and Crimson Seedless and Red Globe (8 percent each). Two newer varieties accounted for 16 percent of acreage: Scarlet Royal and Autumn King (8 percent each). Varieties with the highest shares of non-bearing acres, indicating that acreage is expanding, include Allison, Cotton Candy, and Sugarone.[35] There are at least 79 varieties of table grapes produced commercially. New plantings use fewer inputs and attain higher yields.

The major preharvest hand tasks include pruning vines in the winter, positioning fruiting canes in spring, and removing leaves and thinning grape bunches, which combined require 338 hours an acre (Fidelibus et al. 2018).[36] Harvesting and packing table grapes require another 350 hours an acre, for a total of 688 hours. This means that California's 121,000 acres of table grapes require 83 million hours of hand labor, equivalent to 83,000 workers who average 1,000 hours each.[37]

Table grape vineyards are harvested when grape sugar levels reach 21 or 22 percent (brix). Trios or teams typically include both pickers and a packer. Two pickers cut bunches of grapes and place them into plastic bins or lugs, then use a wheelbarrow to convey the full bins to a packer at the end of the row. Packers take bunches of grapes from these field bins, trim them, and place them into bags or clamshells, working on portable tables at the end of the row.[38]

Boxes of table grapes often include nine 2-pound containers and are cooled to 31.5 degrees F before being shipped to supermarkets. A typical yield is sixteen hundred 19-pound boxes an acre, and with a grower price of $19 a box or $1 a pound, revenues are $30,400 an acre.

The table grape workforce is local and diverse, dominated by Mexican-born workers but including Mexican Americans and US-born Filipinos. Many couples and extended families harvest table grapes.[39] FLCs often provide harvesting crews of 60, including 40 pickers and 20 packers, plus a crew supervisor and assistants to ensure that supplies are available, packed grapes are moved to coolers quickly, and toilets and shade structures are moved with the workers. Crew supervisors ensure that their crews are fully staffed and act as quality control inspectors. FLCs receive a commission of 30 percent to 40 percent above harvester wages to cover the cost of recruitment, payroll taxes, field sanitation, and record keeping.

When California's minimum wage was $9 an hour in 2014, many growers offered harvest workers $9.25 an hour plus $0.33 a box, so a trio of two pickers and one packer who packed 10 cartons an hour earned $10.35 an hour, since the three workers shared the $3.30 total per-box bonus.[40] The largest table grape grower, Sun Pacific, paid a $3.50-per-box piece rate in 2020, so trios picking and packing 12 cartons an hour shared earnings of $42, equivalent to $14 an hour or $1 more than the state's $13 minimum wage.

Table grapes are harvested for 10 weeks from May through July in the Coachella Valley and from July through November in the San Joaquin Valley, the source of 85 percent of California's table grapes. Coachella grape harvesters earned about $15 an hour or $6,500 to $7,000 harvesting grapes in 2022, while those in the San Joaquin Valley have longer seasons and often earn over $15,000 a year After being laid off, legal workers collect unemployment insurance benefits.

Table grapes played a central role in California farm labor disputes. As noted briefly in Chapter 3, Mexican bracero guest workers were paid $1.40 an hour to harvest grapes during the last year of the bracero program in 1964. There was no minimum wage for US farm workers, so when the grape harvest began in May 1965, Coachella Valley growers offered $1.25 an hour. A strike by the Filipino-dominated Agricultural Workers Organizing Committee (AWOC) persuaded Coachella growers to restore the $1.40 an hour rate, although the growers did not recognize AWOC as the representative of their workers (Martin 2003).

When the grape harvest moved north to the San Joaquin Valley, growers offered $1.25 plus $0.15 a box, prompting an AWOC strike in support of its demand for $1.40 an hour plus $0.25 a box. Cesar Chavez's National Farm Workers Association (NFWA), which later became the United Farm Workers union, joined the AWOC strike, Growers refused to recognize the NFWA-AWOC as the representative of their grape harvesters and used labor contractors to get their grapes harvested.

Chavez assumed leadership of the effort to persuade table grape growers to raise wages and recognize the union. Chavez's key insight was to switch from going on strike during the harvest and watching labor contractors break the strike, instead waiting till the off-season and then organizing a boycott of the products of conglomerates that had grape farms.[41] The first major boycott target was the Schenley liquor firm, which had 3,350 acres of vineyards near Delano in the mid-1960s. Chavez enlisted students and clergy to picket stores selling Schenley products during the Christmas season of 1965, and kept the pressure on Schenley with a march from Delano to Sacramento in March 1966. Schenley agreed to raise wages from $1.25 to $1.75 and pay $0.25 a box. As a result, grape workers earned significantly more than the federal minimum wage of $1.30 an hour.[42]

Chavez next targeted the DiGiorgio Fruit Corporation, which responded that its farm workers were already represented by the Teamsters union. Since farm workers were not covered by federal or state labor laws, there was no need to hold elections to determine if workers wanted to be represented by unions. Pressure on DiGiorgio led to an August 1966 election that the UFW won, with 530 votes versus 331 for the Teamsters. DiGiorgio negotiated an agreement with the UFW in April 1967 and went out of business in 1968.

Chavez sent letters to other table grape growers in 1967 asserting that the UFW represented their workers and asking growers to recognize the UFW and sign the UFW's standard contract or to negotiate a contract. The growers did not respond, prompting the UFW to launch a nationwide boycott of grapes that was known as La Causa and made the UFW and Cesar Chavez household names.

The 1968–70 grape boycott is considered one of the most successful union-called consumer boycotts in US history. A September 1975 Harris poll found that 15 percent of Americans avoided grapes in the late 1960s, and per capita grape consumption fell 24 percent. Chavez was hailed as the Latino Martin Luther King Jr. and featured on the cover of *Time* magazine's July 4, 1969, issue under the headline "The Grapes of Wrath: Mexican-Americans on the March."

Lionel Steinberg, owner of the David Freedman Company in Coachella, signed a contract with the UFW in April 1970. Other grape growers soon followed, signing UFW contracts that guaranteed grape harvesters $1.75 an hour plus $0.25 per box of grapes picked. The UFW soon had 150 contracts covering 20,000 workers and joined the AFL-CIO in 1972. The UFW lost most of its table grape contracts in the 1980s and has no table grape contracts today.

Table Grape Alternatives and Outlook

The major challenge in the table grape industry is to develop new varieties that have higher yields and lower production costs and that satisfy consumers. Newer varieties often save on preharvest labor because they require less pruning and thinning.

There are no table grape harvesting machines in development.[43] Instead, some growers are adopting robots to move six to eight lugs of table grapes from pickers to packers, increasing worker productivity. Robots are most useful when workers are harvesting long rows and grapes are packed at a central station, enabling harvest workers to pick and pack grapes faster and leaving workers less tired at the end of the day.

Robot developers want their devices to do more, such as capturing data on grape yields as the machine moves along vineyard rows and spraying and thinning grape bunches in the spring. Early users emphasize that the robots need longer-lasting batteries and other refinements to function reliably under dusty field conditions while traveling 100+ miles a day.

Some table grapes are put into cold storage and some are packed in sheds, a procedure similar to that in apples. Under such systems, robots could convey tubs of grapes from vineyards to packing sheds, where it is easier to use technology to replace hand workers.

Table grapes are grown in areas with relatively low-cost housing and many farm workers, so few table grape growers employ H-2A workers. Some California table grape growers also have operations in Sonora and other areas of Mexico, which would make it possible to bring workers who complete the harvest in Mexico to California via the H-2A program in the event of labor shortages.

Trade could affect the California table grape industry. The world produces about 26 million tons of table grapes each year, including 11 million tons in China, 2 million tons in Turkey, 1.2 million tons in the EU, and 1 million tons in the United States. The United States exports a third of the 100 million boxes of table grapes produced each year, half to Canada and Mexico, and imports from Chile, Peru, and Mexico half of the fresh grapes consumed by Americans.

Most table grape imports arrive in the United States during the winter and spring, but imports from Mexico are increasing during the April-July period, competing with the Coachella harvest.[44] Most US table grape exports are sent abroad during the summer and fall months, when US production peaks. Harvesting seasons are lengthening both in the United States and abroad.

Wine Grape Labor

Producing wine grapes requires pruning grape vines in winter, removing leaves and thinning bunches of grapes in spring, and harvesting grapes in fall.[45] Pruning and thinning are largely mechanized, and over 85 percent of California's wine grapes are harvested by machine (Alston et al. 2020; Kurtural and Fidelibus 2021).[46]

Grape vines are trained to grow on wires that are parallel to the plant or on wires that form a Y above the plant. The vines are pruned and tied so that the foliage is contained within six to eight inches of wires, allowing bunches of grapes to grow at the bottom of the plant's canopy and making them accessible to the rods and fingers of harvesting machines that dislodge berries and convey them to gondolas traveling alongside the harvester. Since the grapes are crushed soon after harvest for their juice, there is less concern about damage to the berries.

The grower price of wine grapes varies by variety, region where the grapes were grown, and other factors. California's vineyards are divided into districts. District 4 Napa growers received an average $5,669 a ton for wine grapes in 2019, including $3,000 a ton for Chardonnay and $8,000 a ton for Cabernet Sauvignon grapes,[47] while District 13 growers around Fresno received an average $300 a ton for wine grapes.

The tasks required to produce Cabernet Sauvignon grapes in the southern San Joaquin Valley are mostly mechanized. Labor costs are less than $500 per acre, including $325 to machine-harvest the grapes. With yields of 12 tons an acre and a grower price of $325 a ton, gross revenue is $3,900 an acre and machine harvesting costs are less than 10 percent of revenues.[48]

Hand harvesting raises costs. A typical fee for hand-harvesting Chardonnay grapes in Sonoma is $250 a ton and, with yields of seven tons an acre, the total cost of hand labor is $25 an hour (a total of $1,750 for workers paid $18 an hour, plus payroll taxes). Preharvest labor costs are $2,500 an acre for pruning, suckering, and thinning, all tasks done by hand. With yields of seven tons an acre and a price of $2,000 a ton, gross revenues are $14,000 an acre and harvesting costs are $1,750 an acre (12.5 percent of gross revenue).[49]

Hand-harvesting wine grapes involves workers cutting bunches of grapes into tubs that hold 40 to 50 pounds of grapes and dumping the tubs into bins or gondolas that take them to the winery for destemming and crushing. Photo 7.2 shows a crew of workers who pick into shared bins or gondolas and divide the per-ton piece rate; most earn $20 to $25 an hour.

Finding harvest workers is mostly a concern in the Napa and Sonoma Valleys, where high housing costs reduce the availability of local workers. The 40th-percentile fair market rent for a two-bedroom apartment in Napa County was $1,880 in 2020.[50] A worker employed full-time at $20 an hour would earn $3,200 a month, and so if a family had only one earner, 60 percent

Photo 7.2 Hand-Harvesting Wine Grapes
Source: Philip Martin

of gross earnings would be devoted to rent. Many low-wage workers who are employed seasonally in Napa live in crowded local housing or endure lengthy commutes from lower-cost housing an hour or more away.

A survey of Napa vineyard workers found that two-thirds of the year-round workers and 85 percent of seasonal workers lived outside Napa County, including some who commuted from 100 miles away. Most earned $15 to $20 an hour in 2018, when the state's minimum wage was $11 an hour, and their major concern was high housing costs and/or long-distances commutes.[51]

The key figure in the premium wine industry is the winemaker, and many winemakers whose wines sell for at least $50 a bottle insist that vineyard work must be done by hand. However, the University of California's Oakville Experiment Station in Napa planted a "no-touch" vineyard designed for mechanization that produces higher yields of better-quality fruit with machines.[52] When asked why more Napa vineyards are not fully mechanized, Kaan Kurtural of the University of California, Davis, said that perhaps it was that "it [a machine] doesn't look romantic. I don't see any other reason."[53]

Wine Grape Alternatives and Outlook

As labor costs rise, there is likely to be more mechanization in wine grape vineyards. Harvesting wine grapes is mostly mechanized, as are pruning, leafing, thinning, and other preharvest tasks. Vineyards planted on steep hills and those not designed for mechanization continue to rely on hand workers, but such vineyards account for a small share of wine grape acreage.

Hand-picking and hauling wine grapes costs $400 a ton, or $3,200 for eight-ton yield, while machine picking and hauling costs $250 to $500 an acre and does not increase as yields rise. Machines that harvest two acres an hour can operate efficiently at night and remove stems and leaves in the field, which reduces labor needs in the winery.

Further vineyard mechanization is likely. Wine production is increasing faster than consumption in the United States and other countries, which puts downward pressure on wine prices. High US interest rates have raised the value of the dollar, which makes imports more attractive. US wine consumption is concentrated: fewer than 20 percent of American adults drink over 80 percent of the wine consumed in the United States, and many are baby boomers in their 60s and 70s (McMillan 2023).

Strawberries

The Romans believed that wild strawberries had medicinal properties, and the French developed modern hybrid varieties in the 1750s from the wild varieties found in the Americas. Today China is the leading producer of strawberries, producing 3.3 million tons in 2020, followed by the United States with 1.1 million tons, Mexico with 560,000 tons, Spain with 270,000 tons, and Poland with 167,000 tons.[54] The leading exporters of fresh strawberries are Mexico, which exported $835 million worth of fresh strawberries in 2022, and Spain, $735 million.[55]

Demand for fresh berries has been rising with their perceived health benefits as well as year-round availability and convenient packaging, making fresh berries worth $8.6 billion in 2022, the highest-value fresh produce item sold in US supermarkets. Strawberries account for about half of US retail fresh berry sales, followed by blueberries that account for a quarter of fresh berry sales, raspberries 15 percent, and blackberries 10 percent.[56]

Table 7.4 Retail Berries, 2017

	Volume Share	Spending Share
Strawberries	65%	47%
Blueberries	21%	27%
Raspberries	7%	14%
Blackberries	5%	9%
Total	98%	97%
Total volume/spending	1.8 billion lb.	$6.4 billion

Source: Cook 2017

Most of the strawberries available to US consumers are produced in the United States, but most blackberries, blueberries, and raspberries are imported. California and Mexico produce the four major berries almost year-round, and berry imports from Mexico are increasing. Four firms market most fresh strawberries: Driscoll's, Naturipe, WellPict, and California Giant.[57]

Production and Trade

The United States produced 2.6 billion pounds of strawberries from 49,400 acres in 2021. The average grower price was $1.28 a pound, making the US crop worth $3.4 billion, second only to apples among US fruits. Strawberry acreage peaked at 60,000 acres in 2013 when production was 3.1 billion pounds; acreage has fallen faster than production due to higher-yielding varieties and improved production practices. Per capita availability of strawberries was 9 pounds in 2021, including 80 percent consumed fresh.

Strawberry acreage in the United States and California is concentrated on a relatively few farms. Some 8,964 US farms had 60,162 acres of strawberries in 2017, including 130 farms that each had 100 or more acres; they accounted for two-thirds of US strawberry acreage (Census of Agriculture 2017, table 38).[58] California had 39,000 acres of strawberries in 2021, including 15 percent that were grown organically. Over 80 percent of California strawberry acreage is planted in the fall for winter, spring, and summer harvesting.[59] About 60 percent of California strawberry acreage is planted with varieties developed by the University of California; the remaining 40 percent are proprietary varieties developed by marketers and leased to growers who are required to sell the berries to marketers.

Labor

Strawberries are the most labor-intensive major crop grown in California, involving 50,000 to 60,000 workers to harvest the state's strawberry fields twice a week during the peak season. The strawberry harvest begins in southern California in winter and moves north in spring and summer. Florida produces fresh strawberries between December and April, when fresh strawberry imports from Mexico peak.

Strawberry fields are picked every 3 days at peak season, so one field may be picked 40 to 50 times. Workers push a light wheelbarrow, containing the plastic clamshells in which strawberries are sold, between two adjacent elevated rows, picking from both rows as shown in Photo 7.3.[60] Pickers take full trays to a checker at the end of the row to receive credit for what was picked, and some workers run with full trays to collection points and return with empty trays to maximize their piece rate earnings.

Most workers are paid piece rate wages of $2 to $2.50 per flat of twelve 12-ounce pints or eight 1-pound clamshells, and are guaranteed at least the California minimum wage of $15 an hour in 2022.[61] Some growers offer workers an hourly wage of $5 an hour and a piece rate of $1.50 for each flat, while others guarantee the minimum wage and offer $0.50 per tray after eight trays an hour. Growers want workers to pick fast and carefully, and most pick 8 to 10 flats an hour, earning $1 to $2 an hour more than the minimum wage. Productivity varies with individual skill, plant yields, type of picking cart, and time of day, with workers often picking slower at the end of the day.

Labor is the major variable cost of producing strawberries, representing 50 to 60 percent of production costs (Bolda et al. 2021). Some growers place slow-moving conveyor belts in front of harvesters, allowing pickers to place full flats of berries on the belt and thus eliminating the need for workers to carry full flats to the end of the row to receive credit for their work. Conveyor belts enable the 20 to 40 pickers in each crew to pick more flats per hour and per day.

Photo 7.3 Harvesting Strawberries
Source: Philip Martin

Many of the workers who harvest strawberries were born in Mexico; half or more are not authorized to work in the United States, including many who are non- or limited-Spanish-speakers from southern Mexican states such as Oaxaca and Chiapas. Picking crews often include several members of a family, making strawberry harvesters more diverse than the solo male work crews that dominate harvest crews in tree fruits such as apples and oranges.

The strawberry labor market is fluid in the sense that pickers often change employers over the season. Piece rates are more similar than yields, so some workers switch to employers whose fields have more ripe berries to maximize their piece-rate earnings. Growers in the past discouraged such worker turnover by refusing to rehire workers who quit during the season, but the slowdown in unauthorized Mexico-US migration after the 2008–9 recession has limited the effectiveness of such policies (Guthman 2019, 142).[62]

Strawberry harvesting crews include 30 to 60 workers. The key figure is the crew supervisor, who is responsible for ensuring that picking crews are at full strength and monitoring the quantity and quality of berries that are picked.

Crew supervisors recruit workers to replace those who quit, and often act as more than employers, sometimes arranging housing for workers or helping them to deal with family issues.

The share of H-2A guest workers in the strawberry workforce is rising despite high housing costs in the coastal areas where strawberries are grown. Berries were the most common type of job filled by H-2A workers in FY19, accounting for 10 percent of all H-2A jobs for which a commodity was identified.[63] Many H-2A workers are housed in motels from which the regular furniture is removed and replaced by bunk beds, so that each room can accommodate four workers. The combination of fewer unauthorized newcomers and more H-2A guest workers, who must be paid an AEWR that is higher than the state's minimum wage, puts upward pressure on farm labor costs.

Average employment in California's strawberry industry (NAICS 111333) has been rising, from 21,600 to 24,900 between 2006 and 2018. The number of farm workers exceeds average employment by a factor of at least 2 due to seasonality and turnover, suggesting over 50,000 unique workers employed in strawberries and over 20,000 employed in other berries (Martin, Hooker, and Stockton 2018).

Other berry employment, primarily blueberries and raspberries, rose much faster, up over 200 percent since 2006. There were seven full-time-equivalent strawberry jobs for each other berry job in 2006, but Table 7.5 shows that the ratio of strawberry to other berry jobs fell to 2.5 in 2018 due to the rapid growth of other berry employment, especially blueberries.

The average weekly wages of other berry workers were 10 percent higher than weekly earnings in strawberries until 2014, when the pattern reversed and strawberry weekly wages began to exceed the wages of other berry workers. There was a major jump in strawberry wages between 2015 and 2016, up 11 percent, reflecting an increase in the state's minimum wage.

Most berry workers are not employed the entire year. Some 38,800 workers had their highest earnings from strawberry farming establishments in 2015 and earned an average $17,850 (Martin, Hooker, and Stockton 2018), and workers whose highest-earning job was with an employer who produced blueberries or raspberries earned an average $16,700 in 2015. There are no data on the commodity of workers who are brought to farms by labor contractors, but some of the 294,000 workers who had their highest earnings with labor contractors in 2015 picked berries and earned an average $9,900, the lowest of any commodity.

Table 7.5 Strawberry and Other Berry Employment and Weekly Pay, 2006–18

	Average Employment		Average Weekly Pay ($)	
	Strawberries	Other Berries	Strawberries	Other Berries
2006	21,622	3,059	366	437
2007	23,652	3,488	393	429
2008	26,165	4,060	391	438
2009	27,211	4,441	392	415
2010	26,934	5,275	406	447
2011	27,088	6,103	423	450
2012	27,073	6,981	462	485
2013	26,727	8,876	480	508
2014	25,939	9,719	518	525
2015	25,975	10,618	531	524
2016	25,501	10,942	588	501
2017	25,376	10,241	591	518
2018	24,897	10,018	604	559
2006–18	15%	227%	65%	28%
2006–12	25%	128%	26%	11%
2012–18	–8%	44%	31%	15%

Source: QCEW, www.bls.gov/cew.
Strawberries: NAICS 111333
Other berries: NAICS 111334

Sharecropping and Unions

There are three key actors involved in getting strawberries from fields to consumers: marketers, growers, and hired workers. Marketers such as Driscoll's develop proprietary strawberry varieties that are planted by growers who sign contracts that require them to deliver their berries to Driscoll's, which deducts 15 to 20 percent of the sales revenue for providing the plants and cooling and marketing services and returns the balance to the grower. Driscoll's and other marketers provide advice on farming practices to growers, who are responsible for growing and harvesting the berries.

Many berry farms are small, and many growers are Hispanic ex-pickers who have made the transition from worker to grower. During the 1970s and 1980s, small berry growers often relied on their family members to harvest berries, a form of sharecropping that permitted younger children to work on family berry farms. A federal lawsuit filed in 1975, *Real v. Driscoll Strawberry Associates*, alleged that 15 sharecropper farmers were employees of Driscoll's and entitled to the minimum wage rather than a share of the revenue from selling the berries. The company prepared the land, provided the plants and irrigation equipment, and monitored the development of the berries, while sharecroppers harvested the berries, delivered them to Driscoll's, and received the net proceeds after deductions for pre-harvest loans and marketing costs. A federal district court dismissed the suit, but after the US Court of Appeals for the Ninth Circuit allowed the case to proceed, the company settled with the 15 sharecroppers in 1981 (Guthman 2019, 137).[64]

Sharecropping was ended soon afterward by a California Supreme Court decision involving S. G. Borello and Sons in Gilroy, where the state labor commissioner in 1985 ordered a stop to the harvesting of cucumbers until Borello obtained workers' compensation insurance for 50 sharecroppers. Borello appealed, noting that it was pickle processor Vlasic that weighed the cucumbers picked by each sharecropper and paid them. However, the California Supreme Court in March 1989 concluded that both Vlasic and Borello had enough control over the sharecroppers' work so that they must provide workers' compensation insurance to anyone picking cucumbers for them (Linder 1989, 250).[65] The court laid out a six-factor test to distinguish employees from independent contractors: who controls the work, the (share) farmer's opportunity for profit or loss, the investment the (share) farmer makes in equipment, the skills required of the (share) farmer, how permanent the relationship is between the (share) farmer and the marketer, and whether the (share) farmer's service is integral to the marketer's business.

The *Real* and *Borello* cases ended sharecropping and increased the number of farm worker employees. Today, hundreds of relatively small growers[66] sign contracts with berry marketers.[67] The practical problem for a small grower with 5 or 10 acres arises when berries are sold at low prices, as checks from marketers may not be sufficient to pay the workers needed to harvest the berries on a timely basis.

Much of the land used to grow strawberries is leased, and many strawberry farms are partnerships that may be reconstituted from year to year, prompting the UFW in the mid-1990s to try to organize all workers in the strawberry industry rather than organizing from farm to farm. In 1996, the UFW's Five Cents for Fairness campaign aimed to raise piece rates from the prevailing $1.20 per flat by $0.05 a pint to $1.80 for a 12-pint flat, a 33 percent wage increase.[68] Workers who picked 10 flats an hour would have earned $10.80 or twice the state's minimum wage.

With the support of the AFL-CIO, the UFW deployed 40 full-time organizers to organize the estimated 15,000 strawberry workers in the Salinas-Watsonville area, the largest US union organizing campaign of the mid-1990s.[69] The UFW was opposed by the grower-friendly Strawberry Workers and Farmers Alliance,[70] which argued that the UFW would not be able to negotiate higher wages and benefits for workers. Union-friendly investors bought the largest strawberry grower, Coastal Berry,[71] but a local union, the Coastal Berry Farm Workers Committee, received more votes than the UFW in the 1998 and 1999 elections.

The UFW had far more clout in the halls of government than with workers in the fields, and it used its influence to win a contract with Coastal Berry, which had operations in northern and southern California. The UFW won the election in Oxnard in 1999 by 311–266 but lost to the Coastal Berry Farm Workers Committee in Watsonville, 268–416. The California Agricultural Labor Relations Board (ALRB) decided that Coastal Berry's northern and southern California farms were separate bargaining units, so the UFW represented Coastal Berry's southern California workers and the Coastal Berry Farm Workers Committee the northern California workers. The UFW eventually won the right to represent all of Coastal Berry's workers before the company was sold to Dole in 2004, and Dole exited berry farming in 2017. Today the UFW has one strawberry contract, with organic grower Swanton Berry.

Instead of union contracts, some berry farms have been certified by the Equitable Food Initiative, an NGO that developed labor, environmental, and worker participation standards that employers must meet for their products to be certified by EFI as "responsibly grown, farm worker assured." EFI standards include full compliance with federal, state, and local labor laws, but their unique feature is the creation of teams that include both workers and supervisors who are trained to ensure that EFI standards are complied with on a day-to-day basis. The EFI has certified several US berry farms (Strom and Greenhouse 2013),[72] while FairTradeUSA certified several US marketers, including Driscoll's.[73] The effects of NGO certification are unclear (Mohan et al. 2018). Workers on certified farms report feeling good about working for an organization that cares about them, but it not clear whether EFI or FairTrade certification reduces worker turnover or raises productivity (Martin 2016).

Alternatives and Outlook

The strawberry industry is at a crossroads, coping with rising disease pressures and labor costs in the United States as well as increased imports from Mexico (Holmes, Mansouripour, and Hewavitharana 2020). Growers could cooperate and use some of the assessments raised via a federal marketing order that collects funds to promote strawberries and deal with disease to also mechanize harvesting, but so far growers have not made mechanization a priority (Baum 2005).

Marketers are financially stable and take the long view, breeding and patenting superior plant varieties and developing brand names that allow their berries to command premium shelf space and higher prices in supermarkets. The major marketers are grappling with where to invest to ensure they have strawberries to sell. Should they invest in machines to replace hand workers, in aids to make workers more productive, in housing so that their growers can hire guest workers, or in production in Mexico and other countries?[74]

The most common immediate labor-saving investment are aids that increase worker productivity, such as conveyor belts that travel slowly in front of pickers and take their full trays. Photo 7.4 shows one of the conveyor belts that straddle up to 17 rows of berries are common in Ventura County's strawberry harvest, allowing workers to pick at least 20 percent faster.[75] Some growers reduce piece rates by 10 percent to 20 percent when workers can place full trays on conveyor belts, which has led to worker protests.[76]

There are fewer conveyor belts in the Salinas-Watsonville area, both because of hills that make it more difficult to use them and due to disputes about how much the piece rate should be reduced with increased worker productivity.[77] Conveyor belts are available in many sizes, with some covering only a few rows of berries for up to five workers and others covering a dozen or more rows for 20 to 40 workers.

Robot carriers are an alternative productivity-increasing aid to take full trays of berries from pickers to collection stations. the carriers must be programmed to anticipate when workers will need an empty tray, so that the

Photo 7.4 Conveyor Belts for Strawberry Harvesters
Source: Philip Martin

robot arrives with an empty tray at the right moment so the picker can work without interruption. During one test, half of the pickers averaged 15 trays an hour, a quarter averaged 10 trays an hour, and the remainder were either faster or slower, so five robots would be required to efficiently serve a 25-person picking crew (Peng and Vougioukas 2020).[78]

Several mechanical strawberry harvesters are being developed (Strong and Hernandez 2018). The Agrobot requires that the elevated rows with strawberry plants have hardened sides to allow stems with ripe strawberries to drape over the sides, where cameras identify them and picking arms pick ripe berries.[79] Changing production practices to use the Agrobot raises costs, making the Agrobot most useful for strawberries grown under protective structures.

Other firms are developing machines that harvest berries using current farming systems. As noted earlier, hand-picked berries are placed directly into the containers in which they are sold. Some firms are developing machines that use padded fingers to pick individual berries and place them in clamshells, while others are picking individual berries into 10-pound trays that are taken from the machine to a packing house for sorting and packing in retail containers.

Advanced Farm is using this pick-in-bulk-and-pack-inside strategy with robots that are leased to growers who have flat fields and plants with smaller canopies so that cameras can more easily detect the ripe berries for robotic arms. One worker can operate five machines that move slowly through fields, although hand workers must follow the robots to pick ripe berries that the machine missed.

The challenge for selective harvesting machines is to identify and pick individual berries quickly enough to compete with hand harvesters. With experience, algorithms can improve the performance of machines, but the presence of leaves and other obstacles can make it difficult to detect all of the ripe fruit and to pick it fast enough to compete with hand harvesters.[80]

The second option is more H-2A guest workers, which requires housing in the high-cost coastal areas of California where strawberries thrive. The cost of H-2A workers is higher than the cost of US workers due to requirements to provide housing and transportation, but H-2A workers are usually younger and work faster, which is why they are a rising share of strawberry workers. There are sometimes tensions between H-2A workers and settled Mexican-born workers who arrived several decades ago. They do not receive free housing and transportation from their employers, and they have social security and other taxes deducted from their wages (CIRS 2018). These tensions have not led to union or protest activities, but they do highlight the challenges faced by settled workers and their families in high-cost farming areas.

The third option is to import more fresh strawberries from Mexico, where labor costs are a tenth of US levels. The Mexican berry export season is lengthening as more are grown under CEA structures, and as land that has not been planted previously to berries and thus has fewer pest pressures is brought into production. A third of strawberries grown in Mexico are exported to the United States, as are almost all of Mexico's raspberries and blackberries.

What is the future outlook? Will most fresh strawberries consumed in the United States be produced in the United States and harvested by machines or guest workers, or will most be imported? The outlook is more machines, migrants, and imports over the next five years until the winning strategy becomes clear. The variables that affect which option proves to be the winning strategy include technological breakthroughs and capital to develop and deploy them, changes to guest worker requirements that raise or lower migrant costs, and the cost of producing strawberries abroad. Some observers believe that the improving Mexican infrastructure combined with new varieties bred for Mexican conditions and grown under CEA structures could make Mexico one of the world's most important berry producers and exporters.

8
Vegetables
Alternatives to US Farm Workers

Americans consume a half pound of fresh vegetables daily.[1] Some of the major fresh vegetables are harvested by machine, including carrots, bulb onions, sweet corn, and leaf lettuces, but almost all broccoli, cucumbers, iceberg lettuce, bell peppers, and fresh tomatoes are hand-harvested. The typically large grower-shippers of lettuce use hand workers efficiently, placing machines in front of harvesters who cut and place the heads of lettuce on conveyor belts, with the lettuce packed for consumers in the field. There are fewer mechanical aids in watermelons and cantaloupes, whose US production is shrinking due to rising Mexican and Central American imports. Field production of hand-picked fresh tomatoes is shrinking in the face of rising imports from Mexico and Canada and more production in US greenhouses closer to consumers.

Seven vegetables accounted for over 80 percent of the fresh vegetables consumed by Americans: bell peppers, 11 pounds per person; carrots, 17 pounds; cucumbers, 11 pounds; lettuce, 25 pounds; onions, 22 pounds; sweet corn, 19 pounds; and tomatoes, 20 pounds. A third of fresh vegetables are imported, and import shares range from less than 10 percent of iceberg lettuce to over 80 percent of cucumbers. Import shares are rising: the share of fresh broccoli that is imported quadrupled from 6 to 24 percent between 2000 and 2019, the share of fresh cucumbers that are imported doubled to 82 percent, and the share of fresh tomatoes that are imported doubled to 61 percent.

This chapter focuses on lettuce, watermelons and cantaloupes, and tomatoes. The production of these commodities is dominated by a handful of firms; the largest firm has more than 10 percent of the commodity's acreage, and the largest four may account for half or more of total production.

Bracero 2.0. Philip Martin, Oxford University Press. © Oxford University Press 2024.
DOI: 10.1093/oso/9780197699973.003.0008

Table 8.1 explains that most lettuce and cantaloupes are harvested with labor aids, but declining demand combined with the systemic plant biology and engineering research needed for complete mechanization limit the investment that is required to develop fully mechanized production systems.

Table 8.1 Vegetables: Mechanization, Migrants, and Imports

Commodity	Trends	Machines	H-2A Labor	Imports
Lettuce: *short term,* more preharvest planting, thinning, and weeding machines, and more H-2A workers; *long term,* rising demand for easier-to-mechanize lettuces	Iceberg production down; romaine and leaf lettuces up. Do investments in current systems deter mechanization? Does each firm try to develop its own machine?	Leaf lettuces are harvested by once-over band saw machines. Water jet and knife machines can harvest romaine and iceberg heads, but washing is required before packing.	H-2A workers dominate in Yuma, green-card commuters in Imperial; rising H-2A labor in Salinas	5% of iceberg and 15% of other lettuces are imported; imports are mostly insurance to satisfy bagged salad contracts with supermarkets and restaurants
Melons: *short term,* more H-2A workers and imports; *long term,* mechanization and imports	Watermelons are two-thirds of all melons by volume; cantaloupes are over one-quarter of all melons. Acreage of melons is falling.	Machines can identify and roll ripe watermelons. Once-over harvesters are used for cantaloupes.	Mostly US workers employed for piece rates, but rising H-2A workers	A third of watermelons are imported, and Mexico is the leading source; 40% of cantaloupes are imported, and Guatemala is the leading source
Tomatoes: *short term,* more imports and H-2A workers; *long term,* imports and more tomatoes from protected culture	Mature green production is shrinking in California and Florida. Greenhouse and shade house production is rising.	No active efforts to develop seeding or harvesting machines. California tomatoes are picked once; Florida tomatoes are staked and picked several times.	FLCs and H-2As rising in California and Florida	61% of fresh tomatoes were imports in 2019; imports are vine-ripened and specialty Roma, cherry, and grape tomatoes, with Mexico as the leading source

Source: Author's elaboration

Lettuce

Lettuces, including head (iceberg) and leaf (romaine, butterhead, and other leaf varieties), are the most valuable US vegetable and are produced primarily in California (70 percent of US production) and Arizona (30 percent). The United States produces lettuce year-round, so only 6 percent of iceberg lettuce and 13 percent of romaine, butterhead, and other leaf lettuces were imported in 2019. Americans have been shifting from head to other lettuces, so each type was about half of the 25 pounds per person available in 2019.

Production and Trade

Most US lettuce is produced by fewer than 50 vertically integrated grower-shippers who plant, harvest, and sell lettuce year-round to major supermarket chains, restaurants, and food service firms. The longest period of production is in the US "Salad Bowl," the Salinas Valley, where lettuce is harvested between May and October. Some equipment and workers move to the San Joaquin Valley for the November harvest before production shifts to Yuma, Arizona, and the Imperial Valley of California between December and March. Lettuce is harvested again in the San Joaquin Valley in April before returning to Salinas.

There are limited government data on the size and structure of farms in the lettuce industry. Cook (2011) estimated that the four largest iceberg lettuce producers accounted for 60 percent of production, and the eight largest for 80 percent. New entrants are deterred by the scarcity of high-quality land for year-round production and the need to obtain contracts with supermarkets and food service buyers.

The United States produced 4.1 billion pounds of head lettuce in 2019, imported 260 million pounds, and exported 244 million pounds, for a total supply of 4.2 billion pounds or almost 13 pounds per US resident. Some US grower-shippers plant lettuce in Mexico in order to fulfill their US contracts if disease or weather problems interrupt the supply of US-grown lettuce. Head lettuce production has been trending downward, but grower prices are rising.

The United States produced 4 billion pounds of leaf and romaine lettuce in 2019, imported 529 million pounds, and exported 439 million pounds, for 4.1 billion pounds available or almost 12 pounds per US resident. Leaf and romaine lettuce production has been increasing and grower prices are trending downward.

The demand for lettuce is changing. Iceberg or head lettuce has been the dominant lettuce; in 2000 head lettuce was almost three-fourths of the 32 pounds of lettuce per person available but is now only half of US lettuce. One reason is the growing consumption of baby lettuces, which can be harvested by a machine that uses a band saw to cut the immature lettuce in one pass through the field and convey it to bins for transport to packing and salad plants. Band-saw lettuce harvesters can cut up to 15,000 pounds of lettuce an hour, equivalent to a crew of over 100 hand workers.

A major change in the lettuce industry is the growth of bagged or prepackaged salads. The interstate highway system reduced the time needed to transport commodities from the West to the East Coast in the 1960s, when most supermarkets added refrigerated sections for perishable commodities. The share of women working for wages rose in the 1970s, increasing the demand for convenient food just when Earthbound Farms developed bagged salads to sell organic produce to restaurants and discovered that consumers would pay premium prices for ready-to-eat salads as well. Fresh Express and Dole became the largest bagged salad firms in the 1980s, though they have since been displaced by Taylor Farms.[2]

Controlled atmosphere technologies developed to preserve apples and other fresh fruit were adapted to preserve leafy green vegetables. What began as a small-scale effort to supply bagged salads to restaurants became the major way to sell lettuce, as marketers developed ready-to-eat salads that have a two-week shelf life. Bagged salads pose trade-offs. For grower-shippers, contracts with retailers and restaurants to provide a consistent supply of bagged salads can stabilize the prices they receive for lettuce. However, mixing heads of lettuce in a packaging plant can spread contaminated lettuces quickly and raise food safety issues.[3]

Labor

Lettuce seeds are inserted into the ground or lettuce seedlings are transplanted when they are about 20 days old. Fields are thinned and weeded by machine or by hand, and the lettuce is ready to harvest 60 to 90 days later, depending on the time of the year and the weather. Growers plant lettuce each week so that there is always a crop to harvest, and two and sometimes three crops can be harvested each year from one piece of land in the Salinas area.

Many innovations reduced the need for preharvest labor. A plant-tape machine puts seedlings in a belt and plants them exactly eight inches apart. This allows a thinning machine to know exactly where plants are located and eliminate any extra plants and weeds (Mohan 2017). Specialized machines use knives, flames, or chemicals to remove weeds that cameras and computers determine are not lettuce plants, reducing preharvest labor needs by two-thirds (Mosqueda et al. 2017).

The harvesting method depends on the type of lettuce and its usage. Iceberg lettuce destined for bagged salads is cut by field workers, who remove the core and unwanted leaves before placing the heads on belts that convey them to bins for transport to salad processing plants. These plants wash the lettuce in a chlorine solution and then spin it dry before the lettuce is cut, mixed, and bagged; the plants are kept at 34 degrees F with 98 percent humidity. About 80 percent of head lettuce is mature during the first harvest, so fields can be harvested a second time if prices justify a second harvest.

Iceberg and romaine lettuces that are not bagged are typically harvested by crews of 20 to 26 workers who walk behind conveyor belts and select and trim mature heads before placing them on a belt that conveys them to packers, who place the heads into plastic sleeves and pack them into cartons, as seen in Photo 8.1. Iceberg lettuce weighs about two pounds a head and is bagged individually or with three or six heads in each plastic sleeve; a carton holds 24 heads and weighs 48 pounds. Full cartons are placed on pallets and taken to vacuum cooling facilities that lower the temperature to 34 degrees F before the lettuce cartons are loaded onto trucks for transport to supermarkets and other buyers.

A crew of 10 cutters and 16 packers, stackers, and drivers can harvest 2,500 to 3,000 cartons of romaine lettuce in an eight-hour day. Growers guarantee all members of the crew the minimum wage, and most offer a bonus that is shared by the crew if they harvest more than a target level of cartons, with the target varying by field and yield. Crew bonus systems allow most lettuce harvesters to earn several dollars an hour more than California's $15-an-hour minimum wage in 2022, often $150 or more a day rather than the $120 guaranteed by the minimum wage.

Baby leaf lettuces and immature romaine lettuce can be harvested with band saw or water jet machines that make one pass through the field. There are several types of machines. One machine that uses water jets to cut the lettuce

Photo 8.1 Harvesting Lettuce
Source: Philip Martin

can harvest 12,000 pounds an hour into totes for packing as heads or 24,000 pounds an hour if the lettuce goes into bulk bins for bagged salads, as seen in Photo 8.2. Similar band saw or water jet machines are used to harvest spinach.

Unions

Lettuce workers have long been a farm worker elite. Most are employed by large and integrated firms whose nonfarm packing and transport employees are represented by unions. Lettuce firms often pay higher-than-average wages to farm workers in the Salinas area, which was the center of farm worker union activities in the 1970s.

The United Farm Workers union achieved its first contracts in table grapes in 1970 and then turned to lettuce. The UFW sent letters to lettuce growers asserting that their employees wanted to be represented by the UFW and asking growers to recognize the UFW and sign the UFW's standard contract; these letters were lawful because farm workers were not covered by any labor relations law until 1975. In response, many lettuce growers whose packing

Photo 8.2 Harvesting Baby Lettuce
Source: Philip Martin

plant workers were represented by the Teamsters union recognized the Teamsters as the representative of their field workers, setting off a three-way struggle between the growers, the Teamsters, and UFW.

The UFW called a strike against Salinas lettuce growers in August 1970 to persuade them to break their Teamster contracts and negotiate with the UFW and asked consumers to boycott lettuce until the growers recognized the UFW.[4] The United Brands (Chiquita) Interharvest subsidiary, which leased land to produce 20 percent of Salinas-area lettuce, was the first lettuce grower to make the switch from the Teamsters to the UFW in September 1972, over the objections of local managers. The UFW-Interharvest contract called for a minimum wage of $2.10 an hour and a piece rate of $0.415 a box for iceberg lettuce, so the fastest cutters and packers could earn $10 an hour at a time when the federal minimum wage for farm workers was $1.30 an hour and $1.60 for nonfarm workers.

Most Salinas growers complained that the Interharvest-UFW contract raised labor costs too much, but local grower D'Arrigo followed

Interharvest and switched from the Teamsters to the UFW. The Teamsters agreed to withdraw from representing most Salinas lettuce field workers in March 1972, and the UFW negotiated contracts with most of the major lettuce growers.

The Teamsters returned to the fields in 1974 and replaced the UFW on 350 farms. The UFW reported 60,000 workers under contract in 1972 and just 5,000 in 1974, when the Teamsters represented 55,000 farm workers.[5] Most growers preferred to deal with the Teamsters, emphasizing that their employees disliked UFW hiring halls, which assigned workers to jobs based on their seniority with the UFW and thus sometimes broke up families who wanted to work together.

California's 1975 Agricultural Labor Relations Act revived the UFW, which won most of the ALRB-supervised elections held in 1975 and 1976 (Martin 2003). The UFW signed contracts with major lettuce growers that raised wages and added employer-paid benefits, including the UFW's Robert F. Kennedy health insurance plan for farm workers and their families. The Teamsters stopped trying to organize field workers in 1977.

As the UFW prepared to renegotiate the two-year lettuce contracts that had been signed in 1976, inflation approached 20 percent, and President Jimmy Carter asked unions to limit their wage demands to a 7 percent increase. The UFW demanded a 42 percent wage increase for lettuce workers in 1978, which would have raised the minimum wage in UFW contracts from $3.70 to $5.25 per hour when the federal minimum wage was $2.90. Growers offered 7 percent a year or a 21 percent wage increase over three years, prompting a UFW strike in January 1979 against the 27 lettuce growers in the Imperial Valley who were negotiating a uniform contract.

Many of the 8,000 Imperial Valley lettuce workers lived in Mexicali, Mexico, and commuted daily to US farm jobs. The UFW and the growers placed competing ads in Mexicali newspapers to persuade workers to stay home or come to work. There violence on the picket lines and a UFW striker was killed.

The Imperial Valley lettuce proved to be a Pyrrhic victory for the UFW because it raised grower prices and revenue. Normal lettuce production in the Imperial Valley in February was 10 million cartons worth $3.75 a carton, for revenue of $38 million. The UFW's partially successful strike in combination with whitefly problems reduced shipments by a third to 6.6 million cartons, and the grower price rose to $12 a carton, generating $70 million in lettuce revenues (Carter et al. 1981).

The wage leader in lettuce was a subsidiary of United Brands (Chiquita) known as Sun-Harvest or Interharvest until 1979. Sun-Harvest agreed to raise its minimum wage to $5.25 an hour in a new UFW contract but then exited the lettuce business, as did several other large Salinas-based lettuce grower-shippers.[6] Smaller growers who operated only in the Imperial Valley did not agree to Sun-Harvest terms, and the UFW charged that they failed to bargain in good faith, as required by California's 1975 Agricultural Labor Relations Act. The ALRB agreed with the UFW that the Imperial-only growers failed to bargain in good faith and ordered them to pay an estimated $100 million to workers for lost wages and benefits.[7] The growers appealed, and a California court of appeal in 1984 reversed the ALRB decision, concluding that "neither party can be said to be solely responsible for the impasse" in bargaining because of the large gap between the UFW's wage demand, which the court estimated would increase labor costs by 123 to 190 percent, and the 21 percent wage hike offered by the employers.[8]

The UFW has one lettuce contract today. Salinas-based D'Arrigo signed a UFW contract in 2007, although most of the workers who voted for UFW representation in 1975 are no longer at D'Arrigo. The UFW-D'Arrigo contract covers about 1,500 workers hired directly by D'Arrigo, but not workers who are brought to D'Arrigo by FLCs.

Alternatives and Outlook

Most workers employed on lettuce farms are guaranteed the California minimum wage or $1 or $2 an hour more; H-2A workers must be paid the higher AEWR. Incentive pay, payroll taxes, and benefits make the cost of US workers $22 an hour or more, while housing and transportation make the cost of H-2A workers $25 or more. H-2A workers dominate harvesting crews in Yuma during the winter months because the Border Patrol frequently checks the buses carrying workers to fields.

There are fewer than 10,000 lettuce harvest workers, and there have been many predictions that this farm worker elite would soon be eliminated by machines. At a time when most lettuce was iceberg and involved 36-member crews of young men who put 24 heads of "naked" or unwrapped lettuce in a carton, Friedland (1994) predicted that over 85 percent of the then 7,000 lettuce workers who earned twice the minimum wage would be displaced by machines within the decade.[9]

Most head or iceberg lettuce and romaine lettuce is hand-harvested by workers who follow conveyor belts, but consumer demand is shifting toward leaf lettuces, which are easier to mechanize. Technical issues have slowed mechanization of iceberg lettuce. At two pounds a head, the head must be lifted before being cut by a machine in order to avoid leaving dirt on the cut head that would require washing before the head of lettuce can be wrapped for sale. If lettuce varieties with longer necks were developed, it would be easier for machines to cut them.[10]

Vegetable grower-shippers tend to be large, privately owned, and competitive. While industry leaders cooperate to deal with federal and state governments on issues ranging from food safety to labor, they can be very competitive in guarding their growing and harvesting techniques. Most lettuce firms are profitable enough that they aim to develop labor-saving machines in-house rather than cooperate with other growers to develop machines that could be used by all growers. This lone-wolf approach to lettuce mechanization is the opposite of what occurred in tomato harvest mechanization in the 1960s, when government-subsidized research at land-grant universities allowed plant scientists and engineers to develop plants and machines that were refined and sold by seed companies and machinery manufacturers to all growers.

Melons

Watermelons, cantaloupes, and honeydews are cucurbits, a plant family that includes cucumbers and pumpkins, squash, and zucchini. Most melons are consumed fresh in summer. Melons are over 90 percent water, and the cost of transporting them long distances can exceed the cost to produce them, especially in summer when there are many fruits and vegetables to transport across the United States from west to east.

Production and Trade

The United States had 8.2 billion pounds of melons available in 2018, or 25 pounds per person, including 15.7 pounds of watermelon, 7 pounds of cantaloupe, and 2.5 pounds of honeydew and other melons. Watermelon per capita availability has been stable over the past decade, but cantaloupe and honeydew availability has declined from 11 and 3 pounds per person in 2000, respectively.

The United States produced 4.4 billion pounds of watermelons in 2018, 1.6 billion pounds of cantaloupes, and 517 million pounds of honeydews from 111,400, 60,700, and 14,900 acres, respectively. The value of watermelons, $657 million in 2018, exceeded the value of cantaloupes, $332 million, and honeydews, $90 million, combined.

Florida, Texas, California, and Georgia are the leading producers of watermelons, and California and Arizona are the leading producers of cantaloupes. Cordele, Georgia, is known as the "Watermelon Capital of the World," and Mendota, California, is the "Cantaloupe Capital of the World." Watermelon consumption peaks on July 4, and cantaloupe consumption also peaks in the summer months.

China produced two-thirds of the world's watermelons and 54 percent of the world's cantaloupes in 2017. The United States ranks sixth, after Turkey, Iran, and other countries, in melon production, and is the only major high-wage melon-producing country. The United States is a net importer of melons, and a third of the melons consumed in the United States are imported. Half of US melon imports are watermelons, primarily from Mexico, and most of the other melon imports are cantaloupes from Guatemala.

US watermelon production is stable at almost 4 billion pounds a year, while imports are increasing and account for a third of US watermelon consumption. Exports have been stable at less than 10 percent of US watermelon production. By contrast, US cantaloupe production is decreasing, down a third over the past two decades to an average of 1.5 billion pounds a year. Imports are stable at 1 billion pounds a year, but they are a rising share of declining US consumption, 40 percent. Mexico accounted for 82 percent of watermelon imports in 2018, and Guatemala accounted for 55 percent of cantaloupe imports.[11] Melons were switched from vegetables to fruits in USDA data after 2011 but remain in NAICS 111219 (Other Vegetable and Melon Farming) in employment data.[12]

Labor

Watermelon seedlings (plugs) are transplanted into raised beds covered with plastic mulch; water and fertilizer are provided by drip irrigation systems. Vines spread and bees pollinate the flowers. Most watermelons are seedless, and smaller personal-size watermelons that weigh 5 to 7 pounds are gaining market share from larger 15- to 20-pound seedless watermelons. Seeded watermelons that weigh more than 20 pounds are losing market share.

When sugar levels near the center of the melon approach 10 percent, cutters walk through fields, identify ripe melons, and use a knife to cut the melons from the stem and roll them into rows with the pale underside up. Loaders pick up these melons and pass them to stackers who ride on trucks or buses that move slowly through the field, loading watermelons five to seven high in the vehicle. Used school buses are lower to the ground than trucks, making them easier to load.[13] Melon trucks and buses often have six inches of straw in the bottom to provide padding, and carpets to cushion the melons from the side walls. Melons are taken to packing sheds, where they are sized and packed in heavy cardboard bins for transport to retailers.

The H-2A job offers of melon farmers guarantee the hourly AEWR but offer a piece rate wage per bus or truck that is shared by a crew of workers. Typical piece rates in 2021 in Florida H-2A job orders were $80 to $100 per busload, a wage that is shared between the field loaders who pass ripe watermelons from one worker to another and the stackers who ride the bus or truck.[14] A member of a crew of 10 loaders and stackers that fill 12 busloads a day or almost two busloads an hour earns $120 for seven hours of work, or $13 an hour.

Harvesting and marketing are 30 to 40 percent of watermelon production costs. Florida harvests watermelons almost year-round, but the harvest peaks in May and June. Levy and Gilchrist Counties in northern Florida account for about 20 percent of Florida's watermelons, but grower prices are highest for watermelons produced during the winter months in southern Florida.

California cantaloupe and muskmelon growers had 35,600 acres in 2017, including 14 growers who each had 500 or more acres (Census of Agriculture 2017, table 36). The acreage of these 14 large growers was not disclosed but appears to be about 20,000, or 55 percent of the state's acreage for this crop. Industry observers say that the seven largest cantaloupe growers dominate the California-Arizona cantaloupe industry.

Cantaloupes are usually planted from seed in raised rows, with drip irrigation installed six inches beneath the surface. Many melon fields are a quarter section, with only 150 of the 160 acres planted to allow room for equipment at the end of rows. In the past, fields were picked daily or every other day during the two weeks that a field was harvested, but newer varieties can be picked in one or two passes through the field.

Harvest workers follow a slow-moving conveyor belt, picking ripe cantaloupes and placing them on the belt, which conveys them to packers who size and pack 9 to 23 melons into 38-pound cartons depending on their size. Cartons are stacked on pallets and placed in trailers, and the fruit is cooled using forced air. Night harvesting reduces the need to cool harvested fruit.

Most cantaloupe fields are picked three or four times during a two-week period by a harvest crew of 21 people, including nine pickers, five packers, two box makers, three loaders, a driver, and a supervisor. Crews pick and pack 200 to 300 cartons an hour and earn about $1 an hour more than the minimum wage.[15] Yields are 800 to 1,000 cartons an acre, and if the grower price is $8.75 a carton,[16] a yield of 900 cartons generates gross revenue of $7,875 an acre. Harvesting costs are $1.50 a carton, almost 30 percent of grower costs of $5.15 a carton.

Some melons are shed-packed, which means that crews of up to 30 pickers follow longer conveyor belts that extend over more rows and place ripe

Photo 8.3 Conveyor Belt Hand-Harvesting of Melons
Source: Philip Martin

melons on a belt that conveys the fruit to a truck or gondola traveling along-side the machine, as seen in Photo 8.3. Harvested melons are transported to a packing shed for washing, grading, and packing.

Alternatives and Outlook

Watermelons are the most valuable melon grown in the United States, and all are hand-harvested, some with the help of mechanical aids such as con-veyor belts.

California cantaloupe growers confront several challenges. First is increased cantaloupe production in other states that have lower trans-port costs to consumers; the California-Arizona share of US production is declining as newer varieties that do not require hot and arid climates are planted east of the Mississippi River. Western cantaloupe varieties are being replaced by long-shelf-life varieties that have a higher sugar content when harvested but do not continue to emit ethylene and thus do not continue to ripen (which reduces their shelf life). There are also newer extended-shelf-life varieties that continue to emit ethylene *and* have a longer shelf life, and they are expected to dominate cantaloupe production.

Harvest labor remains a major challenge. One of California's largest can-taloupe growers developed a mechanical harvester that picks all of the fruit in one pass through the field, so up to 20 percent of the cantaloupes must be discarded because they are unripe. The machine carries seven sorters to re-move unripe melons and dirt clods.

A machine can harvest 12 to 15 acres a day. If machines harvested 15 acres a day or 450 acres over the season, only 70 machines would be needed to har-vest the state's cantaloupes as the harvest moves from southern California to the San Joaquin Valley. The limited number of machines that could be sold limits manufacturer interest in developing and refining machines.

The melon harvest labor dilemma highlights obstacles that slow the mech-anization of many fruits and vegetables.[17] The first obstacle is the need to develop uniformly ripening crops that can withstand machine handling and are desired by consumers. Melons that were bred for yield, flavor, dis-ease resistance, and shelf life may have to be modified for optimal machine harvesting, a process that can take years, and the modified melons must gain consumer acceptance. There may be trade-offs between desirable traits, as when a melon that is sturdy enough for machine harvesting may have less flavor.

Second, the market for mechanical melon harvesters is small, which makes it hard to attract significant investments from private machinery firms. Third, there is no coordinating mechanism to link plant breeders and machinery companies and so enable plant scientists to cooperate with engineers and the rest of the supply chain to promote harvest mechanization.

US cantaloupe production is likely to shrink as imports rise, which further discourages investment in machines due to prospects for few sales. There is rising competition from Central America melon imports due to lower labor costs and cheaper shipping by sea to ports such as Miami and New Orleans that are closer to most US consumers.

Most US watermelons, cantaloupes, and honeydews are likely to continue to be hand harvested for the next decade with more sophisticated mechanical aids that make hand workers more efficient and productive. The major mechanization option is development of uniformly ripening melons and once-over harvesters that resolve the trade-off between lower harvest costs and less marketable fruit in favor of mechanization. However, it is more likely that workers abroad will harvest more of the melons consumed by Americans, so trade in goods substitutes for the migration of melon workers.

Tomatoes

Tomatoes are a nightshade flowering plant, like potatoes and bell peppers. Tomatoes originated in South America and today are one of the world's most widely consumed vegetables. Tomatoes are technically fruits, classified botanically as berries, but they are commonly used as a vegetable ingredient or side dish and included with vegetables in most statistical data. China produced a third of the world's 182 million tons of fresh and processing[18] tomatoes in 2018, followed by India (19 million tons), the United States (13 million tons), and Turkey (12 million tons).

Americans had 88 pounds of tomatoes available per person in 2019, including 20 pounds of fresh tomatoes and 68 pounds of processed tomatoes. The US processing tomato industry is concentrated in California, which produced a record 14.4 million tons from 296,000 acres in 2015, an average 49 tons an acre.

Processing tomatoes are harvested in one pass through the field with a machine developed at the University of California, Davis (see Chapter 6) that cuts the vines, shakes off the tomatoes, and conveys them past electronic sensors that discard green tomatoes and materials other than tomatoes. The machines harvest an acre an hour and convey the tomatoes to twin gondolas traveling alongside the harvester that each hold 12.5 tons. A sample of tomatoes is taken from each gondola to check their quality, and water is used at processing plants to flush the tomatoes from the gondolas; plants turn tomatoes into paste and other products.

Tomatoes that are consumed fresh are grouped in several ways, including by their maturity at harvest. California and Florida produce 80 percent of US field-grown mature green tomatoes, which are picked while green and ripened with ethylene gas, the plant's natural ripening agent. Mature green tomatoes are firm and slice well and are preferred by the food service industry, including fast-food restaurants. Other fresh tomatoes, especially those grown in greenhouses or under other types of protected structures and often imported from Canada and Mexico, are vine ripened, meaning that they are picked after turning red on the vine.

There are many varieties of tomatoes, including Roma, plum, grape, and cherry (Estabrook 2011). Per capita fresh tomato consumption has been rising due to year-round availability, changing consumer preferences,[19] and convenient packaging.

Production and Trade

The United States produced 2.8 billion pounds or 1.4 million tons of fresh tomatoes in 2019 and imported 4.1 billion pounds. After subtracting 173 million pounds of fresh tomatoes that were exported,[20] the US supply of tomatoes was 6.7 billion pounds or 20.3 pounds per person, of which 61 percent were imported. The average US grower price for all types of fresh tomatoes was $0.44 a pound in 2019, but only $0.25 a pound for California mature green tomatoes because they are harvested in summer, when tomato prices are lower.

US tomato production is seasonal, peaking during the summer months. Imports, which have been the majority of fresh tomatoes available to Americans since 2012, peak during the winter months (January through April) and are lowest during the summer months.

Fresh tomatoes are 95 percent water. The combination of high transportation costs and consumer preferences for vine-ripened tomatoes has led to increased production of tomatoes in greenhouses and other CEA structures that are closer to consumers. Protected culture tomato production is more expensive than open-field production, but it also generates higher yields and grower prices. There are limited data on CEA tomato production in the United States, but trade data show a rapid increase in CEA tomato imports, especially from Mexico.

AMHPAC, the Mexican Association of Protected Horticulture, reported that Mexico had 106,000 acres (42,500 hectares) of protected farm structures in 2018, including 27 percent greenhouses, 29 percent hoop or macro tunnels, and 45 percent shade houses.[21] About 70 percent of Mexico's protected agriculture hectares in 2015 were devoted to tomatoes, 16 percent to bell peppers, and 10 percent to cucumbers. Over 80 percent of the vegetables produced under Mexico's protective farm structures were exported to the United States.

Labor

California's mature green tomatoes are determinate varieties with bush-like plants and uniformly ripening tomatoes that are hand-harvested in one pass through the field. Florida relies on indeterminate varieties that continue to produce tomatoes over several months, so Florida fields are picked multiple times.

Workers with two 5-gallon or 20-liter buckets that each hold about 25 pounds of tomatoes harvest mature green tomatoes. The 30-person crew is divided in half, with 15 workers on each side of a gondola that moves slowly through the field. Workers fill two buckets every 2 to 2.5 minutes and carry them to dumpers on the gondola, who credit pickers for their work and dump the full buckets into the gondola.

Most of California's mature green tomatoes are picked by crews of workers brought to farms by labor contractors who charge about $120 a ton for harvesting. California yields average 36 tons an acre, making harvesting costs $4,300 an acre. Harvest workers were paid $0.74 a bucket in 2020, and most fill 24 buckets an hour, meaning 12 two-bucket trips to the dumper each hour, to earn $18 an hour.[22] The tomato picking season is relatively short, and harvest workers average 200 to 400 tomato-picking hours a year.[23]

Florida mature green tomatoes cost more to produce and generate higher grower prices because they are harvested during the winter and spring months (Guan et al. 2018a). Some 26 million 25-pound boxes of round tomatoes were shipped in 2018–19. Grower prices are $15 to $20 a box between October and February but decline toward $10 a box as the season winds down in the spring.

Florida harvest crews have 24 pickers and two dumpers, with 12 pickers covering six rows on each side of a truck- or tractor-pulled gondola that moves through the field. Pickers receive tokens from the dumper for each bucket picked to record their productivity and earnings.

Filling two buckets, carrying them to the dumper, and returning to pick again requires two to three minutes, depending on the yield and the picker's proximity to the truck or gondola. During the first harvest, when yields are highest, pickers average 30 buckets an hour or 180 buckets in a six-hour day. Piece rates rise as yields decline, from $0.55 to $0.60 per bucket on the first pick to $0.70 to $0.75 a bucket for later picks. Pickers averaged $18 to $20 an hour or $108 to $120 for a six-hour day in 2015, while dumpers earned $100 a day and drivers $120 a day (Guan et al. 2018a).

Guan et al. (2018b) interviewed Florida strawberry pickers and found that a third worked in blueberries and a third worked in tomatoes before working in strawberries. After picking strawberries, over 40 percent of the workers expected to work in blueberries and 30 percent in tomatoes, suggesting that workers move between these three commodities to maximize their piece rate earnings.

The Coalition of Immokalee Workers (CIW) has for a quarter century sought to improve wages and working conditions for workers who pick tomatoes and other vegetables in southwestern Florida. By organizing a boycott of the fast-food chains that buy many of Florida's tomatoes, the CIW persuaded restaurant and supermarket chains to sign onto its Fair Food Program (FFP), which adds a penny a pound to the piece rate wage for picking round tomatoes and makes the tomato growers, who are required to participate in the FFP in order to sell to McDonald's or Walmart, responsible for compliance with labor laws on their farms (Brudney 2016).

Payroll records from one FFP farm found that pickers averaged 22 buckets of mature green tomatoes per hour (Ku 2019). The FFP bonus added 8 percent to earnings, and faster pickers gained the largest share of FFP bonuses. However, most of the tomatoes picked by the workers who were studied were not purchased by FFP buyers, so workers did not receive a bonus for picking them.

Alternatives and Outlook

Some fresh-market tomato growers used the mechanical harvester developed for processing tomatoes to harvest mature green tomatoes in the 1960s and 1970s but soon returned to hand harvesting. The major reason was that machine-harvested fields could be picked only once, which lowered the pack-out rate.

The fact that California tomatoes are harvested only once and that the state has machines to harvest processing tomatoes should make California mature green tomatoes amendable to machine harvesting. However, machine-handled fruit can be bruised, setting in motion fungal decay that shows up a week or two after the harvest and shortens the shelf life of machine-harvested fresh tomatoes. Mechanization in Florida would be even more difficult because Florida tomatoes are staked and are picked several times, so a cut-and-shake machine could not be used unless Florida growers developed determinate tomato varieties that ripened uniformly and were not staked.

There are no active efforts to develop machines to harvest fresh market tomatoes. A major obstacle to private investment in a fresh tomato harvesting machine is the small number likely to be sold. California has 25,000 acres of mature green tomatoes and seven major grower-shippers.[24] If machines harvested an acre an hour, slightly slower than the machines that harvest processing tomatoes, and they worked 15 hours a day to harvest 15 acres a day, each machine could harvest 1,500 acres over a 100-day harvest season, and 17 machines would be needed to harvest the entire California crop. Such a limited market reduces private sector incentives to tackle the plant breeding and technical challenges that have stymied mechanization to this point.

The major labor savings in the US fresh tomato industry are from rising imports (Baskins, Bond, and Minor 2019). Mexican president Salinas urged the United States to approve NAFTA in 1990 by asserting that Mexico can export either tomatoes or tomato pickers to the United States. Although it took far longer than Salinas predicted to develop a tomato export industry,

Mexico is now the world's leading exporter of fresh tomatoes, accounting for a quarter of the world's tomato exports.[25] Canada also exports tomatoes to the United States, mostly vine-ripe tomatoes grown in greenhouses around Leamington, Ontario, the tomato capital of Canada, that are picked by Mexican guest workers. The United States could import more fresh tomatoes if there were free trade with Cuba, a major source of fresh tomato imports in the 1950s.

Production of US open-field tomatoes is expected to shrink over the next decade due to competition from imports and greenhouse tomatoes. A shrinking open-field US tomato industry is unlikely to provide the financing for new plant varieties, machines, and packing systems to develop mechanized systems for field-grown tomatoes.

Controlled Environment Agriculture

Tomatoes are the largest-acreage commodity produced in controlled environment agriculture, including greenhouses and other structures that protect growing plants from pests and weather. The United States lacks reliable data on tomato production from greenhouses (Cook and Calvin 2005), but industry sources agree that greenhouse production is rising.[26]

A leading CEA tomato producer is Naturesweet (known as Desert Glory until 2008), which had its origins in efforts by Israeli investors to sell greenhouse technologies by investing in US greenhouses. Naturesweet transplants tomato seedlings into substrate rather than soil and ties the vines so that the tomatoes grow on vertical rope walls. After 10 to 25 weeks, tomatoes are picked every two or three days for 25 to 40 weeks, after which the greenhouse is cleaned and a new production cycle begins. Naturesweet has 9,000 employees in the United States and Mexico and specializes in branded cherry tomatoes (Cherubs) packed in pyramid-shaped clamshells.[27]

Naturesweet aims to produce branded tomatoes year-round and sell them in distinctive containers for premium prices; its "tomatoes raised right" slogan emphasizes that they are picked when ripe by empowered workers who are treated well. Supermarkets have accepted the Naturesweet model, generating revenues of about $1 million a day for the private company.

Many other firms use CEA to produce tomatoes and other vegetables for nearby consumers, including start-ups that raise private funds and emphasize that they are local producers of organic vegetables. Making a profit is hard: Morehead, Kentucky–based AppHarvest has spent over $640 million since 2018 to develop CEA facilities to produce fresh tomatoes but continues to lose money. Gotham Greens, Mucci, Plenty, and Windset are some of the many companies aiming to replace open-field with CEA vegetables.[28]

Greenhouses and other protected culture structures make farm work more akin to factory work, with year-round employment for workers who live near the workplace. The need for more investment, contracts to supply produce year-round, and local employees makes the management of labor in greenhouses different from managing open-field tomato pickers.

9
Protecting Farm Workers

Enforcing farm labor laws is difficult and complicated by agricultural exceptionalism, the practice of exempting farm workers from laws setting minimum wages, requiring overtime pay, or prohibiting child labor. Federal investigators visit 1 percent of US farm employers each year and find violations on two-thirds of the farms investigated. The enforcement data reveal a bad-apple problem: the 5 percent of berry, vegetable, and orange farms with labor law violations account for half to three-fourths of all violations found in these commodities. If the worst violators could be eliminated, total labor law violations could drop sharply.

One way to identify and target labor law violators is to adapt the food safety model that requires farms to identify possible hazards to food safety, train workers, and monitor data on water quality and other items that could contaminate produce. Similar labor compliance plans, worker and supervisor training, and analysis of data from electronic and other record keeping could improve labor law compliance.

This chapter focuses on US efforts to encourage compliance with farm labor laws and H-2A regulations. Enforcement encourages compliance by punishing violators, but the lack of investigators calls for a proactive approach motivated by produce buyers. Employers could improve compliance by putting in place systems to prevent, detect, and remedy labor law violations, just as they have been required to do by buyers to ensure that their fresh produce is safe.

The fresh produce industry's so-called 9/11 moment occurred on September 15, 2006, when *E. coli* in bagged spinach was blamed for killing three people and injuring several hundred, prompting recalls of spinach (Calvin 2007; Calvin et al. 2017). The source of the *E. coli* contamination was traced to a 50-acre field in San Benito County, California, leased by a cattle rancher to a spinach grower; the *E. coli* got into the spinach via irrigation water. Supermarkets and other buyers demanded that growers develop systems to prevent, detect, and remedy contamination, and their voluntary efforts culminated in the Food Safety Modernization Act (FSMA) of

Bracero 2.0. Philip Martin, Oxford University Press. © Oxford University Press 2024.
DOI: 10.1093/oso/9780197699973.003.0009

2011, which requires produce safety protocols derived from science-based standards, government and private enforcement, and civil litigation and grower-purchased insurance to improve food safety.

What lessons does the food safety system hold for labor law enforcement? Labor laws establish minimum wage and working conditions standards, and are usually enforced when workers complain of violations to government investigators. This complaint-and-investigation system is less effective if vulnerable workers do not complain, highlighting the importance of workers having the power to say no to poor wages and working conditions to ensure labor law compliance; when employers must pay higher wages and offer benefits in order to recruit and retain workers, they do. As we have seen, local workers tend to exit the seasonal farm labor market in search of opportunity, and their replacement with migrant workers from lower-wage countries requires more than a complaint-and-investigation system to ensure compliance.

Labor Law Enforcement

The US Department of Labor's Wage and Hour Division (WHD) aims to "promote and achieve compliance with labor standards to protect and enhance the welfare of the Nation's workforce" by enforcing 13 federal labor laws, including the Fair Labor Standards Act (FLSA), which sets minimum wages and regulates the employment of workers under 18, as well as laws that govern firms with government contracts and regulate employer use of polygraph testing. WHD had 1,700 employees and a budget of $230 million to investigate 7.3 million US establishments with 135 million employees in 2017 (Weil 2018, 339).

WHD enforces two laws specific to agricultural employment: the Migrant and Seasonal Agricultural Worker Protection Act (MSPA), the major federal law that protects US farmworkers, and the laws and regulations that govern the H-2A program. WHD investigators, who normally work in teams of two and spend two weeks in the field to investigate 5 to 10 farms before returning to their offices to prepare reports, can order employers to pay back wages to underpaid employees and assess civil money penalties that aim to remove incentives to violate labor laws.

Figure 9.1 shows that WHD investigators conducted over 31,000 investigations in agriculture between fiscal year 2000 and fiscal year 2019,

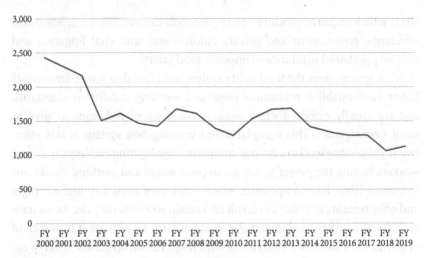

Figure 9.1 WHD Agricultural Investigations, FY00–FY19
Source: Costa et al. 2020

an average of 100 a month in recent years. Seventeen percent of those investigations were in Florida, 12 percent in Texas, and 11 percent in California (Costa, Martin, and Rutledge 2020). North Carolina and New York each had 5 percent of WHD farm investigations, and Georgia, New Jersey, New Mexico, Pennsylvania, and Virginia each accounted for 3 percent.

WHD investigators ordered $66 million to be paid in back wages to 154,000 farm workers, and assessed $56 million in civil money penalties over almost two decades (2019 dollars), including $6 million each in back wages and CMPs in FY19.[1] The number of farm workers found to be owed back wages peaked at 12,000 in FY14, and fell to 9,000 in FY19. Figure 9.2 shows that the amount of back wages owed peaked at $7.7 million in FY13, the same year that CMP assessments peaked at $7.3 million. Annual back wages and CMPs were between $4 million and $7 million over the past five years.

About 45 percent of the agricultural investigations over the past two decades found violations of MSPA, and on farms with MSPA violations, an average 14 violations were found in FY14, higher than the average eight violations found over the past 20 years. Table 9.1 shows that the back wages owed to workers for MSPA violations peaked at $1.3 million in FY19, when CMPs for MSPA violations also peaked at $2.9 million. In FY19, employers were ordered to provide $1.3 million in back pay to 2,253 workers, an average of $570 each. This continues the pattern of the past two decades, when CMPs of $21 million for MSPA violations were more than double the back wages owed of almost $9 million.

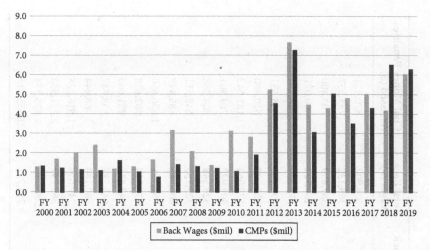

Figure 9.2 Back Wages Owed and CMPs Assessed, FY00–19 (2019 dollars)
Source: US Department of Labor, Wage and Hour Division

The share of farm investigations that find H-2A violations is rising with the expansion of the H-2A program, which tripled in size over the past decade. Table 9.2 shows that WHD found a peak $4.4 million in back wages owed to workers for H-2A violations in FY13, when CMPs for H-2A violations peaked at almost $6 million. However, the number of workers who were found to be owed back wages peaked at almost 5,000 in FY19, when the average affected employee was owed $485 for H-2A violations.

The highest back wage assessment per employee was in FY13, when 4,400 workers were found to be owed $1,000 each. Over the past two decades, total CMPs of $29 million for H-2A violations exceeded total back wages due to US and H-2A workers of almost $22 million, making the ratio of CMPs to back wages lower for H-2A violations than for MSPA violations.

The average amount of back wages found to be owed to workers for H-2A violations fluctuated, from $300 in 2000 to $1,000 in 2013 and $500 in 2019. Most of the back wages assessed in H-2A cases go to H-2A guest workers, who are in the United States for an average of six months and earn $2,000 to $3,000 a month or $12,000 to $18,000 over the course of their stay, making back wages of $500 in 2019 equivalent to 4 percent of average H-2A earnings.

WHD enforces the federal minimum wage specified in the FLSA, but most major agricultural states have minimum wages that are higher than the federal standard, including $15 an hour in California in 2022 for larger employers when the federal minimum wage was $7.25. Most workers who are not paid the minimum wage file complaints with state labor law enforcement agencies.

Table 9.1 WHD MSPA Back Wages and CMPs, Fiscal Years 2000–2019 (in 2019 dollars)

FY	Cases with Violations	Share	Total Violations Under MSPA	Average	Employees Receiving Back Wages	Average Back Wage ($)	Total Back Wages ($)	Civil Money Penalties Assessed ($)
2000	853	35%	4,422	5	1,114	94	104,902	870,421
2001	941	41%	10,745	11	6,356	58	368,132	733,537
2002	948	44%	5,994	6	1,835	211	387,659	783,400
2003	740	49%	6,008	8	1,994	134	266,324	600,071
2004	794	49%	4,295	5	1,129	241	272,540	946,102
2005	616	43%	3,430	6	1,330	74	98,459	588,631
2006	615	44%	3,105	5	1,007	151	152,332	610,890
2007	812	49%	5,350	7	1,497	120	179,564	1,181,543
2008	747	47%	5,275	7	2,557	121	308,923	764,301
2009	636	46%	4,979	8	2,061	158	326,548	804,288
2010	626	49%	4,876	8	1,883	172	323,135	648,311
2011	654	43%	5,578	9	2,558	158	404,961	885,448
2012	767	46%	7,129	9	3,688	205	754,591	1,036,650
2013	822	49%	8,255	10	4,336	147	636,514	902,628
2014	756	53%	10,745	14	6,213	120	742,536	951,669
2015	707	52%	7,802	11	3,569	180	644,187	838,747
2016	608	48%	7,696	13	3,792	179	680,184	968,444
2017	548	42%	3,876	7	1,274	196	249,644	1,613,028
2018	492	46%	4,905	10	2,314	243	562,797	2,751,533
2019	412	37%	4,580	11	2,253	572	1,288,790	2,875,374
Total	14,094	45%	119,045	8	52,760	166	8,752,732	21,355,015

Source: US Department of Labor, Wage and Hour Division, "Agriculture," https://www.dol.gov/agencies/whd/data/charts/agriculture

Table 9.2 WHD H-2A Back Wages and CMPs, Fiscal Years 2000–2019 (2019 dollars)

FY	Cases with Violations	Share	Total Violations Under H-2A	Average	Employees Receiving Back Wages	Average Back Wage ($)	Total Back Wages ($)	Civil Money Penalties Assessed ($)
2000	68	3%	1,100	16	307	299	91,915	136,620
2001	102	4%	9,739	95	1,185	393	466,293	258,540
2002	121	6%	3,606	30	1,043	195	203,347	173,385
2003	76	5%	3,440	45	937	385	360,788	311,025
2004	79	5%	1,910	24	560	249	139,367	178,350
2005	73	5%	2,415	33	947	383	363,032	285,900
2006	86	6%	1,084	13	265	824	218,421	57,900
2007	95	6%	3,270	34	1,826	241	440,085	77,412
2008	114	7%	3,314	29	1,064	602	640,472	440,507
2009	117	8%	4,152	35	1,487	270	400,765	309,337
2010	100	8%	3,730	37	954	389	371,221	357,080
2011	170	11%	5,987	35	1,548	525	813,374	780,755
2012	216	13%	10,214	47	3,228	559	1,805,327	3,267,239
2013	232	14%	11,171	48	4,440	1002	4,448,005	5,972,230
2014	173	12%	6,954	40	2,971	464	1,379,230	1,768,000
2015	207	15%	7,935	38	2,496	643	1,605,360	3,921,186
2016	235	18%	6,079	26	3,572	406	1,451,579	2,223,114
2017	330	25%	7,314	22	3,717	640	2,378,157	2,246,526
2018	318	30%	8,438	27	4,328	456	1,971,674	3,064,224
2019	431	38%	11,984	28	4,994	485	2,419,766	2,836,552
Total	3,343	11%	113,836	34	41,869	525	21,968,177	28,665,885

Source: US Department of Labor, Wage and Hour Division, "Agriculture," https://www.dol.gov/agencies/whd/data/charts/agriculture

WHD violation data reveal three major patterns. First, WHD investigates only a small share of US farm employers. There are over 100,000 farm establishments registered with state unemployment insurance agencies. Investigating 100 a month or 1,200 a year means that the probability of being investigated in any year is about 1 percent, helping to explain why some farm employers can develop business models that depend on violating labor laws and assume they will not be detected if their employees do not complain.

Second, the outcomes of WHD investigations have a U-shape, with most farms found at the zero- or one-violation end of the spectrum *or* at the other end with five or more violations. WHD does not provide data on the characteristics of the farms and workers at the extremes of the number-of-violations spectrum, but analyzing such data could make enforcement more efficient by targeting likely violators, who could be offered more education or be subject to more sanctions to increase labor law compliance. For example, crew supervisors who leave farms to become labor contractors who supply workers to the farms where they were employees could become joint employers with their ex-employer, which should make the farm more concerned that their ex-supervisors are operating lawfully.

Third, the share of investigations that find violations of H-2A regulations rose in lockstep with the expansion of the H-2A program, but the amount of back wages and CMPs was a small share of wages paid to H-2A workers. Between 2000 and 2019, farms with H-2A violations owed $22 million in back wages and were assessed $29 million in CMPs, a total of over $50 million a year. Almost all H-2A workers are employed in crops, where combined direct-hire and crop support wages are about $34 billion a year, including 10 percent paid to H-2A workers, making back wages and CMPs of $50 million a minuscule share of the $3.4 billion in wages paid to H-2A workers.

Detailed Enforcement Data

Detailed enforcement data are available for the 15 years between FY05 and FY19, when WHD investigators conducted 20,260 investigations of farms and found 292,400 violations of the major federal farm labor laws affecting farm workers, FLSA (24 percent of all violations found), MSPA (30 percent), and H-2A (32 percent).

Figure 9.3 shows that there was a U-shape of farms and FLCs with violations, meaning that farms and FLCs were grouped at the zero-/one-violation and at the five-or-more-violations ends of the spectrum. Over

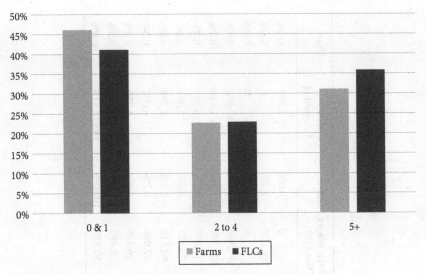

Figure 9.3 Farms and FLCs by Violations, FY05–FY19
Source: US Department of Labor, Wage and Hour Division

45 percent of the farms and 40 percent of the FLCs investigated had zero or one violation of labor laws, which could include failure to have appropriate notices posted to inform workers. At the other end of the spectrum, 30 percent of the farms and 35 percent of the FLCs had five or more violations. About 40 percent of the workers on US crop farms are employees of nonfarm crop support employers such as labor contractors, and they account for over 40 percent of H-2A job certifications.

The fact that many investigations find zero or one violation of labor laws while a third find five or more violations highlights the bad-apple issue: the fact that a minority of the farms and FLCs investigated account for a majority of the labor law violations detected. Table 9.3 highlights the bad-apple issue among FLCs. There were 4,900 investigations of FLCs between FY05 and FY19, an average of 300 a year, that found a total of 65,000 violations. However, the 10 FLCs with the most violations accounted for a sixth of all violations found and 10 percent of the back wages owed. Indeed, the four FLCs with the most violations accounted for almost 10 percent of all violations found in FLC investigations.

Some employers had zero violations each time they were investigated, some were investigated many times and were found to have violations during a few of these investigations, and some had violations almost every time they were investigated. The "bad apple" becomes very visible in Figure 9.4 when

Table 9.3 FLCs with the Most Violations, Fiscal Year 2005–19

Employer	Investigations	Violations	Share	Back Wages Owed ($)	Share	CMPs Assessed ($)	Share
Urenda's Farm and Forest Contractors, Inc.	2	1,645	2.5%	0	0.0%	2,789	0.0%
Global Horizons Inc.	6	1,625	2.5%	164,259	2.3%	0	0.0%
T Bell Detasseling LLC	1	1,413	2.2%	0	0.0%	0	0.0%
Escamilla & Sons, Inc.	1	1,140	1.8%	192,174	2.7%	47,602	0.3%
Overlook Harvesting Company LLC	3	807	1.2%	107,995	1.5%	1,116	0.0%
M & L Contractors, LLC	2	799	1.2%	17,797	0.2%	5,002	0.0%
Cal West Farm Management, Inc.	2	776	1.2%	55,182	0.8%	2,934	0.0%
Sunshine Agricultural Services	2	674	1.0%	64,518	0.9%	1,759	0.0%
EAM Harvesting Inc	1	662	1.0%	47,096	0.7%	6,007	0.0%
Vasquez Citrus & Hauling, Inc.	1	568	0.9%	56,476	0.8%	4,856	0.0%
Total (top 10 FLCs)	21	10,109	15.5%	705,497	9.9%	72,065	0.5%
Total (all FLCs)	4,893	65,135	100.0%	7,150,330	100.0%	13,928,818	100.0%

Note: Dollar amounts are adjusted for inflation to constant 2019 dollars using the CPI-U-RS.

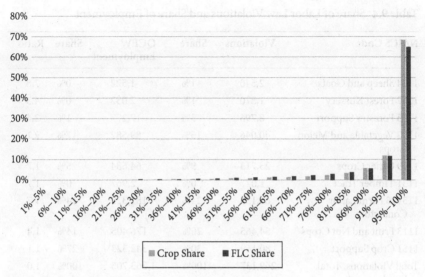

Figure 9.4 Bad Apples: 5 Percent of Crop Farms and FLCs Account for Two-Thirds of Labor Law Violations
Source: US Department of Labor, Wage and Hour Division

violations are cumulated for particular commodities and types of employer. For example, the 5 percent of crop farms with the most violations accounted for almost 70 percent of all violations between FY05 and FY19, and the 5 percent of FLCs with the most violations accounted for two-thirds of all violations found among FLCs. This same pattern of bad-apple employers accounting for two-thirds or more of all violations also applies to particular commodities, including dairies, vegetable farms, and strawberry and grape farms (Costa, Martin, and Rutledge 2020, appendices).

Labor law violations in particular commodities can also be compared to the share of employment in a particular commodity, and a different pattern emerges. In this case, commodities with small shares of agricultural employment can have a much larger share of labor law violations. For example, sheep and goat farming employs a very small share of US farm workers but has a larger share of labor law violations, likely because many shepherds are H-2A guest workers from Peru. Similarly, forest nurseries employ a very small share of farm workers but account for a much larger share of labor law violations. When comparing shares of labor law violations to shares of employment, the lowest ratios are in commodities that offer year-round jobs and do not hire H-2A workers, such as dairy and hog farming.

Table 9.4　Share of Labor Law Violations and Share of Employment

NAICS Code	Violations	Share	QCEW Employment	Share	Ratio
1124 Sheep and Goats	2,540	1%	1,522	0%	7.8
1132 Forest Nursery	1,870	1%	2,052	0%	4.3
1153 Forestry Support	8,796	3%	17,277	1%	2.4
1112 Vegetable and Melon Crops	40,046	15%	89,582	7%	2.1
1119 Other Crops	23,713	9%	64,634	5%	1.7
1131 Timber Tract	1,077	0%	2,967	0%	1.7
115115 Farm Labor Contactors	65,135	24%	181,322	14%	1.7
1113 Fruit and Nut Crops	54,465	20%	176,405	14%	1.4
1151 Crop Support	80,169	30%	342,323	27%	1.1
Total Violations, Total Employment	269,137	100%	1,263,705	100%	1.0
1125 Aquaculture	1,165	0%	7,071	1%	0.8
1129 Other Animal	2,464	1%	20,259	2%	0.6
1114 Nursery Crops	15,094	6%	161,272	13%	0.4
1142 Hunting and Trapping	146	0%	1,908	0%	0.4
1111 Grain Crops	3,572	1%	54,657	4%	0.3
1133 Logging	2,522	1%	48,257	4%	0.2
1141 Fishing	311	0%	6,665	1%	0.2
1122 Hogs and Pigs	948	0%	31,004	2%	0.1
1152 Animal Support	924	0%	30,622	2%	0.1
1121 Cattle and Dairy	1,954	1%	159,234	13%	0.1

Violations are between FY05 and FY19; employment is the share of QCEW employment in 2019

Source: US Department of Labor, Wage and Hour Division, and Quarterly Census of Employment and Wages

Table 9.4 compares the share of labor law violations by commodity over 15 years to that commodity's share of agricultural employment in 2019, and finds the highest ratios of violation shares to employment shares in commodities that employ H-2A workers, as in sheep and goats,[2] or involve FLCs who employ H-2A guest workers, as in forest nurseries and forestry support. The lowest ratios are in commodities that are not allowed to participate in the H-2A program because they offer year-round jobs, including animal operations such as dairies and hog farms as well as grain and nursery crops.

Enforcement Lessons

The analysis of labor law violation data generates three major findings: the bad-apple issue, FLCs, and the link between H-2A workers and violations. First, as noted earlier, only 1,200 of the 100,000+ US farm employers are investigated each year, making the probability of being investigated less than 1 percent in any year. Most investigations respond to complaints, and almost half of investigations find zero or one violation, including a few farms that are investigated multiple times in one year with no violations found. When violations are found, the third of farms with five or more violations account for almost of all violations found in a particular commodity or among FLCs. Indeed, the 5 percent of farms with the most violations account for half to three-fourths of all violations found in particular commodities and areas, raising the question of how to deal with the worst violators of labor laws. Those whose business models depend on violating labor laws need to be reformed or put out of business, which requires monitoring to ensure that they do not reoffend. Current remedy procedures, which involve determining how much in back wages is owed and assessing CMPs, may not change behavior if employers dispute WHD charges and eventually settle for smaller payments or go out of business without paying.

Second, the farm employers most likely to be associated with labor law violations are expanding fastest—nonfarm crop support employers who bring workers to farms. The FLCs who account for two-thirds of crop support employment are expanding their share of total farm employment, which promises a more difficult task ahead for labor law compliance and highlighting the need to develop effective mechanisms to regulate FLCs, such as certifying "good" FLCs or requiring "bad" FLCs to prove compliance on an ongoing basis, as by requiring them to submit certified employment and earnings data to provide early warning of violations.

Third, the H-2A guest worker program is associated with more labor law violations than is the hiring of US workers, and this combination of more guest workers and more labor contractors poses a dilemma for a labor law compliance system based on enforcement agencies responding to worker complaints. With enforcement agencies already short-staffed, who will take on the task of improving compliance?

A wide range of NGOs are trying to fill the compliance gap by creating labor standards that must be satisfied so that employers can gain certification and advertise their certification to gain market share, thus expanding production and employment. Fair trade and similar certification schemes have been tried in many countries and commodities, where they have gained significant market share in a few commodities, such as chocolate and coffee. However, the effects of the programs on the workers they aim to help are mixed, and there are no examples of certification programs that have transformed seasonal farm labor markets.

There is no substitute for government enforcement of labor laws, making it vital to improve the efficiency and efficacy of labor law enforcement with more staff and better targeting of investigations. Enforcement agencies can improve efficiency by combining and analyzing violation and employment data to highlight what experienced investigators already know, which is that FLCs that hire H-2A guest workers and have been found to violate labor laws in the past are most likely to violate again. Efficacy means changing the behavior of the bad apples who commit most labor law violations by increasing penalties for repeat violators and requiring them to submit employment data electronically to enforcement agencies so that apparent violations can be detected without field visits. Similarly, comparing the provisions of H-2A job offers to benchmarks for wages and working conditions in various commodities and areas could provide early warning of likely labor law violations.

The longer-term goal is to change the mindset of employers so that compliance with farm labor laws is a key goal of farms, with systems in place to measure compliance on a continuous basis and remedy violations. This means, inter alia, electronically recording worker hours worked and units of work accomplished, so that algorithms can spot deviations from norms in particular crews. Workers could be encouraged to record their hours and units of production on phone-based apps to generate employee data that can be compared with employer records.

Collecting and analyzing employment and wage data on a continuous basis is only a first step to ensure compliance with labor laws. The evolution of food safety models in fresh produce shows that collecting and analyzing data can help to change behavior, especially when coupled with buyer pressure, government enforcement, and peer pressure for compliance. If there were a similar evolution to collect and analyze employment and earnings data, an ecosystem of consultants and trainers would likely emerge to help farm managers to understand the risks of noncompliance in their operations, as has already occurred in food and worker safety. Extending this employer prioritization of compliance with improved government enforcement and continuous private monitoring and assistance promises to improve protections for farm workers.

The Food Safety Model

Food safety systems provides a model for improving protections for farm workers. Such systems for fresh fruit and vegetables emerged as defensive reactions to food-borne illnesses that sickened consumers and reduced the demand for and the prices of affected commodities (Cook 2011). Consumers do not want to get sick from the food that they eat, retailers do not want to be sued for selling bad produce, and farmers want fellow growers to be in compliance with food safety protocols so that one producer's unsafe lettuce does not reduce the overall demand for and price of lettuce.

There was little government or industry concern with the safety of fresh produce until the 1990s. The death of several children in 1993 who ate undercooked Jack in the Box hamburgers contaminated with E. coli prompted a change in food safety efforts. Instead of investigating to discover the source of the food that made people sick, food suppliers were encouraged to use Hazard Analysis and Critical Control Point (HACCP) plans to identify and correct potential food safety problems, in order to prevent contaminated food from being sent to supermarkets and sold to consumers.

Fresh produce suppliers developed voluntary guidelines to train workers, monitor irrigation water, and test produce regularly, and to use traceback systems so that any problems could be quickly tracked to their source. The Food Safety Modernization Act of 2011 incorporated many of these privately developed best practices into law by governing how US fruits and vegetables are grown, harvested, cooled, and transported. The FSMA gave the Food and Drug Administration new powers to require food producers to take steps to prevent contamination by monitoring the water used to irrigate and wash produce and by ensuring that workers do not contaminate produce, and required farmers to document their on-farm food safety efforts (Collart 2016; Bovay, Ferrier, and Zhen 2018).

Food Safety Systems

Three interacting systems aim to ensure that fresh produce is safe: government regulation; market pressure or supply chain management, as when buyers set standards and require audits to ensure compliance; and civil litigation that involves consumers who sue the growers of the food that sickened them and the retailers who sold the food. These regulatory, standard and audit, and litigation systems interact. Research and experience inform the development of government and private standards, such as how much bacteria is allowable in irrigation water, and underwriters of liability insurance set premiums that reflect their claims experience by commodity and grower.

An example highlights these interactions. Listeria on the Sweet Rocky Ford cantaloupes produced by the Jensen farm in Colorado led to at least 33 deaths in 2011. Previously, the Jensens had dunked harvested cantaloupes in chlorinated water, earning them a 95 (superior) rating in a food safety audit in 2010. In 2011, the brothers who owned the farm replaced the dunk tank with spray-washing equipment in 2011, earning them a 96 (superior) rating despite their failure to add antimicrobial solution to the water, allowing the spray wash machine to spread listeria from one cantaloupe to the next. Within a year of the outbreak, the Jensens filed for bankruptcy, and in 2013 they pled guilty to selling contaminated food, resulting in a sentence of six months' probation (Lytton 2019).

Victims' families sued the Jensens, their auditor, Primus Labs, and the stores, such as Kroger and Walmart, that sold the contaminated cantaloupes. Primus defended itself by arguing that it provided the audit that the Jensens had requested and paid for—an announced audit to ensure compliance with FDA food safety standards, not best-practice standards. Primus argued that it was liable only for the losses suffered by the Jensens, not those suffered by consumers who ate Jensen cantaloupes. But after courts handed down decisions asserting that consumers should have reasonably been able to rely on Primus certification to assume the cantaloupes were safe, Primus and the supermarket chains settled.

The Jensen case illustrates how governments and buyers set standards, audits help ensure compliance, and litigation provides private incentives to comply. Some analysts suggest that the third element, litigation to compensate victims, is a missing key to labor law compliance, where government agencies typically require violators to pay the wages they should have paid and perhaps penalties to deter future violations. They point to workers' compensation insurance that employers buy to cover the cost of workplace injuries, with employer-paid premiums reflecting the risks that the insurance firm will incur with a particular farm.

Could a similar system of government regulation, standards and audits, and litigation improve compliance with labor laws? The major labor compliance tool today are government investigations prompted by worker complaints. Workers can also complain to unions, although less than 1 percent of US farm workers are employed under union contracts. Many produce buyers require their suppliers to abide by standards embodied in labor codes of conducts, many of which require suppliers to abide by labor laws.[3]

Market interdependence between firms differs in food safety and labor. In food safety, growers and buyers have a shared incentive to ensure that their produce is safe. The costs of contaminated food include reduced sales of the contaminated commodity as well as significant payouts to consumers who get sick, giving growers, buyers, and insurers incentives to prevent contamination. The major role of government in food safety is more often to locate the source of the contamination than to levy fines.

Compliance with labor laws is different. Labor violations are usually employer-specific rather than commodity-wide, with exceptions such as Thai seafood or Bangladeshi garments,[4] so a violation on one farm does not affect consumer demand for the commodity. Employers and buyers believe that labor violations are episodic rather than systemic. Aggrieved workers can normally recover only the wages and benefits they should have received—a sharp contrast to food safety litigation, which can produce large payments to victims and their families.

The goals of producing safe food and protecting farm workers are best achieved by creating cultures of safety and compliance, as when farms implement systems to prevent contamination by monitoring water and fertilizer and worker hygiene, and ensure labor compliance through the use of systems to record worker hours accurately and measures to avoid side payments to or harassment by supervisors.

It is hard to create top-down systems that provide what could be called a motion-picture view of labor law compliance in the same way that testing irrigation water creates a record of water quality. Audits provide a snapshot of labor conditions, but they often become checklists that confirm whether an employer has a policy on a particular item, not whether the policy is adhered to continuously. Some employers consider rectifying individual worker complaints a cost of doing business rather than a reason for systemic change.

Lessons

The evolution of food safety standards suggests three lessons for labor compliance systems. First, food safety protocols have both bottom-up and top-down qualities. Good Agricultural Practices (GAPs) were a bottom-up response to food safety issues on individual farms, were quickly mandated by produce buyers, and were adopted by the relative handful of large farms that produce most fresh produce. When these private GAPs proved to be effective, a top-down law, the FSMA, made them the minimum standards for all producers.

Similarly, labor compliance systems can be the result of top-down pressure, as when the threat of federal and state penalties for violations or the inability to sell produce to preferred buyers induces growers to comply with labor laws. Labor compliance can also be bottom-up, as when a union organizes workers and negotiates higher wages, or growers find that they cannot recruit or retain workers until wages and working conditions are improved.

Second, whether inspected by governments or third parties, audits are snapshots of food safety and workplace practices at a point in time. More important is a motion-picture model of compliance, to ensure that the systems governing food safety protocols and labor laws are obeyed consistently. A snapshot audit can certify a farm as compliant one day, but this same farm can have food safety and farm labor violations the next day. Systems to collect data and record responses to problems are needed to create a motion-picture record of compliance with food safety and farm labor protocols (Mortimore and Wallace 2015).

Management responses to worker complaints influence day-to-day farming operations. If managers ignore worker complaints, they send a signal that production is more important than compliance, which may erode respect for labor compliance over time. If managers discipline supervisors who violate labor laws, they send a signal that compliance is a top priority.

Third, food safety audits and certifications were developed primarily as a defensive reaction to illnesses that impose negative externalities on all producers. Some of the first food safety certification systems offered preferred access to particular buyers and sometimes price premiums to certified growers, but these premiums often disappeared after "everyone complied." Buyers and consumers expect food to be safe, making it hard to sustain premium prices for compliant farms (Crespi and Marette 2001).

Farm labor compliance systems today are in the premium-price, seal-of-approval phase, meaning that the relatively few growers who participate often receive preferred access to particular buyers and sometimes premium prices. However, if all farmers comply with labor laws, these benefits are likely to disappear, since only the early adopters of food safety and labor compliance systems typically receive special benefits.

Epilogue: What's Next

Human history is a story of rising agricultural productivity allowing fewer people to feed more. All countries with more than 50 percent of their workers employed in agriculture are poor, and all countries with less than 5 percent of their workers employed in agriculture are rich. As countries get richer, a higher share of those employed on the remaining fewer and larger farms are hired workers rather than farm operators and their family members. In the 21st century, these hired farm workers are increasingly migrants from lower-wage countries.

This farm labor "prosperity paradox" highlights the fact that farm workers can become more vulnerable as the total workforce in agriculture shrinks (Martin 2021). Instead of farm labor problems fading away as the agricultural share of the workforce shrinks, the challenge of protecting farm workers can become more challenging because migrant workers arrive from farther afield.

The farming systems of Canada, Mexico, and the United States rely on 5 million Mexican-born hired farm workers, including 50,000 in Canada, 3 million in Mexico, and 2 million in the United States. Almost all of these workers were raised in rural Mexico, and this book has explored the implications of employing rural Mexicans in seasonal farm jobs at home and abroad.

Poverty has been declining in rural Mexico for reasons that range from smaller families to more employment opportunities and a more inclusive social safety net. Government transfer payments now provide almost as much income to the poorest 10 percent of rural Mexicans as they earn from working for wages. Poverty is declining fastest in the areas of Mexico with the most farms that export fresh fruits and vegetables to the United States, creating jobs for workers with little education who can earn two or three times Mexico's minimum wage.

The expansion of fruit and vegetable exports from Mexico raises questions. Will declining rural poverty in Mexico increase labor costs and choke off the further expansion of Mexico's export agriculture, or will higher worker productivity offset rising labor costs and allow Mexican producers to export even more fresh produce? Will Canadian and American farmers outbid Mexican farmers for the best Mexican workers or look farther afield for guest workers, recruiting Guatemalan, Caribbean, or Asian workers? If the Canadian and American governments allow guest workers to stay longer and fill year-round farm jobs, will farm employers recruit guest workers in Asian countries, returning to the pre–World War I era of Chinese and Indian farm workers dominating seasonal farm workforces in western Canada and the United States?

North America's fruit and vegetable agriculture depends on rural Mexicans to fill seasonal farm jobs for three major reasons. First, consumers want fresh fruits and vegetables year-round, creating a demand for seasonal farm workers. Second, farmers and marketers decide where to produce fruits and vegetables, weighing factors that include climate and soils, infrastructure, labor costs, and ease and cost of transport to consumers. Third, just-in-time guest workers allow farms to hire seasonal workers when they are needed.

Workers who migrate earn more in all three countries than they would earn if they stayed home, but it is difficult to protect migrants during recruitment and while they are employed away from their usual homes. Media exposés, government enforcement, and pressure from grower associations and produce buyers have led to improvements in wages and working conditions. However, regular exposés of child labor, trafficking, and other abuses reinforce the perception that many farm workers are vulnerable to exploitation.

Worker advocates emphasize the low wages and hard work of vulnerable farm workers and call for policies and programs to empower them. Such calls often obscure two realities. First, most seasonal farm workers want to exit the seasonal farm labor market. While they may welcome higher farm wages, many farm workers are seeking year-round nonfarm jobs that offer higher wages and more opportunities for upward mobility. Second, the demand for labor in agriculture is elastic, meaning successful efforts to raise wages also speed labor-saving changes such as faster labor-saving mechanization or increased imports.

There is considerable confusion and contradiction in laws and policies that aim to protect migrant workers (Martin and Ruhs 2019). If employers are required to pay all of the recruitment costs of guest workers, and there are more workers than jobs, how should the limited number of high-wage jobs abroad be rationed among workers eager to migrate? Many employers want migrants to pay something for jobs abroad to demonstrate that the migrant is serious about working away from home, and some migrants believe that paying recruitment fees will give them priority to get high-wage jobs.

The COVID pandemic prompted most governments to open otherwise closed borders to farm guest workers, often justifying such exceptions by noting that food is essential. Food, water, and oxygen are essential to life, but which foods? USDA's food pyramid urges consumers to eat more fruits and vegetables and less red meat and processed foods.[1] Within fruits and vegetables, should those that rank higher in nutrition or calories also rank higher when making immigration exceptions to admit guest workers—so, for example, mechanically harvested potatoes may rank higher than hand-picked berries? US tobacco growers employ H-2A workers; should immigration exceptions be made so that guest workers can harvest tobacco?

Agriculture is an economic sector regulated by government for a simple reason: ensuring an adequate supply of food has long been essential for government legitimacy. Most rich-country governments subsidize their relatively few farmers, who are generally richer than the nonfarm residents whose taxes support farm incomes. Most poor-country governments tax their relatively numerous farmers, who are generally poorer than the urban residents who benefit from subsidized food.

Thinking about farm worker protections raises three considerations. First, labor law violations need to be detected, which is difficult when workers do not complain and enforcement agencies are understaffed. Private labor certification programs educate workers and operate hotlines to receive complaints, but there are surprisingly few worker calls to program hotlines, and many worker concerns deal with personal problems such as caring for children or commuting to work rather than labor law violations.

Second, when workers do complain or labor law inspectors charge that employers violated labor laws, the employer may contest the complaints and charges. Not all worker complaints and charges are valid; complaints and charges are often withdrawn or reduced if misunderstandings are resolved or employers remedy problems, the ultimate goal of compliance. If buyers refuse to buy from farms where workers complain or where inspectors file charges, they are presuming that these farms are guilty before farmers have an opportunity to defend themselves. Allowing offending farms to remedy problems, as is permitted under most private labor certification programs, preserves jobs for workers but may weaken incentives for continuous compliance.

The third issue is the most difficult. Farmers need workers, and workers need jobs, so refusing to buy produce from farms that are charged with or convicted of violating labor laws penalizes both the employer and the employees who may have endured poor conditions. For this reason, most labor laws include penalties for violations and provide incentives for compliance by allowing employers to make changes that maintain production and employment.

This means that the usual response to labor law violations is "mend rather than end"—to require farmers to remedy violations rather than to stop production or terminate the buyer-farmer relationship, raising the question of how to monitor farmers to ensure the violation is fixed and does not recur. Options for continuous compliance include appointing monitors (as is done after firms are convicted of violating antitrust laws, to ensure that these firms do not reengage in anticompetitive behavior), requiring the offending firm to submit certified payroll data regularly to provide early warning of labor law violations, and stiffening requirements for employers who need licenses, such as labor contractors, after convictions for labor law violations.

One model for such a labor compliance system is the food safety audit and certification system, which includes worker training as well as continuous monitoring of water, pesticide residues, and other potential hazards. There are similarities and differences between food safety and labor compliance data. Most food safety violations likely go unreported, but investigators who identify a cluster of illnesses look for one item consumed by all of those who became sick. Similarly, labor violations can go unchecked in the absence of complaints, investigations, and audits, but compiling a database of violations by commodity, size of employer, and area could help investigators to detect patterns and target investigations.

The alternative to negative pressure on employers that are in violation, such as refusal to buy, is positive encouragement, offering certified producers preferential treatment or premium prices, the approach of most fair-trade NGOs. Growers are willing to pay for NGO certification if the cost of compliance is low and certification gives them preferred access to particular buyers or higher prices.

Employer compliance with labor laws means understanding where and why violations occur, developing policies to combat violations, and ensuring that employer compliance systems are respected on a day-to-day basis. The best way to ensure day-to-day compliance is bottom-up pressure from workers who refuse to work on noncompliant farms, forcing employers to comply in order to obtain workers. When there are more workers than jobs, and when workers have few other job options, workers cannot exert bottom-up pressure.

Top-down pressure from governments and produce buyers to encourage compliance may offer more promise, but it is important to be realistic. Government labor law enforcement agencies are unlikely to have sufficient resources to make the threat of enforcement sufficient to ensure compliance when labor costs can be up to half of production costs and less than 1 percent of employers are investigated each year. Produce buyers often send inspectors into fields to check on food safety, but most avoid the extra responsibility of ensuring compliance with labor laws. Systems that generate data on labor law compliance that can be monitored remotely by buyers may be the most promising low-cost means to monitor adherence to labor laws.

One last issue is whether labor laws need to be strengthened; that is, are violations of labor laws that protect farm workers isolated or systemic? Most farm employers emphasize the paucity of worker complaints and the fact that seasonal workers vote with their feet each year to return to their farms, suggesting that the workers are satisfied with farm wages and working conditions. Migrant advocates counter that labor law violations are systemic and remain hidden because vulnerable workers have no choice but to accept farm wages and conditions without complaint, justifying more enforcement and tougher penalties.

There are no data to prove whether farmers or advocates are correct. One violation is one too many. When fresh spinach sickened and killed consumers in September 2006, industry leaders recognized that the entire fresh produce industry needed to improve food safety standards so that growers collectively do not suffer when one farmer ships contaminated produce. Labor law violations are different in the sense that they typically affect workers on one farm rather than all farms. When labor violations become so commonplace that buyers or consumers associate particular commodities with exploited workers, an entire industry can be motivated to act, as after the *Los Angeles Times* articles in December 2014 on labor law violations in Mexican export agriculture led to government and peer pressure to improve compliance.

There have been few recent exposés in Canadian or US agriculture like the 1960 documentary *Harvest of Shame*. Farm employers say that the reason is simple: most employers comply with labor laws, so there are no systemic violations to uncover. Worker advocates point to the growing number of vulnerable guest workers in Canada and the United States, the rising share of such workers who are brought to farms by farm labor contractors, and difficulties monitoring these merchants of labor. In this sense, farm labor markets remain on a knife edge, pulled by forces upward toward continuous compliance by buyer pressure and downward toward more violations by more labor contractors and migrant workers.

Notes

Prologue: Mexicans in the Fields

1. Canada assembles 2 million vehicles a year and exports 85 percent of them; the United States produces 11 million vehicles a year and exports one-sixth.

Chapter 1

1. Some of these criticisms have a perfect-is-the-enemy-of-the-good flavor, especially in comparison to US management of foreign-born farm workers. Half of US crop workers are unauthorized, and 10 percent are legal guest workers.
2. The Dominion Lands Act remains in effect but today is limited to Canada's northern territories.
3. Eighty percent of the Agri-Food Pilot workers are in the meat- and food-processing industries. See Government of Canada, "Agri-Food Pilot: Eligible Industries and Occupations," last modified May 8, 2023, https://www.canada.ca/en/immigration-refugees-citizenship/services/immigrate-canada/agri-food-pilot/eligible-industries.html#industry.
4. Within the tree fruit sector, there has been a shift from hand-harvested apples to machine-harvested blueberries and cranberries.
5. 2016 Census of Agriculture: www150.statcan.gc.ca/t1/tbl1/en/tv.action?pid=321 0015401.
6. The share of cash receipts from grains and oil seeds rose sharply between 2006 and 2016, from 21 to 37 percent, while the share from fruits and vegetables fell from 15 to 11 percent.
7. See Ministry of Agriculture, Food, and Rural Affairs, Ontario, "Statistical Summary of Ontario Agriculture," last modified March 7, 2023, http://www.omafra.gov.on.ca/english/stats/agriculture_summary.htm#labour.
8. Some 264 Jamaican workers were admitted in 1966; the Caribbean SAWP was extended to Barbados and Trinidad and Tobago in 1967, and expanded to other Caribbean islands in 1976.
9. The MOUs between Canada and Mexico, Jamaica, and other Caribbean countries are intergovernmental administrative arrangements, not binding international treaties. Government of Canada, "Hire a Temporary Worker Through the Seasonal Agricultural Worker Program: Overview," last modified March 21, 2023, www.can

ada.ca/en/employment-social-development/services/foreign-workers/agricultural/seasonal-agricultural.html.

10. Farm employers receive a positive Labor Market Impact Assessment that allows them to recruit foreign workers. Most discussions of available Canadian workers refer to insufficient "reliable" local workers—that is, there may be unemployed Canadians, but they do not want to fill seasonal farm jobs.

11. For details, see "Canada: SAWP," *Rural Migration News* 14, no. 3 (July 2008), http://migration.ucdavis.edu/rmn/more.php?id=1328.

12. British Columbia does not allow farmers to recoup transportation costs from SAWP workers but does allow farmers to deduct 6 percent of gross wages or a maximum of C$450 to cover housing costs. The Mexican consulate in British Columbia handles employer requests for SAWP workers and arranges for workers to travel to the province.

13. The Jamaican Liaison Service is at http://jamliser.com/.

14. Some workers and NGOs say that government liaison officers in Canada generally favor Canadian employers rather than their citizen workers because they value high-wage jobs and remittances more than worker complaints.

15. The Jamaican government required Jamaican workers coming to the United States with H-2A visas to agree to have 25 percent of their wages deducted, and promised to return 23 percent. The United States ended this forced savings scheme before Canada did (Mize 2019, 137–38).

16. The dispute over the Jamaican forced savings program is described in Teresa Wright, "Minister Urged to Press Jamaica over Wage Deductions of Migrant Workers in Canada," *National Post*, September 28, 2018, https://nationalpost.com/pmn/news-pmn/canada-news-pmn/minister-urged-to-press-jamaica-over-wage-deductions-of-migrant-workers-in-canada.

17. Most Caribbean countries allow returning workers to bring $500 worth of electronics and other goods home duty free at the end of their contracts; many pack these goods in barrels to send home. See "Canada: SAWP, BC," *Rural Migration News* 10, no. 1 (January 2004),http://migration.ucdavis.edu/rmn/more.php?id=824.

18. Government of Canada, "Hire a Temporary Foreign Worker Through the Agricultural Stream: Program Requirements," last modified May 19, 2023, www.canada.ca/en/employment-social-development/services/foreign-workers/agricultural/agricultural/requirements.html.

19. If they then leave Canada for at least four years, NOC guest workers can return for another four years.

20. The Guatemalan government appears incapable of regulating recruitment. After announcing that all private recruiters must register and pay Q3,000 or C$500, the government failed to establish a registry of recruiters, so neither workers nor employers could check the list of registered recruiters (Gabriel and Macdonald 2017, 1719).

21. Canadian Press, "Migrant Farm Worker Review Prompts Renewed Calls for Reforms, Protections," OHS Canada, March 18, 2019, www.ohscanada.com/migrant-farm-worker-review-prompts-renewed-calls-reforms-protections/.

22. Government of Canada, "What We Heard: Primary Agriculture Review," last modified February 12, 2019, https://www.canada.ca/en/employment-social-development/services/foreign-workers/reports/primary-agriculture.html.

23. See "Canada: Unions and Migrants," *Rural Migration News* 15, no. 4 (2009), http://migration.ucdavis.edu/rmn/more.php?id=1488.

24. See "Canada, Mexico," *Rural Migration News* 21, no. 2 (April 2015), https://migration.ucdavis.edu/rmn/more.php?id=1893.

25. Secretaría del Trabajo y Previsión Social, "2015 Season of the Mexico-Canada Seasonal Agricultural Workers Program Begins," last updated May 10, 2016, https://embamex.sre.gob.mx/canada/index.php/press/press-releases/1292-jan15/11465-ptat15begins.

26. Researchers disagree on whether returned migrants prefer to rest in preparation for working abroad again or are shunned by local employers who fear that work abroad may prompt returned migrants to expect higher wages and benefits. Some argue that many returned migrants try to launch small businesses that frequently fail (Castell Roldán and Alvarez Anaya 2022).

27. Mark Kelley, Karen Wirsig, and Virginia Smart, "Bitter Harvest," CBC News, November 29, 2020, https://newsinteractives.cbc.ca/longform/bitter-harvest-migrant-workers-pandemic.

Chapter 2

1. The proximate cause of fighting was the failure of the 31-year-long regime of President Porfirio Díaz to manage the presidential succession. Francisco Madero challenged Díaz in the 1910 presidential election. Diaz rigged the results, Madero and Pancho Villa led a revolt that toppled Diaz, and Madero was elected president in 1911. Madero was soon attacked by conservatives who saw him as too liberal and by revolutionaries who saw him as too conservative, and he was forced out in 1913. Civil war that led to the deaths of 10 percent of the 15 million Mexicans followed until the new constitution of 1917.

2. Few private banks serve rural areas, in part because some past Mexican presidents won elections by promising to cancel farmers' debts. President Enrique Peña Nieto won the national election in 2012 by 3 million votes, but won by a margin of 5.4 million votes among farmers.

3. Hufbauer and Schott report 3.5 million ejidatarios and 103 million hectares of ejido land in 2005. Five hectares is 12.3 acres.

4. Subsistence farmers and landless workers can be hurt by high corn prices if they (1) do not produce a surplus of corn to sell and (2) do not have access to the subsidized tortillas made from government-bought corn.

5. Economic Research Service, US Department of Agriculture, "Mexico: Policy," last modified November 17, 2022, https://www.ers.usda.gov/topics/international-markets-u-s-trade/countries-regions/usmca-canada-mexico/mexico-policy/.

6. Galvez (2018) reported that much of her field work was done in rural areas of Puebla, which has sent many residents to New York City.

7. AHMPAC, "Simposio de Responsabilidad Social Agrícola AMHPAC," accessed June 2023, http://www.amhpac.org/es/index.php/descripcion.

8. Some researchers say that workers in protected culture structures complain of hot working conditions during some times of the year and the presence of cameras and other control devices that require them to strictly observe food safety and other protocols.

9. The United States is the largest importer of avocados, followed by the Netherlands, but over 80 percent of avocados imported to the Netherlands are reexported to other European countries, explaining why the Netherlands is also a large exporter of avocados.

10. Kate Linthicum, "Inside the Bloody Cartel War for Mexico's Multibillion-Dollar Avocado Industry," *Los Angeles Times*, November 21, 2019, https://www.latimes.com/world-nation/story/2019-11-20/mexico-cartel-violence-avocados.

11. Christian Wagner, "Are Mexican Avocados the Next 'Conflict Commodity'?," Verisk Maplecroft, December 5, 2019, https://www.maplecroft.com/insights/analysis/are-mexican-avocados-the-next-conflict-commodity/.

12. Mexicali growers must compete with US growers for labor and so they pay the highest wages, an average $510 a month.

13. Some researchers decry Mexican exports of "luxury crops" from water-scarce regions of Mexico, including the water incorporated in berries exported to the United States (Hartman et al. 2021). However, high-value berries are often grown under protective cover, so if drip irrigation in greenhouses displaced flood-irrigated field crops, agricultural water use may decrease as farm revenues and employment increase.

14. The Coalition of Immokalee Workers used boycotts to persuade many buyers of mature green tomatoes, such as fast-food restaurant chains, to pay a penny a pound more for tomatoes and pass this extra penny on to workers under the CIW's Fair Food Program; the goal was to double the piece rate from $0.35 to $0.70 a bucket (Marquis 2017).

Chapter 3

1. Cash receipts from the sale of crops and livestock were $358 billion in 2020, down from $370 billion in 2019, due to lower prices associated with trade disputes with China and the global recession. Net farm income nonetheless exceeded $100 billion, due to government aid of $50 billion.

2. New York City, the largest US city in 1800, had 60,000 residents.

3. The Union Pacific and Central Pacific railroads met May 10, 1869, in Promontory Summit, Utah, reducing the trip across the United States from months to days and integrating California with the other states.

4. More than 1,000 Chinese died building the railroad, especially during the winter of 1868–69 in the Sierra Nevada. Chinese workers were not included in the photo commemorating the completion of the railroad. The Union Pacific, which was building the railroad from east to west, relied on Irish workers, many of whom were Civil War veterans.

5. Immigrants are sometimes called green card holders because immigrant visas used to be printed on green paper.

6. Until the American Revolution in 1776, bound labor, which tied to an employer in the colonies upon arrival, was most common for whites, while Blacks were slaves.

7. Some contract laborers had to work additional time because upon arrival they signed additional contracts promising to pay for their room and board. Most reports say that only a few thousand contract laborers were admitted and that many broke their contracts.

8. Chinese contract workers were barred in 1882.

9. The DOL consultants' report concluded that "wage levels tend to become fixed [and not increase] in areas and activities where Mexicans are employed" (US Department of Labor 1959, 273).

10. Day labor markets bring workers and employers together in parking lots and other locations. Employers with buses post or announce the piece rate wages being paid, and workers decide which bus to board, expecting to be paid at the end of the day but not necessarily having a job with the same employer the next day.

11. The Senate Committee on Labor and Public Welfare had a Subcommittee on Migratory Labor, chaired by Senator Harrison Williams (D-NJ), while the House Committee on Education and Labor had a Select Subcommittee on Labor. See National Archives, "Records of the Committee on Labor and Public Welfare, 80th–90th Congresses (1947–1968)," https://www.archives.gov/legislative/guide/sen ate/chapter-14.html#CmtLabor1947; House Committee on Education and Labor, *Migratory Labor: Hearings Before the Select Subcommittee on Labor of the Committee on Education and Labor, House of Representatives, Eighty-Seventh Congress, First Session* (Washington, DC: GPO, 1961), https://books.google.com/books/about/Migr atory_Labor.html?id=So635N03Z-kC.

12. Reisler (1976, 25–26) reported that many Mexicans left the United States in the spring of 1917 because of rumors that all persons in the United States, including foreigners, could be drafted into the US Army.

13. Scruggs noted that before the Border Patrol was created in 1924, 60 mounted men patrolled the 2,000-mile Mexico-US border.

14. The Weedpatch migrant camp in Arvin (today the Sunset Migrant Center) provided the backdrop for *The Grapes of Wrath*. After the book's publication, farmers accused Steinbeck of having Communist sympathies, Steinbeck received death threats, and the FBI investigated the author.

15. Vialet and McClure (1980, 20) says that US unions were mollified by promises to ensure that Mexican farm workers left the United States when their seasonal jobs ended.

Mexican Americans were more ambivalent, fearing that importing Mexicans would have an adverse effect on their wages.

16. Mexico, which declared war on Germany, Italy, and Japan on June 1, 1942, considered its workers in the United States a contribution to the war effort.

17. The federal minimum wage was set at $0.25 an hour on October 24, 1938, and raised to $0.30 an hour a year later. If farmers paid piece rate wages, the average worker had to earn $0.30 or the prevailing wage, whichever was higher (Vialet and McClure 1980, 23). In 1946, the federal minimum wage was raised to $0.37 an hour or $33.60 every two weeks.

18. Intergovernmental agreements were also signed with Barbados and British Honduras.

19. The agreement also required that the housing provided to braceros be the same as that provided to US farm workers, and prohibited requiring workers to make purchases from company stores.

20. Suits filed after 2000 alleged that lost bracero savings were $30 million to $50 million. "Braceros: Lost Savings?," *Rural Migration News* 7, no. 2 (April 2001), https://migration.ucdavis.edu/rmn/more.php?id=508.

21. PL 45 was followed by PL 229 (1944) and PL 80 (1947), which had similar provisions forbidding the US government from setting minimum wages for US farm workers.

22. Joon Kim and some other historians divide the World War II bracero program into three phases: the wartime program of 1942–46, the chaos of 1947–51 when unauthorized Mexican "wetbacks" were "dried out" by the INS by issuing work permits to those who had arrived illegally, and the PL-78 era between 1952 and 1964 when DOL and INS first cooperated to make it easier to employ legal braceros and then, in the early 1960s, tightened regulations to make braceros more expensive.

23. Both admissions and apprehensions count events rather than unique individuals, so a bracero admitted twice in one year is counted twice, as is an unauthorized foreigner caught several times. The 4.5 million bracero admissions between 1942 and 1964 may represent 1.5 million unique persons. The number of unique persons represented by 5.3 million apprehensions between 1942 and 1964 is unknown.

24. Representative W. R. Poage (D-TX) argued that the lack of a minimum wage for US farm workers was "one of the greatest safeguards that you can provide for American labor. If it, in fact, costs the employer more to bring in foreign labor," employers would prefer US workers (Vialet and McClure 1980, 35).

25. Swing created and led the 11th Airborne Division during World War II and is credited with helping to achieve victories in Sicily in 1943 and in the Pacific War in 1944–45. Swing was INS commissioner from 1954 to 1962.

26. "Mexican Braceros and US Farm Workers," *Rural Migration News* blog, July 10, 2020, https://migration.ucdavis.edu/rmn/blog/post/?id=2441.

27. Farms are defined as places that normally sell at least $1,000 worth of farm commodities a year. Over half of farm operators report that they are retired or primarily work off the farm.

28. "Fewer and Larger Farms Produce Most Farm Output," *Rural Migration News* blog, March 29, 2018, https://migration.ucdavis.edu/rmn/blog/post/?id=2136.

29. NAICS 113 covers forestry and 114 covers fishing, hunting, and trapping.

30. "Fewer and Larger Farms Produce Most Farm Output," *Rural Migration News* blog, March 29, 2018, https://migration.ucdavis.edu/rmn/blog/post/?id=2136.

31. Data are not collected on which commodities FLC employees work in.

32. The QCEW collects data on farm employers who pay unemployment insurance taxes, while the COA reports farms with expenses for hired farm labor. Some farm operators transfer money to family and relatives in good years to reduce their income tax liability, giving them expenses for hired farm labor but not registration in unemployment insurance systems.

33. Within California, five counties accounted for 43 percent of the state's direct-hire and contract farm labor expenses. Fresno had $1.2 billion in total farm labor expenses, Monterey $1.1 billion, Kern $867 million, Tulare $852 million, and Santa Barbara $595 million.

34. The COA double-counts workers employed on two farms, and it does not collect data on the number of workers brought to farms by labor contractors and other intermediaries.

35. COA data on the number of workers hired by state are in table 7 of the state data.

36. US employers who pay cash wages of $20,000 or more for agricultural labor during any calendar quarter of the current or preceding year, or who employ at least 10 workers during some portion of the day in each of 20 different weeks of the current or preceding year, must enroll in state unemployment insurance systems and pay taxes that provide benefits to their laid-off workers (the 10-20 rule).

37. In 2017, the Bureau of Labor Statistics estimated that total wage and salary employment in agriculture averaged 1.7 million, including 1.3 million (76 percent) that was reported by employers to state UI systems.

38. Two percent of nonfarm establishments during the second quarter of 2019 had 100 or more employees, and they collectively employed 45 percent of all California workers. Five percent of agricultural businesses had 100 or more employees, and they collectively employed 65 percent of agricultural employees.

39. Workers employed in both grapes and strawberries are assigned to grapes if their highest earnings were from grape employers. Commodity information is not available for workers brought to farms by nonfarm employers such as labor contractors.

40. The sample of farm employers was expanded to over 30,000 in 2019 but has since returned to 12,000.

41. The ALS questionnaire collects data for the week containing the 12th of the current month (April) and for the same week of the previous quarter (January).

42. US Department of Agriculture, National Agricultural Statistics Service, "Surveys: Farm Labor," last modified October 17, 2022, https://www.nass.usda.gov/Surveys/Guide_to_NASS_Surveys/Farm_Labor/.

43. "USDA's Farm Labor Survey," *Rural Migration News* blog, December 20, 2019, https://migration.ucdavis.edu/rmn/blog/post/?id=2371.

44. "The H-2A Program and AEWRs," *Rural Migration News* blog, September 9, 2019,https://migration.ucdavis.edu/rmn/blog/post/?id=2336.

45. "Temporary Agricultural Employment of H-2A Nonimmigrants in the United States," FR Doc. 2019-15307, *Federal Register*, July 26, 2019, 36168–301, https://www.federalr

egister.gov/documents/2019/07/26/2019-15307/temporary-agricultural-employm
ent-of-h-2a-nonimmigrants-in-the-united-states.

46. The name was changed from OES to OEWS in May 2021. The OEWS surveys 200,000 nonfarm firms twice a year to obtain employment and wage data by job title or occupation, and uses three years or six employer surveys of 1.2 million establishments to generate wage estimates for 800 occupations. Data can be found at US Bureau of Labor Statistics, "Occupational Employment and Wage Statistics," www.bls.gov/oes/home.htm.

47. For example, the ALS regional wage for California crop workers (SOC 45-2092) was $11.49 in 2016, $12.33 in 2017, and $12.92 in 2018, compared with the AEWRs of $11.89, $12.57, and $13.18; that is, the new AEWRs by job title are up to 3.5 percent lower than the old statewide AEWRs. The new AEWR for first-line supervisors (SOC 45-1011) would be $19.48, $20.38, and $22.11, or 65 to 68 percent higher than with the current statewide AEWR.

48. For example, California's OES wage for first-line supervisors (SOC 45-1011) was $19.48, $20.38, and $22.11 in 2016, 2017, and 2018, respectively, including the 2017–18 jump of 8.4 percent. By contrast, the 2017–18 increase for California crop workers (SOC 45-2092) in the FLS was 4.8 percent.

49. The National Council of Agricultural Employers, whose 300 members (including associations) employ 85 percent of all H-2A workers, sued DOL to prevent the 2019 AEWRs from going into effect, citing the 20 percent increase in the AEWR in the mountain states. The NCAE argues that DOL should be required to first find that H-2A workers adversely affect US workers before it is permitted to establish an AEWR. "The H-2A Program and AEWRs," *Rural Migration News* blog, September 9, 2019, https://migration.ucdavis.edu/rmn/blog/post/?id=2336.

50. The worker side of these 3 Rs are job search, reservation wages and effort on the job, and quits and turnover (worker willingness to leave one job to find another).

51. These NGOs have websites outlining requirements for certification and the advantages for those that are certified: https://www.stronger2gether.org/us/ and http://www.equitablefood.org/.

52. Two 2013 California appellate court decisions, *Gonzalez v. Downtown LA Motors* and *Bluford v. Safeway Stores*, encouraged many employers to switch from piece rate to hourly wage systems. *Gonzalez* held that workers who are paid piece rate wages must be paid at least the minimum wage when not they are doing piece rate work, while *Bluford* held that employees who are paid piece rate wages must be paid for the rest periods required by law at their average piece rate earnings. Most piece rate workers earn more than the minimum wage, and before these decisions many employers did not pay piece rate workers for waiting and rest time. See "California: Piece Rates, Marijuana," *Rural Migration News* 22, no. 1 (January 2016), https://migration.ucda vis.edu/rmn/more.php?id=1939.

53. Chapter 6 discusses how Florida sugar mills were able to use a piece rate system that they called a task rate to terminate slower US and Jamaican cane cutters. When the

workers won a suit in the early 1990s that their piece rate wage was too low and they were owed back wages, the mills quickly mechanized the harvest.

54. Farm workers employed on farms that used fewer than 500 person-days of labor in any quarter of the preceding year are exempt from the federal minimum wage, and all farm workers are exempt from federal overtime pay requirements. The Fair Labor Standards Act allows youth 16 and older to work in any farm job at any time, and those 12 and older to work in nonhazardous farm jobs outside of school hours with the consent of their parents.

55. The Phase-In Overtime for Agricultural Workers Act (AB 1066) requires overtime pay for California farm workers on larger farms after 8 hours a day or 40 hours a week, beginning in 2022. The other states that require overtime for farm workers usually require 1.5 times pay only after exceeding 40 hours a week. For example, New York requires overtime pay for farm workers after 60 hours a week in 2024 and after 40 hours a week in 2032. "California: Overtime, H-2A," *Rural Migration News* 22, no. 4 (October 2016), http://migration.ucdavis.edu/rmn/more.php?id=1995.

56. The UFW sometimes included in its contract count farms where it was certified to represent workers but no contract was negotiated, and farms where contracts expired and were expected to be renegotiated. A careful count found 65 UFW contracts with California farms in 1975, 108 in 1978, 84 in 1981, and 28 in 1985 (Martin, Egan, and Luce 1988).

57. Sarah Klearman, "Forty Years from the UFW Heyday, Unionized Farmworkers Are Sparse in Napa Valley," *Napa Valley Register*, December 18, 2020, https://napavalleyr egister.com/news/local/forty-years-from-the-ufw-heyday-unionized-farmworkers-are-sparse-in-napa-valley/article_9cf29261-4f4a-584f-acfc-ad3b75f6a01a.html.

Chapter 4

1. Using the same definitions, the OECD reported that the US labor force was 157.1 million in 2015, including 83.6 million men and 73.5 million women; some 8.3 million of these US workers were unemployed. Of the 148.8 million employed persons, 139.2 million were employees and 9.5 million were self-employed (own account). Mexico has relatively fewer women in its labor force and a much higher share of self-employed and unpaid family workers.

2. Some worry that Mexico will "run out of" rural workers willing to fill jobs in US agriculture that pay 10 times Mexican wages (Charlton and Taylor 2016), but so far there have been more Mexicans eager to come to the United States as guest workers than there are jobs available to them.

3. "National Survey of Occupation and Employment (ENOE), Population Aged 15 Years and Over," INEGI, last modified February 20, 2023, https://en.www.inegi.org. mx/programas/enoe/15ymas/.

Chapter 5

1. See United States Census Bureau, "American Community Survey (ACS)," https://www.census.gov/programs-surveys/acs.
2. See United States Census Bureau, "Current Population Survey (CPS)," https://www.census.gov/programs-surveys/cps.html.
3. The number of migrant workers was last reported for 1985, when there were an estimated 159,000, or 6 percent of all hired farm workers.
4. During the years when the NAWS sampling strategy was first being developed, NAWS reported that 30 percent of crop workers were legalized under the SAW program and 13 percent were unauthorized. All crop workers reported an average 26 weeks of farm work for 1.7 farm employers, and three-fourths were employed on fruit and vegetable farms.
5. Some 2,154 California crop workers were interviewed in 2015–16 and 1,100 in 2017–18.
6. Foreign-born newcomers were in the United States less than one year before being interviewed. Even if they had only one US residence and farm job since their arrival, all newcomers are considered migrants.

Chapter 6

1. Machines often damage plants, complicating multiple passes through fields.
2. Hanna also bred tomato plants to be smaller, so that they could be planted closer together, and to ensure that tomatoes easily dislodged from the vine. The shape of the tomato was altered from round to pear-shaped to help tomatoes at the bottom of trucks to better withstand pressure from the tomatoes on top.
3. The California Tomato Growers Association negotiates the price of each year's tomato crop with processors.
4. Tomato processors initially resisted machine-picked tomatoes because of required adjustments in their plants, such as accepting bulk loads of tomatoes and doing more of the sorting that had been done by hand pickers.
5. Charles Paul, California's director of agriculture, responding to a question in 1963 about what would happen to the price of processing tomato products without braceros, said that the price "could double . . . triple . . . quadruple . . . and easily put the price of tomatoes out of the range of the average housewife" (US House of Representatives 1963, 66).
6. California harvested almost 12 million tons of processing tomatoes from 235,000 acres in 2022.
7. Then USDA Secretary Bob Bergland in December 1979 said: "I do not think that federal funding for labor-saving devices is a proper use of federal money . . . we will not put federal money into research . . . where the major effect of that research will be the replacing of an adequate and willing workforce with machines" (Marshall, 1980, 579).

8. "Alternatives to Hand Labor in US Melons," *Rural Migration News* blog, December 18, 2020, https://migration.ucdavis.edu/rmn/blog/post/?id=2503.

9. Working holidaymakers are youth in a country for work and tourism. The US calls working holidaymakers exchange visitors and issues them J-1 visas. Australia relies on working holidaymakers to fill many seasonal farm jobs, and allows them to stay longer and find nonfarm jobs if they do farm work during their first year in Australia.

10. Any out-of-area US workers hired in response to employer recruitment efforts receive the same travel and housing benefits as H-2A workers.

11. The Fair Labor Standards Act of 1938, which sets minimum wages and restricts child labor, exempted farm workers until 1966; the federal minimum wage for farm workers was lower than the federal minimum wage for nonfarm workers until 1978.

12. Newly hired workers must present work authorization documents that employers see but do not verify. E-Verify is a government program that allows employers to check the authenticity of worker-presented documents.

13. "3 Decades of NAWS Data," *Rural Migration News* blog, September 13, 2021, https://migration.ucdavis.edu/rmn/blog/post/?id=2643.

14. California has almost a third of these jobs—425,000 year-round-equivalent farm jobs, including 390,000 in crops.

15. The job offer and other information are completed on Agricultural and Food Processing Clearance Order Form ETA-790A and the Application for Temporary Employment Certification ETA Form 9142A. US Department of Labor, "H-2A Temporary Agricultural Program Details," last modified January 6, 2020, www.foreignlaborcert.doleta.gov/h-2a_details.cfm.

16. Jobs are posted at https://seasonaljobs.dol.gov/.

17. NPC analysts must explain what employers must do to make their deficient applications acceptable rather than simply reject them.

18. The SWA or NPA verifies that if US workers have been found for the job but not offered the job, the employer has provided a valid reason for the choice.

19. DOL certifies employers to fill about 97 percent of the jobs they want to fill with H-2A workers.

20. SWA prevailing wage and practice surveys are posted at US Department of Labor, "Agricultural Online Wage Library," last modified February 1, 2023, https://www.foreignlaborcert.doleta.gov/aowl.cfm. In June 2022, there were no prevailing wage results published for California for 2020 and 2021.

21. California and a few other states require farm employers to pay overtime to workers on an 8/40 basis. See "The H-2A Program and Nonfarm Jobs," *Rural Migration News* blog, June 21, 2021, https://migration.ucdavis.edu/rmn/blog/post/?id=2606.

22. Employers prepare a job order for the local, intrastate, and interstate recruitment of US workers. Job orders are posted on private job search sites as well as a government website, https://seasonaljobs.dol.gov/, and interested U.S. workers may apply directly to the employer or to the closest SWA. Employers must also contact former US workers to advise them of the seasonal jobs available and continue to engage in "active recruitment" of US workers until the H-2A workers depart for the United States, usually three days before the scheduled start of work.

23. Employers have testified in many congressional hearings on the difficulty of recruiting and retaining US farm workers in jobs they want to fill with H-2A workers. See "Testimony of Bill Brim Before the U.S. House of Representatives, Committee on the Judiciary, Subcommittee on Immigration and citizenship, Hearing, 'Securing the Future of American Agriculture,'" April 3, 2019, https://www.congress.gov/116/meet ing/house/109235/witnesses/HHRG-116-JU01-Wstate-BrimB-20190403.pdf.

24. "H-2A; H-2B," *Rural Migration News* 20, no. 2 (April 2014), https://migration.ucda vis.edu/rmn/more.php?id=1824.

25. Some US employers and associations ask arriving H-2A workers if they paid fees in Mexico for their jobs and then reimburse the costs. Since no receipts are required, there are suspicions of workers learning to falsely report they paid recruitment fees.

26. Article 28 of Mexico's 1970 labor law, revised in 2019, requires that contracts for foreign jobs be registered with the Ministry of Labor. Mexico had 433 registered labor recruiters in 2019, including nine registered to recruit workers for foreign jobs. The ministry conducted 81 inspections of recruiters between 2009 and 2019 and found no violations of Article 28.

27. Some US employers and associations ask arriving H-2A workers if they paid fees in Mexico for their jobs and then reimburse the costs. Since no receipts are required, there are suspicions of workers learning to falsely report they paid recruitment fees.

28. *Elton Orchards, Inc. v. Brennan*, 508 F. 2d 493, Court of Appeals, 1st Circuit, 1974, https://scholar.google.com/scholar_case?case=4116686416235579922&hl= en&as_sdt=6&as_vis=1&oi=scholarr.

29. Employment, hours, and earnings from the Current Employment Statistics survey, seasonally adjusted.

30. USDA asks farm operators to report the total earnings of different types of employees, such as workers employed in crops, those involved with animals, and equipment operators, for the week that includes the 12th of the month. Employers also report the total hours worked by each type of employee during the survey week, and the FLS divides these two numbers to calculate the average hourly earnings of all hired farm workers, nonsupervisory workers, crop workers, livestock workers, equipment operators and other occupations. Mean wages can be pulled up by high-wage workers.

31. The federal UI tax is 0.7 percent of the first $7,000 in worker earnings. State UI taxes vary and are often 5 percent for employers of seasonal farm workers.

32. US Bureau of Labor Statistics, "Occupational Employment and Wage Statistics," www. bls.gov/oes/home.htm.

33. "H-2A; H-2B," *Rural Migration News* 27, no. 1 (January 2021), https://migration.ucda vis.edu/rmn/more.php?id=2558.

34. For details and examples, see "The Iron Triangle and a Piece Rate-Productivity Standards Database," *Rural Migration News* blog, December 21, 2017, https://migrat ion.ucdavis.edu/rmn/blog/post/?id=2102.

35. In *NAACP v. Donovan*, 558 F. Supp. 218 (D.D.C. 1982), https://law.justia.com/cases/ federal/district-courts/FSupp/558/218/1811083/, federal district judge Charles Richey blocked DOL's certification of West Virginia apple growers to employ

H-2 workers because they raised the minimum productivity standard from 80 to 90 bushels in an eight-hour day. Richey ruled that apple picking piece rates must increase in tandem with AEWRs.

36. The United States produced about 5.1 million short tons, raw value (STRV) sugar from beets and 4.2 million STRV from cane in 2020/21. An additional 8 million tons of high fructose corn syrup (HFCS) was produced from the wet milling of corn.

37. For more details, see "H-2 Guest Workers and Florida Sugar," *Rural Migration News* blog, February 24, 2021, https://migration.ucdavis.edu/rmn/blog/post/?id=2567.

38. Fauconnier's global survey (1993, 119) estimated cane cutters averaged four tons of cane a day, or a half ton an hour.

39. For comparison, a football field is 100 by 40 yards (300 by 120 feet), or 36,000 square feet—about 0.8 of an acre.

40. There were questions about the productivity standard. Was it a minimum or average standard? Over what time period should the mills enforce the standard—an hour, day, a pay period, or the season?

41. More background on the Florida sugarcane issue is at "H-2 Guest Workers and Florida Sugar," *Rural Migration News* blog, February 24, 2021, https://migration.ucda vis.edu/rmn/blog/post/?id=2567.

42. The Fanjuls, through their American Sugar Refining, own about 400,000 acres of sugar cane land, half in south Florida and half in the Dominican Republic, where they own the 7,000-acre Casa de Canpo. Guy Rolnik, "Meet the Sugar Barons Who Used Both Sides of American Politics to Get Billions in Subsidies," Promarket, September 19, 2016, https://www.promarket.org/2016/09/19/sugar-industry-buys-academia-politicians/.

43. US Department of Labor, "Agricultural Online Wage Library," https://www.foreignla borcert.doleta.gov/aowl.cfm.

44. Washington H-2A provider WAFLA was accused in 2015–16 of advising the state's farmers to report only the state's minimum wage or AEWR as the guaranteed hourly wage rather than report a piece rate wage on state PWR surveys so there would not be sufficient data to establish PWR piece rates. WAFLA reproduced the SWA's survey form in 2015 and suggested that respondents specify they do not provide housing for nonemployees, that they do require at least three months experience and expect employees to satisfy a productivity standard, and that they specify the minimum wage guaranteed to workers rather than average hourly earnings.

45. DOL requires at least three employers and 30 workers for employer-conducted H-2B PWRs

46. Roberto Suro, "Migrants' False Claims: Fraud on a Huge Scale," *New York Times*, November 12, 1989; "Agricultural Guest Workers," *Rural Migration News* 5, no. 4 (October 1999), https://migration.ucdavis.edu/rmn/more.php?id=406.

47. In a July 2000 report, the inspector general of the Department of Justice noted that in 1995, management at the Immigration and Naturalization Service estimated that 70 percent of SAW applications were fraudulent. See "Grassley Opening Remarks at Hearing on Immigrant Farm Labor Reform," US Senate Committee on the Judiciary, July 21, 2021, https://www.judiciary.senate.gov/grassley-opening-remarks-at-hear ing-on-immigrant-farm-labor-reform.

48. "House Rejects Guest Workers," *Rural Migration News* 2, no. 2 (April 1996), https://migration.ucdavis.edu/rmn/more.php?id=111.

49. "Congress: Farm Workers," *Rural Migration News* 5, no. 8 (August 1998), https://migration.ucdavis.edu/mn/more.php?id=1595.

50. Quoted in https://migration.ucdavis.edu/mn/more.php?id=1595.

51. Most of the labor-intensive agriculture is in metro counties. The 40th percentile fair-market monthly rent for a two-bedroom apartment varied from $1,200 in Fresno and similar central valley counties to $2,400 in Napa and Sonoma Counties.

52. "AgJOBS: Round 2," *Rural Migration News* 9, no. 4 (October 2003), https://migration.ucdavis.edu/rmn/more.php?id=778

53. "AgJOBS: Provisions, Eligibility," *Rural Migration News* 15, no. 3 (July 2009), https://migration.ucdavis.edu/rmn/more.php?id=1466_0_4_0.

54. For details, see "House Approves HR 5038, the Farm Workforce Modernization Act," *Rural Migration News* blog, December 20, 2019, https://migration.ucdavis.edu/rmn/blog/post/?id=2370.

55. CAWs in the United States for 10 or more years before the enactment of the FWMA could become immigrants by doing at least 100 days of farm work a year for four years; those in the United States less than 10 years would have to do farm work for eight more years. CAWs could get credit for days not worked due to illness, pregnancy, COVID, unfair termination, severe weather, and other factors.

56. Mexico exported $5 billion worth of beer in 2021, making Mexico the world's leading beer exporter. Heineken, Anheuser-Busch InBev, and Constellation Brands have plants in northern Mexico, where water is scarce (about 2.5 liters of water are required to make a liter of beer) but transport costs to the United States are lower.

57. There are two major reference prices: a higher price between October 22 and June 30, when US imports of Mexican tomatoes are highest, and a lower price between July 1 and October 22, when there are fewer tomato imports. Renegotiations have added reference prices for open-field and protected-culture tomatoes, cherry and grape tomatoes, and tomatoes packed in clamshells.

58. "Alternatives to Hand Labor in US Tomatoes," *Rural Migration News* blog, November 20, 2020, https://migration.ucdavis.edu/rmn/blog/post/?id=2498.

59. USMCA Chapter 23, Annex A, includes a rapid-response labor mechanism that allows private parties to file complaints about violations of labor laws at specific workplaces and promises quick government responses. See "Canada, Mexico," *Rural Migration News* 26, no. 4 (October 2020), https://migration.ucdavis.edu/rmn/more.php?id=2489.

Chapter 7

1. US Bureau of Labor Statistics, "Consumer Expenditure Surveys," www.bls.gov/cex.

2. The United States has more acres of oranges, about 450,000 acres, but most of Florida's 300,000 acres of oranges are processed into juice.

3. DOL defines year-round work as 52 weeks at 40 hours a week, or 2,080 hours a year.

4. Imported table grapes are available almost year-round rather than only during the winter months, when there is little US production.

5. R. Karina Gallardo and Suzette P. Galinato, "2019 Cost Estimates of Establishing, Producing and Packing Honeycrisp Apples in Washington," Washington State University Extension, April 2020, https://research.wsulibs.wsu.edu/xmlui/handle/2376/17724.

6. The QCEW data assign farms or establishments to the NAICS code of their major commodity, which means that some cherry workers may be included with apple workers on farms that have both apples and cherries. On the other hand, a farm with grapes and apples may be classified with grapes or, if there are multiple fruit crops, with other noncitrus fruit. Washington had 870 establishments classified as other noncitrus fruit farming (111339) that employed an average 10,300 workers in 2019. Average annual employment represents employment during the payroll period that includes the 12th of the month, summed and divided by 12, and so misses workers who were hired only in other weeks of the month, but the wages paid to these other workers are included in the wage bill.

7. WAFLA says that some H-2A workers are employed in other commodities, but all H-2A workers do some work in apples. WAFLA expected to bring 20,000 H-2A workers into the state in 2020 for 200 growers. WAFLA flies Mexican workers to Tijuana so they can obtain H-2A visas and buses them to farms in Washington.

8. https://civileats.com/2020/03/25/farmworkers-are-in-the-coronavirus-crosshairs/.

9. R. Karina Gallardo and Suzette P. Galinato, "2019 Cost Estimates of Establishing, Producing and Packing Honeycrisp Apples in Washington," Washington State University Extension, April 2020.

10. Apple spurs develop into blossoms and fruitlets; thinning small fruitlets leads to fewer and larger apples. https://intermountainfruit.org/thinning/apple-thinning#:~:text=Thinning%20the%20crop%20will%20maximize,30%20days%20after%20full%20bloom.

11. R. Karina Gallardo and Suzette P. Galinato, "2019 Cost Estimates of Establishing, Producing and Packing Honeycrisp Apples in Washington," Washington State University Extension, April 2020, https://research.wsulibs.wsu.edu/xmlui/handle/2376/17724.

12. Nonfarm employers also bring workers to apple farms, including firms engaged in other postharvest crop activities (NAICS 115114) such as fruit sorting, grading, and packing, where employment was over 21,000 workers in June and July and less than 15,000 from January through May, a peak-trough ratio of 1.5. Cherries and pears have the most seasonality, while sorting and packing are the least seasonal activities.

13. More expensive platforms can level themselves for use on hills.

14. WAFLA was created in 2011 as an employer association to assist employers seeking H-2A workers. WAFLA has evolved to provide a wide range of services, from being a co-employer of some H-2A workers that houses workers and moves them between employers to an agency that helps employers bring H-2A workers to a farm and then bows out of the relationship. Some large employers who used WAFLA in the past to

obtain H-2A workers now do so without WAFLA assistance; WAFLA believes it is involved in the employment of about three-fourths of the 20,000 H-2A workers in the state. A company called másLabor also helps Washington employers to obtain H-2A workers.

15. PWRs are posted at US Department of Labor, "Agricultural Online Wage Library," https://www.foreignlaborcert.doleta.gov/aowl.cfm.

16. Charlie, "Federal Court Tosses Out Flawed Wage Survey That Would Have Drastically Reduced Crucial Harvest Wages for Farm Workers," Columbia Legal Services, March 2, 2021, https://columbialegal.org/federal-court-tosses-out-flawed-wage-survey-that-would-have-drastically-reduced-crucial-harvest-wages-for-farm-workers/.

17. Peru produces blueberries year-round, but production peaks in October and November.

18. Michigan tame or cultivated blueberry acreage is suppressed; this is total acreage.

19. The low wild berry plants are "raked" with a frame grasped with both hands and dragged through the bushes, and the dislodged berries are picked off the ground. "Oregon, Washington," *Rural Migration News* 20, no. 3 (July 2014), https://migration.ucdavis.edu/rmn/more.php?id=1837.

20. Allan Brettman, "Judge Rules U.S. Labor Department Can't Appeal Ruling That It Wrongly Punished Blueberry Farmers," *The Oregonian*, August 29, 2014, https://www.oregonlive.com/playbooks-profits/2014/08/judge_rules_us_labor_depart men.html.

21. Bill Trotter, "Micmacs Find Fellowship—and Good Money—on Maine Blueberry Barrens," *Bangor Daily News*, August 19, 2016, https://bangordailynews.com/2016/08/19/news/blueberry-harvest-sustains-annual-tradition-for-micmac-rakers/.

22. "East: Blueberries, Housing, Tomatoes," *Rural Migration News* 7, no. 4 (October 2001), https://migration.ucdavis.edu/rmn/more.php?id=543.

23. The RAC required handlers or processors to "set aside" 47 percent of the raisin crop in 2002–3 and 30 percent in 2003–4. Set-aside raisins are typically exported or sold as food ingredients at low prices. Growers receive a blended price, a high price for "free tonnage" sold to retail buyers and a low price for reserve or set-aside raisins.

24. The percentage of sugar in grapes is called brix, so 20 brix means that the grape juice is 20 percent sugar.

25. Mason (1998) found that 60 percent of raisin growers used labor contractors to obtain harvest workers.

26. Mason's (1998) survey found that 94 percent of raisin harvesters were born in Mexico, were a median 28 years old, had five years of schooling, and were in the United States less than a decade before being interviewed; 60 percent to 70 percent were unauthorized.

27. "California Raisins Commercial Compilation," YouTube, posted by CavitySam, September 24, 2016, https://www.youtube.com/watch?v=JL3eTqsB73I.

28. https://www.nass.usda.gov/Statistics_by_State/California/Publications/S.

29. Ezra David Romero, "Sunpreme: The Grape That Could Revolutionize the Raisin Industry," National Public Radio, October 7, 2015, https://www.npr.org/sections/thes

alt/2015/10/07/446590533/sunpreme-the-grape-that-could-revolutionize-the-rai sin-industry.

30. Newly planted Sunpreme vineyards have more vines per acre and higher yields, since there is no need to leave space between the rows for drying grapes.

31. "Mechanical Harvesting of Grapes for Raisin Production," YouTube, posted by raisinsales, December 11, 2009, https://www.youtube.com/watch?v=6Chv rWXW1TY.

32. "Raisins, Mexican Food, and Parlier's Future; Parlier, September 9–10, 2004 Report," Changing Face Project, https://migration.ucdavis.edu/cf/more.php?id=176.

33. Sun-Maid reported in 2005 that 60 percent of its raisin growers were over 60 and farmed an average 70 acres; a third have a second nonfarm job; only 5 percent were under 40. "California: Raisins, Parlier," *Rural Migration News* 11, no. 2 (April 2005), https://migration.ucdavis.edu/rmn/more.php?id=976.

34. "Media," California Table Grape Commission, https://www.grapesfromcalifornia. com/media/.

35. California Department of Food and Agriculture/USDA National Agricultural Statistics Service, "California Grape Acreage Report, 2019 Crop," table 3, https:// www.nass.usda.gov/Statistics_by_State/California/Publications/Specialty_and_Oth er_Releases/Grapes/Acreage/2020/202004gabtb00.pdf.

36. Fidelibus et al. (2018) assumed that labor costs for hand labor were $15.46 an hour. Hours per acre were calculated by dividing labor costs per acre by $15.46.

37. USDA NASS provides data on bearing acres of California table-type grapes, not bearing acres of grapes that are actually harvested for table grapes.

38. Most table grapes are picked and packed in the field, but some are packed in packing sheds. This means that pickers cut bunches of grapes and place them into lugs, and the lugs are taken to packing houses to be packed.

39. Personal interviews, summer 2020.

40. "California Agriculture and Labor 2014," *Rural Migration News* 20, no. 4 (October 2014), https://migration.ucdavis.edu/rmn/more.php?id=1862.

41. Captain Charles Boycott was an English land agent for Lord Erne. He was ostracized by his local Irish community in 1880 as a result of activists encouraging seasonal workers to refuse to harvest Erne's crops, in a bid for fair rent and fixed-term contracts on the plots Erne provided them, with the result that the British government and others spent £10,000 to harvest £500 worth of crops for Erne. His name gave rise to the verb "to boycott."

42. Farm workers were not covered by the federal minimum wage until 1967.

43. Ryan Zaninovich, farm manager for Vincent B. Zaninovich & Sons (VBZ) in Delano, noted in 2013 that it would be difficult for a machine to differentiate between various colors and sizes of grapes and for it to cut bunches in a way that does not shatter the grapes. Some of VBZ's 6,000 acres were sold to Wonderful in March 2019, which is replacing table grape vineyards with tree nuts. Lisa Lieberman, "Minimum Wage Hike Will Hurt California Growers," Fruit Growers News, November 27, 2013, https://fruit growersnews.com/article/minimum-wage-hike-will-hurt-california-growers/.

264 NOTES

44. The Coachella harvest is shrinking. It was 2.4 million boxes in 2020, down from 3.4 million boxes in 2019,
45. Other hand labor tasks performed in some vineyards including tying vines to cordon wires and removing leaves to allow the sun to ripen grapes.
46. Henry Lutz, "With Vineyard Labor Scarce, Napa Growers Warm Up to Machines," *Napa Valley Register*, June 23, 2018, https://napavalleyregister.com/news/local/with-vineyard-labor-scarce-napa-growers-warm-up-to-machines/article_19f7f5c5-995f-5f21-ba6c-66af1fe6ce11.html.
47. USDA, National Agricultural Statistics Service, California Field Office, "Grape Crush Reports Listing," https://www.nass.usda.gov/Statistics_by_State/California/Publicati ons/Specialty_and_Other_Releases/Grapes/Crush/Reports/index.php.
48. University of California Agriculture and Natural Resources Cooperative Extension, Agricultural Issues Center, UC Davis Department of Agricultural and Resource Economics, "2019 Sample Costs to Establish a Vineyard and Produce Winegrapes," 2019, https://coststudyfiles.ucdavis.edu/uploads/cs_public/2d/10/2d10450b-f265-45db-85d6-5b15a0fde6c0/19winegrapessjvsouthcabernet.pdf.
49. University of California Agriculture and Natural Resources Cooperative Extension, Agricultural Issues Center, UC Davis Department of Agricultural and Resource Economics, "Sample Costs to Produce Winegrapes," amended September 2017, https://coststudyfiles.ucdavis.edu/uploads/cs_public/c6/28/c6287d1a-64b9-4ba6-b8ff-d83d6c0d0a64/amendedwinegrapessonomafinaldraft91817.pdf.
50. Office of Policy Development and Research, US Department of Housing and Urban Development, "FY 2023 Fair Market Rent Documentation System," https://www.huduser.gov/portal/datasets/fmr/fmrs/FY2020_code/2020summary.odn.
51. "California: Virus, Overtime," *Rural Migration News* 26, no. 2 (April 2020), https://migration.ucdavis.edu/rmn/more.php?id=2414.
52. The vineyard is planted to allow canopies to spread so that fruit is pulled downward as bunches form, allowing sunlight into the middle of the canopy.
53. Henry Lutz, "With Vineyard Labor Scarce, Napa Growers Warm Up to Machines," *Napa Valley Register*, June 23, 2018, https://napavalleyregister.com/news/local/with-vineyard-labor-scarce-napa-growers-warm-up-to-machines/article_19f7f5c5-995f-5f21-ba6c-66af1fe6ce11.html.
54. http://data.un.org/Data.aspx?d=FAO&f=itemCode%3A544.
55. The US was the third leading fresh strawberry exporter $600 million, followed by the Netherlands, $300 million. https://www.opportimes.com/top-strawberry-exporters-mexico-displaces-spain-from-the-lead/.
56. https://www.statista.com/statistics/1164980/sales-share-of-fresh-fruit-in-the-us-by-product/#:~:text=For%20the%2052%20weeks%20ended,billion%20dollars%20in%20the%20U.S.
57. Driscoll's, which has its origins in the 1896 partnership of brothers-in-law Joseph "Ed" Reiter and Richard "Dick" Driscoll, markets about a third of US fresh berries and two-thirds of organic fresh berries. Driscoll helped to create the Central California Berry Grower Association in 1917 to negotiate better prices for Japanese and white berry growers, which evolved into Naturipe in 1922 and Naturipe Berry Growers in 1958

(Guthman 2019, 157). After World War II, Driscoll's began to develop its own straw-berry varieties. Driscoll's Strawberry Associates was formed in 1953, and a decade it later merged with the Strawberry Institute, which was a developer of new plant varieties. Driscoll's had a reported 5,000 employees in administration, marketing, and nursery operations in 2018, and 800 independent growers who lease Driscoll plants and deliver their harvested berries to Driscoll's coolers. Driscoll's growers range in size from a few acres to 10,000 acres, and they hire a peak 30,000 farm workers in the United States and 40,000 in Mexico. Driscoll's reported returning an average 85 per-cent of the selling price of strawberries to its growers. "California: Berries, Nuts, Cannabis," *Rural Migration News* 24, no. 3 (July 2018), https://migration.ucdavis.edu/rmn/more.php?id=2190.

58. The midpoint acreage of strawberry farms was 180 in 2012, meaning that half of US strawberry acres were on farms with 180 acres or more and half of the straw-berry acreage was on farms with less than 180 acres (MacDonald, Hoppe, and Newton 2018).

59. Short-day varieties produce berries in the fall and early spring, when there is less than 14 hours of sun per day and temperatures are below 60 degrees F, while day-neutral varieties produce fruit throughout the growing season.

60. Strawberries must be at least two-thirds red to be picked and packed; non-salable berries are discarded in a bucket attached to the picking cart or on the ground

61. Piece rates are higher near the end of the season, when there are fewer berries to pick, and in Florida, where growers receive higher prices for their winter berries, so piece rates can be $2.50 a flat.

62. *Real v. Driscoll Strawberry Associates Inc D J*, 603 F. 2d 748, Calif. 79-3000, 1979, https://openjurist.org/603/f2d/748/ca-79-3000-real-v-driscoll-strawberry-associa tes-inc-d-j.

63. The most common job certified was general farm worker, 12 percent of certifications, followed by 10 percent for berries, 6 percent for tobacco, and five percent each for apples and melons. Selected statistics by program at US Department of Labor, Employment and Training Administration, "Performance Data," https://www.forei gnlaborcert.doleta.gov/performancedata.cfm.

64. Alonzo Real and each of the other sharecroppers who sued received $1,600 after attorneys' fees (Linder 1989, 239).

65. *S. G. Borello & Sons, Inc. v. Department of Industrial Relations*, No. S003956. Supreme Court of California, March 23, 1989, https://law.justia.com/cases/california/supr eme-court/3d/48/341.html.

66. There are no official data, but industry observers say that 55 percent of strawberry growers (not acreage) are Hispanic, 25 percent are of Japanese ancestry, and 20 per-cent are non-Hispanic white. Guthman (2019, 167) reports that 20 percent of straw-berry growers are Japanese and other Asians (especially Hmong). Before World War II, Japanese farmers grew more than 90 percent of California's strawberries, but plant and soil diseases and the internment of Japanese during the war took many Japanese out of the industry.

67. Guthman (2019, 169) describes partnerships in which a managing partner and non-farm intermediaries seek out entrepreneurial supervisors and provide 70 percent of the capital, and the supervisor growers put up 30 percent of the capital, at least $25,000 for a 20-acre farm. The managing partner deals with land and marketing contracts, and the supervisor grower farms and harvests the crop. Reiter Affiliated Companies and Ocean Breeze Ag Management (Oxnard) are examples of managing partners.

68. Many strawberries are picked into flats or trays that contain 12 dry pints, each weighing 12 ounces, for a total of 144 ounces or 9 pounds of strawberries; full trays weigh 10 to 11 pounds, including the weight of the tray. Some strawberries are picked into eight 1-pound clamshells.

69. "UFW Educates on Strawberries," *Rural Migration News* 3, no. 1 (January 1997), https://migration.ucdavis.edu/rmn/more.php?id=167.

70. Carey Goldberg, "The Battle of the Strawberry Fields," *New York Times*, July 3, 1996, http://www.nytimes.com/1996/07/03/us/the-battle-of-the-strawberry-fields.html.

71. "UFW: Strawberry Campaign," *Rural Migration News* 3, no. 3 (July 1997), https://migration.ucdavis.edu/rmn/more.php?id=210.

72. Most EFI certified farms are in Mexico. Equitable Food Initiative, "EFI Certified Farms," https://equitablefood.org/efi-certified-farms/.

73. https://www.fairtradecertified.org/search/fair-trade-products?product_type=143&name=&page=1.

74. Some growers say that Driscoll's and WellPict have such high quality standards that up to 30 percent of their fruit must be culled, so the higher prices offered by some marketers are offset by less marketable fruit (Guthman 2019, 168).

75. GK Machine Inc., "Berry Ferry," https://www.gkmachine.com/products/ag-equipment/175-berry-transport.

76. "California: Strawberries, Vegetables, Water," *Rural Migration News* 14, no. 3 (July 2008), https://migration.ucdavis.edu/rmn/more.php?id=1330.

77. "California: Strawberries, Vegetables, Water," *Rural Migration News* 14, no. 3 (July 2008), https://migration.ucdavis.edu/rmn/more.php?id=1330

78. Fresh Harvest, the largest employer of H-2A guest workers, includes language in its job orders that require strawberry harvesters to pick fast enough to achieve at least 70 percent of the crew average. This means that if the crew averages 10 flats or trays an hour, the minimum productivity standard is seven trays an hour.

79. Ilan Brat, "Robots Step into New Planting, Harvesting Roles," *Wall Street Journal*, April 23, 2015, https://www.wsj.com/articles/robots-step-into-new-planting-harvesting-roles-1429781404.

80. There are 3,600 seconds in an hour. Hand-picked strawberries are typically packed in one pound clamshells that hold 15 to 20 berries, so each an eight-pound tray has 120 to 160 berries. Workers who pick 10 trays an hour are picking 1,200 to 1,600 berries an hour, or one berry every two or three seconds at a piece rate of $2 to $2.50 per tray and, with payroll taxes and supervision costs, a total of $4 a tray. Robots must increase their harvesting efficiency, the share of ripe berries that are detected and picked, to 80 percent or more, and reduce the time required to pick each berry to two seconds or less, to be cost competitive with hand pickers.

Chapter 8

1. Americans had 409 pounds of vegetables and melons available per person in 2019, including about 153 pounds of fresh vegetables (excluding melons); USDA moved melons from vegetables to fruits in 2012.
2. Johnny Bowman, "The History of Packaged Salad in 5 Minutes," Horti Daily, October 25, 2018, https://www.hortidaily.com/article/9035568/the-history-of-packaged-salad-in-5-minutes/.
3. The three C's of food safety are clean, cold, and no cross-contamination. Harvested lettuce is cooled and held at 34 degrees F and kept at 98 percent humidity to minimize water loss.
4. This was also when the UFW moved its headquarters away from most farm workers to an ex-sanitarium southeast of Bakersfield in Keene called La Paz. Movie producer Eddie Lewis purchased La Paz in 1971 for the UFW at the suggestion of LeRoy Chatfield.
5. The *New York Times* published a lengthy article in 1974 that concluded that the Teamsters would displace the UFW in California farm fields. Winthrop Griffith, "He Started a Kind of Revolution Among Migrant Workers—but a Rival Union Is Now Reaping the Harvest," *New York Times*, September 15, 1974, https://www.nytimes.com/1974/09/15/archives/is-chavez-beaten-he-started-a-kind-of-revolution-among-migrant.html.
6. Sun Harvest in the early 1980s owned no farmland; it went out of business by not renewing its leases.
7. The ALRB cited an ad placed by growers in a Mexicali newspaper as evidence of unlawful bargaining: "The contract is complete in each of its clauses and it is already accepted and signed by the 27 affected companies. Now, the Union must sign it so that you can return to work."
8. *Carl Joseph Maggio, Inc. et al., Petitioners, v. Agricultural Labor Relations Board, Respondent*, Court of Appeal of California, Fourth Appellate District, 154 Cal. App. 3d 40, April 2, 1984.
9. The invention of vacuum cooling in 1956 led to the field packing of lettuce. Before 1956, iceberg lettuce was harvested mostly by braceros and packed in sheds by white and unionized workers. Bud Antle introduced vacuum tube coolers, and by 1960 over 90 percent of iceberg lettuce was field packed and vacuum cooled (Bardacke 2012, chap. 19).
10. Long-neck lettuce and tall-stalk broccoli are examples of the biological breakthroughs that, coordinated with engineering research, can lead to the mechanization of tasks now performed by hand.
11. ERS Fruit Yearbook, table E-15, https://www.ers.usda.gov/data-products/fruit-and-tree-nuts-data/fruit-and-tree-nuts-yearbook-tables/. Mexican watermelons are trucked into the United States, while Central American cantaloupes typically travel by ship at a cost of $2 a carton for ocean freight, followed by $4 to $5 a carton in trucking costs to reach US buyers. Del Monte and Dole are the major importers of Central American cantaloupes, and they often own the ships bringing melons to the United States.

12. ERS Fruit Yearbook, https://www.ers.usda.gov/data-products/fruit-and-tree-nuts-data/fruit-and-tree-nuts-yearbook-tables/.

13. School buses are often taken out of service after a decade and can be purchased by farmers for about $2,500. Many used school buses are exported from the United States to Latin America, where they are used in public transport systems in rural areas.

14. Double J Harvesting, Inc., Moore Haven, FL, H-2A job offer for 2021, https://seaso naljobs.dol.gov/jobs.

15. Harvest crews in the California-Arizona desert areas are typically paid a piece rate rather than hourly wages. Some desert growers in 2020 complained that vegetable harvesters who were normally available to harvest melons after lettuce production ended in March and April were not available in 2020 because of regular and pandemic unemployment insurance benefits that raised their total UI benefits to $1,000 a week or more, above the $800 a week they could earn harvesting melons. Border-area farm workers are usually legal US workers and eligible for UI benefits.

16. The season average grower price of US cantaloupes in 2018 was almost $23 per hundredweight or $8.75 per 38-pound carton.

17. Rebecca Plevin, "Meet 'The Melonater,' a Harvesting Machine Developed to Counter California Minimum Wage Increase, Farmworker Shortage," *Desert Sun*, July 13, 2018, https://www.desertsun.com/story/news/2018/07/13/california-grower-devel ops-harvesting-machine-reduce-need-workers/764128002/.

18. About 40 million tons of processing tomatoes that are made into catsup and sauces are harvested each year, including a quarter in the United States and an eighth each in Italy and China.

19. Hispanics, who were 19 percent of US residents in 2020, consume more fresh tomatoes than other ethnic and racial groups.

20. Almost all US tomato exports go to Canada.

21. "Simposio de Responsabilidad Social Agrícola AMHPAC," n.d., AMHPAC, http://www.amhpac.org/es/index.php/descripcion.

22. With yields of 36 tons an acre and buckets weighing an average 25 pounds, there are 80 buckets per ton, and workers who are paid $0.74 per bucket earn $59 a ton, about half what FLCs charge to harvest tomatoes.

23. Bardacke (2012, chap. 23) reported that mature green tomatoes were picked into wooden boxes for hourly wages until 1973, when growers switched to five-gallon or 20-liter buckets and offered a piece rate of $0.20 a bucket. In August 1973, some tomato pickers went on strike to demand a $0.25-a-bucket piece rate; the growers agreed and then reneged, prompting another strike and a $0.30-a-bucket piece rate.

24. Six firms accounted for 80 percent of California's fresh tomatoes in 2012: Ace Tomato Co., DiMare Company, Gargiulo, Live Oak Farms, Pacific Triple E, and San Joaquin Tomato Growers; "California Tomato Farmers Ready for 2012 Season," press release, June 13, 2012, https://www.farmprogress.com/vegetables/california-tom ato-farmers-ready-2012-season. In 2020, there were eight California fresh tomato packers: Central Cal Tomato Growers, DiMare, Gargiulo, Gonzales Packing, Lipman, Live Oak, OP Murphy and Sons, and Red Rooster; these growers each have 1,200 to 2,000 acres of tomatoes. All of the California tomato growers rely on FLCs to harvest

their tomatoes, and all rely on two to four FLCs except Lipman and OP Murphy, which each rely on one FLC.

25. The Netherlands is the second-leading tomato exporter, with exports worth $2 billion in 2019, followed by Spain at $1.1 billion. Daniel Workman, "Tomatoes Exports by Country," World's Top Exports, 2022, http://www.worldstopexports.com/tomatoes-exports-country/.

26. Cook and Calvin (2005) estimated that 40 percent of North American greenhouse tomatoes were produced in Canada and 30 percent each in Mexico and the United States. Today Mexico is the leading producer of tomatoes grown under protective structures,

27. Naturesweet in 2014 paid $30 million for the largest US greenhouse, the 250-acre EuroFresh facility in Willcox, Arizona, that was built with Dutch technology at a cost of $300 million. The Willcox area has 330 days of sunlight a year, but it is subject to high temperature swings that raise the cost of heating and cooling. The major challenge was finding 1,200 workers in this remote area, and EuroFresh relied on legal Mexican immigrants who commuted 75 miles one-way from homes in Agua Prieto, Mexico. However, the result was high employee turnover and low productivity, which led to experiments including state prisoners to supplement the labor force.

28. "US: Farm Bill, CEA," *Rural Migration News* 29, no. 1 (2023), https://migration.ucdavis.edu/rmn/more.php?id=2825.

Chapter 9

1. These summary data are at US Department of Labor, Wage and Hour Division, "Agriculture," https://www.dol.gov/agencies/whd/data/charts/agriculture.

2. Many sheep and goat operations are small and located in states that do not require smaller employers to participate in the unemployment insurance program, the source of the employment share data. The United States had 344 establishments in sheep and goat farming (NAICS 1124) in 2019 that had average employment of 1,522, including 83 sheep and goat establishments with an average 370 employees in California.

3. The *Los Angeles Times* in December 2014 published a four-part series entitled "Product of Mexico" that highlighted child and forced labor on Mexican farms that export fruits and vegetables to the United States. In response, US buyers called on their Mexican suppliers to comply with labor laws, Mexican exporters formed associations such as AHIFORES to promote compliance, and the Mexican government stepped up enforcement of labor laws.

Two US-based associations, United Fresh and PMA, developed an Ethical Charter on Responsible Labor Practices that called on employers in the fresh produce industry to comply with applicable labor laws and to treat employees with respect. The Ethical Charter has 13 standards grouped into three categories: labor laws, human rights, and professional conduct. See "Codes of Conduct and Labor Law Compliance," *Rural*

Migration News blog, July 8, 2022, https://migration.ucdavis.edu/rmn/blog/post/?id=2765.

4. Europeans threatened to stop buying Thai fish and seafood unless the Thai government forced improvements in wages and working conditions for fishery and seafood workers. The ILO became the agency that monitored working conditions, and Thai exports continued. See "Labor in Thai Agriculture," *Rural Migration News* blog, July 8, 2022, https://migration.ucdavis.edu/rmn/blog/post/?id=2763.

Epilogue: What's Next

1. https://naldc.nal.usda.gov/download/CAT40000642/PDF

Bibliography

Agriculture and Agri-Food Canada. 2017. "An Overview of the Canadian Agriculture and Agri-Food System 2017." https://www.agr.gc.ca/eng/canadian-agri-food-sector/an-overview-of-the-canadian-agriculture-and-agri-food-system-2017/?id=1510326669269.

Alston, Julian M., James T. Lapsley, and Olena Sambucci. 2020. "Grape and Wine Production in California. California Agriculture." https://giannini.ucop.edu/publications/cal-ag-book/.

Bardacke, Frank. 2012. "Trampling Out the Vintage. Cesar Chavez and the Two Souls of the United Farm Workers. Verso." https://www.versobooks.com/products/2213-trampling-out-the-vintage.

Baskins, Sarah, Jennifer Bond, and Travis Minor. 2019. "Unpacking the Growth in Per Capita Availability of Fresh Market Tomatoes." US Department of Agriculture, Economic Research Service, Vegetables and Pulses Outlook, VGS-19C-01. https://www.ers.usda.gov/publications/pub-details/?pubid=92441.

Basok, Tanya. 2007. "Canada's Temporary Migration Program: A Model Despite Flaws." Migration Policy Institute. www.justicia4migrantworkers.org/bc/pdf/SAWP-A_Model_Despite_Flaws.pdf.

Baum, Herbert. 2005. *Quest for the Perfect Strawberry; A Case Study of the California Strawberry Commission and the Strawberry Industry: A Descriptive Model for Marketing Order Evaluation*. n.p.: iUniverse.

Beckman, Jayson 2017. "The Global Landscape of Agricultural Trade, 1995–2014." US Department of Agriculture, Economic Research Service, EIB 181. www.ers.usda.gov/webdocs/publications/85626/eib-181.pdf?v=0.

Bolda, Mark et al. 2021. "Sample Cost to Produce and Harvest Strawberries. Central Coast Region." UCCE. https://coststudyfiles.ucdavis.edu/uploads/pub/2022/01/04/strawberrycentralcoastfinaldraft-121321.pdf.

Bovay, John, Peyton Ferrier, and Chen Zhen. 2018. "Estimated Costs for Fruit and Vegetable Producers to Comply with the Food Safety Modernization Act's Produce Rule." US Department of Agriculture, Economic Research Service, EIB 195. https://ageconsearch.umn.edu/record/276220/.

Briggs, Vernon. 1992. *Mass Immigration and the National Interest*. ME Sharpe. https://books.google.com/books/about/Mass_Immigration_and_the_National_Intere.html?id=hGiOAAAAMAAJ.

Brudney, James. 2016. "Decent Labor Standards in Corporate Supply Chains: The Immokalee Workers Model." In *Temporary Labour Migration in the Global Era: The Regulatory Challenges*, edited by Joanna Howe and Rosemary Owens, 351–76. Oxford: Hart.

Calvin, Linda. 2007. "Outbreak Linked to Spinach Forces Reassessment of Food Safety Practices." *Amber Waves*, June. www.ers.usda.gov/amber-waves/2007-june/outbreak-linked-to-spinach-forces-reassessment-of-food-safety-practices.aspx.

Calvin, Linda, Helen Jensen, Karen Klonsky, and Roberta Cook. 2017. "Food Safety Practices and Costs Under the California Leafy Greens Marketing Agreement." US Department of Agriculture, Economic Research Service, EIB 173, June. www.ers.usda.gov/webdocs/publications/83771/eib-173.pdf?v=42893.

Calvin, Linda, and Philip Martin. 2010. "The US Produce Industry and Labor: Facing the Future in a Global Economy." US Department of Agriculture, Economic Research Service, ERR 106. http://www.ers.usda.gov/Publications/ERR106/.

Canada Agriculture and Agrifood. 2016. "An Overview of the Canadian Agriculture and Agri-Food System 2016." https://foodsecurecanada.org/sites/foodsecurecanada.org/files/aafcaac-an_overview_of_the_canadian_agriculture_and_agri-food_system_2016.pdf.

Cargill, B.F., and G.E. Rossmiller. 1970. *Fruit and Vegetable Harvest Mechanization*. DOL-MSU. https://books.google.com/books/about/Fruit_and_Vegetable_Harvest_Mechanizatio.html?id=sDt6xgEACAAJ.

Carter Colin, Darrell L. Hueth, John W. Mamer and Andrew Schmitz. 1981. "Labor Strikes and the Price of Lettuce." *Western Journal of Agricultural Economics*. https://econpapers.repec.org/article/agswjagec/32084.htm.

Casey, Rebecca, Eric Tucker, and Leah Vosko. 2019. "Enforcing Employment Standards for Temporary Migrant Agricultural Workers in Ontario, Canada: Exposing Underexplored Layers of Vulnerability." *International Journal of Comparative Labour Law and Industrial Relations*. https://kluwerlawonline.com/journalarticle/Internatio nal+Journal+of+Comparative+Labour+Law+and+Industrial+Relations/35.2/IJCL 2019011.

Castell Roldán, E. Zoe, and Yessenia Alvarez Anaya. 2022. "Migration and Dependency: Mexican Countryside Proletarianization and the Seasonal Agricultural Worker Program." *Dialectical Anthropology* 46: 163–82.

Castillo, Marcelo, Philip Martin, and Zach Rutledge. 2022. "The H-2A Program in 2020." US Department of Agriculture, Economic Research Service, EIB 238. https://www.ers.usda.gov/publications/pub-details/?pubid=104605.

CAW. 1992. *Report of the Commission on Agricultural Workers*. Washington, DC: Commission on Agricultural Workers.

Census of Agriculture. 2017. US Department of Agriculture, National Agricultural Statistics Service. https://www.nass.usda.gov/Publications/AgCensus/2017/index.php.

Centro de los Derechos del Migrante. 2020. "Ripe for Reform: Abuse of Agricultural Workers in the H-2A Visa Program." https://cdmigrante.org/wp-content/uploads/2020/04/Ripe-for-Reform.pdf.

Chang, Gordon. 2019. *Ghosts of Gold Mountain: The Epic Story of the Chinese Who Built the Transcontinental Railroad*. New York: Houghton Mifflin Harcourt.

Charlton, Diane, and Edward Taylor. 2016. "A Declining Farm Workforce: Analysis of Panel Data from Rural Mexico." *American Journal of Agricultural Economics* 98, no. 4: 1158–80.

Charlton, Diane, Edward Taylor, Stavros Vougioukas, and Zachariah Rutledge. 2019. "Innovations for a Shrinking Agricultural Workforce." *Choices*, quarter 2.

Choudry, Aziz, and Adrian Smith, eds. 2016. *Unfree Labor? Struggles of Migrant and Immigrant Workers in Canada*. Oakland, CA: PM Press.

CIRS. 2018. "Farmworker Housing Study and Action Plan for Salinas Valley and Pájaro Valley." https://cirsinc.org/wp-content/uploads/2021/11/Farmworker-Housing-Ass essment-and-Action-Plan-Salinas-Pajaro-Laborshed-2018.pdf.

Collart, Alba. 2016. "The Food Safety Modernization Act and the Marketing of Fresh Produce." *Choices*, quarter 1.

Cook, Roberta. 2011. "Fundamental Forces Affecting the US Fresh Berry and Lettuce/Leafy Green Subsectors." *Choices* 26, no. 4.

Cook, Roberta, and Linda Calvin. 2005. "Greenhouse Tomatoes Change the Dynamics of the North American Fresh Tomato Industry." US Department of Agriculture, Economic Research Service, Report 2. ucce.ucdavis.edu/files/datastore/234-447.pdf.

Commision on Agricultural Workers. Conrad, Alfred, and John Meyer. 1958. "The Economics of Slavery in the Ante Bellum South." *Journal of Political Economy* 66, no. 2: 95–130.

Costa, Daniel, Philip Martin, and Zachariah Rutledge. 2020. "Federal Labor Law Enforcement in Agriculture." Economic Policy Institute. https://www.epi.org/publication/federal-labor-standards-enforcement-in-agriculture-data-reveal-the-biggest-violators-and-raise-new-questions-about-how-to-improve-and-target-efforts-to-protect-farmworkers/.

Crespi, John, and Stephan Marette. 2001. "How Should Food Safety Certification Be Financed?" *American Journal of Agricultural Economics* 83, no. 4: 852–61. https://onlinelibrary.wiley.com/doi/abs/10.1111/0002-9092.00214.

Daria, James. 2022. "Fairwashing and Union Busting: The Privatization of Labor Standards in Mexico's Agro-Export Industry." *Mexican Studies* 38, no. 3: 379–405.

De Lone, Sarah. 1992. "Farmworkers, Growers and the Department of Labor: The Inequality of Balance in the Temporary Agricultural Worker Program." *Yale Journal of Law and Liberation* 11, no. 3: 100–144.

Escobar, Agustin, Philip Martin, and Omar Starbridis. 2019. "Farm Labor and Mexico's Export Produce Industry." Wilson Center. www.wilsoncenter.org/publication/farm-labor-and-mexicos-export-produce-industry.

Estabrook, Barry. 2011. *Tomatoland: How Modern Industrial Agriculture Destroyed Our Most Alluring Fruit*. New York: Andrews McMeel.

Falconer, Robert. 2020a. "Grown Locally, Harvested Globally: The Role of Temporary Foreign Workers in Canadian Agriculture." *University of Calgary School of Public Policy Publications* 13: art. 70510.

Falconer, Robert. 2020b. "Family Farmers to Foreign Fieldhands: Consolidation of Canadian Agriculture and the Temporary Foreign Worker Program." *University of Calgary School of Public Policy Publications* 13: art. 70741.

Fidelibus, M., L. Ferry, G. Jordan, D. Zhuang, D. Sumner, and D. Stewart. 2016. "Sample Costs to Establish a Vineyard and Produce Dry-on-Vine Raisins, Open Gable Trellis System, Early Maturing Varieties, San Joaquin Valley." https://coststudyfiles.ucdavis.edu/uploads/cs_public/ec/ba/ecba9b89-f1e9-401c-9044-4afa2c060093/2016dovraisinsohtsjvfinaldraft111716.pdf.

Fidelibus, M et al. 2018. "Sample Costs to Establish and Produce Table Grapes." San Joaquin Valley. South. https://coststudyfiles.ucdavis.edu/uploads/cs_public/03/e8/03e8865f-2b6b-4859-90c6-84414cd9d3f4/2018tablegrapessjvflameseedlessfinaldraft.pdf.

Fisher, Lloyd. 1953. *The Harvest Labor Market in California*. Cambridge, MA: Harvard University Press.

Friedland, William. 1994. "The Global Fresh Fruit and Vegetable System." In *The Global Restructuring of Agro-Food Systems*, edited by Philip McMichael, ch. 7. Ithaca, NY: Cornell University Press.

Fuller, Varden. 1967. "A New Era for Farm Labor?" *Industrial Relations* 6, no. 3: 285–302.

Fuller, Varden. 1991. "Hired Hands in California's Farm Fields." Giannini Foundation https://giannini.ucop.edu/publications/historic/special-reports/.

Fuller, Varden, and Bert Mason. 1977. "Farm Labor." *Annals of the American Academy of Political and Social Science* 429, no. 1: 63–80.

Gabriel, Christina, and Laura Macdonald. 2017. "After the International Organization for Migration: Recruitment of Guatemalan Temporary Agricultural Workers to Canada." *International Migration* 44, no. 10: 1706–24.

Gale, H. Frederick, Jr., Linda Foreman, and Thomas Capehart. 2000. "Tobacco and the Economy: Farms, Jobs, and Communities." US Department of Agriculture, Economic Research Service, AER 789, https://www.ers.usda.gov/webdocs/publications/41156/14942_aer789a_1_.pdf?v=0.

Galindo, Jose. 2019. "Some Aspects on the Failure of Agrarian Reforms in Mexico and Other Latin American Countries." *Forum for Development Studies* 46, no. 1: 131–46.

Gallardo, R. Karina, Eric T. Stafne, Lisa Wasko DeVetter, Qi Zhang, Charlie Li, Fumiomi Takeda, Jeffrey Williamson, Wei Qiang Yang, William O. Cline, Randy Beaudry, and Renee Allen. 2018. "Blueberry Producers' Attitudes toward Harvest Mechanization for Fresh Market." https://www.researchgate.net/profile/Fumiomi-Takeda/publication/323406692_Blueberry_Producers%27_Attitudes_toward_Harvest_Mechanization_f or_Fresh_Market/links/5ac786a14585151e80a3a54e/Blueberry-Producers-Attitudes-toward-Harvest-Mechanization-for-Fresh-Market.pdf.

Gálvez, Alyshia. 2018. *Eating NAFTA: Trade, Food Policies and the Destruction of Mexico.* Berkeley: University of California Press.

GAO. 1988. "The H-2A Program: Protections for US Workers." US Government Accountability Office. https://www.gao.gov/assets/pemd-89-3.pdf.

GAO. 2017. "H-2A and H-2B Visa Programs: Increased Protections Needed for Foreign Workers." US Government Accountability Office. https://www.gao.gov/products/gao-15-154.

González, Humberto. 2020. "What Socioenvironmental Impacts Did 35 Years of Export Agriculture Have in Mexico (1980–2014): A Transnational Agri-Food Field Analysis." *Journal of Agrarian Change* 20: 163–87.

Gonzalez, Humberto, and Alejandro Macias. 2017. "Agrifood Vulnerability and Neoliberal Economic Policies in Mexico." *Review of Agrarian Studies* 7, no. 1: 72–106.

Gordon, Jennifer. 2016. "Roles for Workers and Unions in Regulating Labor Recruitment in Mexico." In *Temporary Labour Migration in the Global Era: The Regulatory Challenges*, edited by Joanna Howe and Rosemary Owens, 329–50. Oxford: Hart.

Guan, Zhengfei, Trina Biswas, and Feng Wu. 2018a. "The U.S. Tomato Industry: An Overview of Production and Trade: FE1027, 9/2017." https://journals.flvc.org/edis/article/view/105009.

Guan Zhengfei, Berdikul Qushim, Feng Wu, and Alicia Whidden. 2018b. "The Migration Pattern of Florida Seasonal Farmworkers." https://edis.ifas.ufl.edu/publication/FE1040.

Guthman, Julie. 2019. *Wilted: Pathogens, Chemicals, and the Fragile Future of the Strawberry Industry.* Berkeley: University of California Press.

Hartman, Sarah, et al. 2021. "A Growing Produce Bubble: United States Produce Tied to Mexico's Unsustainable Agricultural Water Use." *Environmental Research Letters* 16, no. 10: art. 5008.

Hawley, Ellis. 1966. "The Politics of the Mexican Labor Issue, 1950–1965." *Agricultural History* 40, no. 3: 157–76.

Haythorne, George. 1960. *Labor in Canadian Agriculture*. Cambridge, MA: Harvard University Press.

Hernández-León, Ruben. 2020. "The Work That Brokers Do: The Skills, Competences and Know-How of Intermediaries in the H-2 Visa Programme." *Journal of Ethnic and Migration Studies* 47, no. 10: 2341–58.

Hennebry, Jenna. 2012. "Permanently Temporary? Agricultural Migrant Workers and Their Integration in Canada." Institute for Research on Public Policy, study no. 26. http://irpp.org/research-studies/study-no26/.

Hennebry, Jenna, and Kerry Preibisch. 2012. "A Model for Managed Migration? Re-examining Best Practices in Canada's Seasonal Agricultural Worker Program." *International Migration* 50: S319–40.

Hightower, Jim. 1972. *Hard Tomatoes, Hard Times: A Report of the Agribusiness Accountability Project on the Failure of America's Land Grant College Complex*. Cambridge, MA: Schenkman.

Holmes, Gerald, Seyed Mojtaba Mansouripour, and Shashika Hewavitharana. 2020. "Strawberries at the Crossroads: Management of Soilborne Diseases in California Without Methyl Bromide." *Phytopathology* 110, no. 5: 956–68.

Hufbauer, Gary and Jeffrey Schott. 2005. *NAFTA Revisited: Achievements and Challenges*. Peterson Institute for International Economics. https://www.piie.com/bookstore/nafta-revisited-achievements-and-challenges.

IMF. 2018. "Mexico: Selected Issues." https://www.imf.org/en/Publications/CR/Issues/2018/11/07/Mexico-Selected-Issues-46344.

INEGI. 2016. "Estadisticas del dia del trabajador agricola." May 15. http://www.inegi.org.mx/saladeprensa/aproposito/2016/agricola2016_0.pdf.

Jamieson, Stuart. 1945. "Labor Unionism in American Agriculture." US Department of Labor, Bureau of Labor Statistics, Bulletin 836. https://fraser.stlouisfed.org/docs/publications/bls/bls_0836_1945.pdf.

Jensen, Heather. 2014. "A History of Legal Exclusion: Labour Relations Laws and British Columbia's Agricultural Workers, 1937–1975." *Labour / Le Travail* 73: 67–95.

Jia, Weikuan, Yan Zhang, and Chengjiang Li. 2020. "Apple Harvesting Robot under Information Technology: A Review." *International Journal of Advanced Robotic Systems*. https://journals.sagepub.com/doi/full/10.1177/1729881420925310.

Kim, Joon. 2004. "The Political Economy of the Mexican Farm Labor Program, 1942–64." *Aztlan: Journal of Chicano Studies* 2: 13–53.

Kiser, George. 1973. "The Bracero Program: A Case Study of Its Development, Termination, and Political Aftermath." University of Massachusetts, PhD Thesis. https://scholarworks.umass.edu/dissertations_1/1874/.

Kitroeff, Natalie, and Geoffrey Mohan. 2017. "Wages Rise on California Farms. Americans Still Don't Want the Job." *Los Angeles Times*, March 17.

Ku, Hyejin. 2019. "The Effect of Wage Subsidies on Piece Rate Workers: Evidence from the Penny per Pound Program in Florida." *Journal of Development Economics* 139: 122–34.

Kuruvilla, Sarosh, ed. 2021. *Private Regulation of Labor Standards in Global Supply Chains: Problems, Progress, and Prospects*. Ithaca, NY: Cornell University Press.

Kurtural, Kaan, and Matt Fidelibus. 2021. "Mechanization of Pruning, Canopy Management, and Harvest in Winegrape Vineyards." *Catalyst*. https://www.asevcatalyst.org/content/early/2021/04/20/catalyst.2021.20011.

Levy, Santiago. 2018. "Under-Rewarded Efforts: The Elusive Quest for Prosperity in Mexico." IADB. https://publications.iadb.org/en/under-rewarded-efforts-elusive-quest-prosperity-mexico.

Linder, Marc. 1989. "The Joint Employment Doctrine: Clarifying Joint Legislative-Judicial Confusion." https://nationalaglawcenter.org/publication/linder-the-joint-employm ent-doctrine-clarifying-joint-legislative-judicial-confusion-10-hamline-j-public-law-policy-321-345-1989/.

Lloyd, Jack, Philip Martin, and John Mamer. 1988. "The Ventura Citrus Labor Market." Giannini Foundation, Information Series 88-1. https://s.giannini.ucop.edu/uploads/ giannini_public/b1/be/b1bece70-3b5d-4504-953a-1942f47be586/881-citruslabor.pdf.

Lytton, Timothy. 2019. *Outbreak: Foodborne Illness and the Struggle for Food Safety.* Chicago: University of Chicago Press.

MacDonald, James, Robert Hoppe, and Doris Newton. 2018. "Three Decades of Consolidation in US Agriculture," US Department of Agriculture, Economic Research Service, EIB-189. https://www.ers.usda.gov/publications/pub-details/?pubid=88056.

Mamer, John, and D. O. Rosedale. 1975. "Labor Management for Seasonal Farmworkers." *Hilgardia* 29, no. 2: 8–9.

Marosi, Richard. 2014. "Hardship on Mexico's Farms, a Bounty for U.S. Tables." *Los Angeles Times,* December 7–14. http://graphics.latimes.com/product-of-mexico-camps/.

Marosi, Richard. 2016. "A Year After a Violent and Costly Strike, Baja Farm Laborers See Uneven Gains." *Los Angeles Times,* May 21. https://www.latimes.com/world/mexico-americas/la-me-baja-farm-labor-snap-story.html.

Marquis, Susan. 2017. *I Am Not a Tractor! How Florida Farmworkers Took on the Fast Food Giants and Won.* Ithaca, NY: Cornell University Press.

Marshall, Elliot. 1980. "Bergland Opposed on Farm Machine Policy." *Science.* https:// www.science.org/doi/10.1126/science.208.4444.578.

Martin, Philip. 1994. "Good Intentions Gone Awry: IRCA and US Agriculture." *Annals of the Academy of Political and Social Science* 534: 44–57.

Martin, Philip. 2003. *Promise Unfulfilled: Unions, Immigration, and Farm Workers.* Ithaca, NY: Cornell University Press.

Martin, Philip. 2008. "Evaluation of the H-2A Alien Certification Process and the US Farm Labor Market." KRA Corporation. https://wdr.doleta.gov/research/FullText_Do cuments/ETAOP_2013_04.pdf.

Martin, Philip. 2009. *Importing Poverty? Immigration and the Changing Face of Rural America.* New Haven, CT: Yale University Press.

Martin, Philip, 2014. "The H-2A Program; Evolution, Impacts, and Outlook." In *(Mis)managing Migration: Guestworkers' Experiences with the North American Labor Market,* edited by David Griffith, 33–62. Ithaca, NY: SAR Press.

Martin, Philip. 2016. "Labor Compliance in Fresh Produce: Lessons from Food Safety." *Choices,* quarter 3.

Martin, Philip. 2017a. *Merchants of Labor: Recruiters and International Labor Migration.* New York: Oxford University Press.

Martin, Philip. 2017b. "Immigration and Farm Labor: Challenges and Issues." Giannini Foundation. https://giannini.ucop.edu/publications/historic/infoseries/.

Martin, Philip. 2019. "The Role of the H-2A Program in California Agriculture." *Choices,* quarter 1.

Martin, Philip, Daniel Egan, and Stephanie Luce. 1988. "The Wages and Fringe Benefits of Unionized California Farmworkers." Giannini Foundation, Information Series 88-4. https://s.giannini.ucop.edu/uploads/giannini_public/e2/cc/e2cc8176-51e3-4c91-9325-d6ddd2842d16/884-farmworkers.pdf.

Martin Philip, Brandon Hooker, Zach Rutledge, and Marc Stockton. 2023. "California Has 882,000 Farm Workers to Fill 413,000 Jobs." *California Agriculture*.

Martin, Philip, Brandon Hooker, and Marc Stockton. 2018. "Employment and Earnings of California Farm Workers in 2015." *California Agriculture* 72, no. 2.

Martin, Philip, and David Martin. 1994. *The Endless Quest: Helping America's Farm Workers*. Boulder, CO: Westview Press.

Martin, Philip, and Bert Mason. 2003. "Mandatory Mediation Changes Rules for Negotiating Farm Labor Contracts." *California Agriculture* 57, no 1: 13–17.

Martin, Philip, Richard Mines, and Angela Diaz. 1985. "A Profile of California Farmworkers." *California Agriculture*.

Martin, Philip, and Martin Ruhs. 2019. "Labour Market Realism and the Global Compacts on Migration and Refugees." *International Migration* 57, no. 6: 80–90.

Martin, Philip, and Zach Rutledge. 2021. "Proposed Changes to the H-2A Program Would Affect Labor Costs in the United States and California." *California Agriculture* 75, no. 3.

Martin, Philip L., and Alan L. Olmstead. 1985. "The Agricultural Mechanization Controversy." *Science* 227, no. 4687 (February): 601–06. http://science.sciencemag.org/content/227/4687/601.

Martin, Susan. 2021. "A Nation of Immigrants." Cambridge. https://www.cambridge.org/core/books/nation-of-immigrants/6066550BE3CDCF7FE1972F635539530A.

Mason, Bert. 1998. "The Raisin Grape Industry." https://migration.ucdavis.edu/cf/more.php?id=124.

McKinsey. 2015. "Four Fundamentals of Workplace Automation." https://www.mckinsey.com/capabilities/mckinsey-digital/our-insights/four-fundamentals-of-workplace-automation.

McMillan, Rob. 2023. "State of the US Wine Industry 2023." Silicon Valley Bank. https://www.svb.com/trends-insights/reports/wine-report.

McWilliams, Carey. 1939. *Factories in the Field: The Story of Migratory Farm Labor in California*. Berkeley: University of California Press.

Mines, Rick. 2010. "Jornaleros in Mexico's Agro-export Industry: Changes and Challenges." *Word Press*. https://rickmines.files.wordpress.com/2011/12/jornaleros-in-mexicos-agro-export-industry-unpublished-2010.pdf.

Mize, Ronald. 2019. "The State Management of Guest Workers: The Decline of the Bracero Program, the Rise of Temporary Worker Visas." In *A Nation of Immigrants Reconsidered: US Society in an Age of Restriction, 1924–1965*, edited by Maddalena Marinari, Madeline Hsu, and María Cristina García, 123–43. Champaign: University of Illinois Press.

Mohan, Geoffrey. 2017. "As California's Labor Shortage Grows, Farmers Race to Replace Workers with Robots." *Los Angeles Times*, July 21.

Mohan, Sushi, Arvind Upadhyay, Nikolaos Daskalakis, and Ridhima Durham. 2018. "Fair Trade as a Social Enterprise: Oversold, Misunderstood or Unethical?" *Strategic Change* 28, no. 5: 423–33.

Mortimore, Sara, and Carol Wallace. 2015. *HACCP: A Food Industry Briefing*. 2nd ed. Chichester, UK: Wiley Blackwell.

Mosqueda, Elizabeth, Richard Smith, Dave Goorahoo, and Anil Shrestha. 2017. "Automated Lettuce Thinners Reduce Labor requirements and Increase Speed of Thinning." California Agriculture. https://doi.org/10.3733/ca.2017a0018.

NAWS. n.d. "National Agricultural Worker Survey." Department of Labor, Employment and Training Administration. https://www.dol.gov/agencies/eta/national-agricultural-workers-survey/research/data-tables.

OECD. 2020. "Agricultural Policy Monitoring and Evaluation 2020." https://www.oecd-ilibrary.org/docserver/928181a8-en.pdf.

Olivera, Vic. 1989. "Trends in the Hired Farm Work Force, 1945–87." US Department of Agriculture, Economic Research Service, AIB 561. https://naldc.nal.usda.gov/downl oad/CAT89917698/PDF.

Pawel, Miriam. 2009. *The Union of Their Dreams: Power, Hope, and Struggle in Cesar Chavez's Farm Worker Movement.* New York: Bloomsbury.

Pawel, Miriam. 2014. *The Crusades of Cesar Chavez.* New York: Bloomsbury.

Peng, Chen and Stavros Vougioukas. 2020. "Deterministic Predictive Dynamic Scheduling for Crop-Transport Co-robots Acting as Harvesting Aids." https://www.sciencedirect.com/science/article/abs/pii/S0168169920317130.

Pratt, Lawrence, and Juan Manuel Ortega. 2019. "Protected Agriculture in Mexico: Building the Methodology for the First Certified Agricultural Green Bond." Inter-American Development Bank. https://publications.iadb.org/en/protected-agri culture-mexico-building-methodology-first-certified-agricultural-green-bond.

Rasmussen, Wayne. 1968. "Advances in American Agriculture: The Mechanical Tomato Harvester as a Case Study." *Technology and Culture* 9, no. 4: 531–43.

Rauconnier, R. 1993. *Sugar Cane.* London: Macmillan.

Rural Migration News. 1999. "Guest Workers: Advocates Change." *Rural Migration News* 5, no. 3.

Rural Migration News. 2018a. "California: Travel, Housing." *Rural Migration News* 24, no. 4.

Rural Migration News. 2018b. "Goodlatte H-2C; H-2B." *Rural Migration News* 24, no. 2.

Rural Migration News. 2019. "COA 2017: Direct-Hire Farm Workers." *Rural Migration News* blog, June 17. https://migration.ucdavis.edu/rmn/blog/post/?id=2303.

Rural Migration News. 2020a. "QCEW: Who Employs California Farm Workers?" *Rural Migration News* blog, May 19. https://migration.ucdavis.edu/rmn/blog/post/?id=2431.

Rural Migration News. 2020b. "US Farm Employment and Farm Workers." *Rural Migration News* blog, June 24. https://migration.ucdavis.edu/rmn/blog/post/?id=2435.

Rural Migration News. 2020c. "QCEW: The H-2A Program and AEWRs." *Rural Migration News* blog, December 18. https://migration.ucdavis.edu/rmn/blog/post/?id=2506.

Rural Migration News Blog. 2020. "The CAW at 30." https://migration.ucdavis.edu/rmn/blog/post/?id=2469.

Rural Migration News. 2022a. "Alternatives to Hand Labor in Blueberries." *Rural Migration News* blog, February 28. https://migration.ucdavis.edu/rmn/blog/post/?id=2701.

Rural Migration News. 2023. "DOL Changes AEWRs and PWRs." *Rural Migration News* blog, April 7. https://migration.ucdavis.edu/rmn/blog/post/?id=2838.

Russo, Robert. 2018. "Collective Struggles: A Comparative Analysis of Unionizing Temporary Foreign Farm Workers in the United States and Canada." *Houston Journal of International Law* 41, no. 1: 5–55.

Sarig, Yoav, James F. Thompson, and Galen K. Brown. 2000. "Alternatives to Immigrant Labor." Center for Immigration Studies. https://cis.org/Report/Alternatives-Immigr ant-Labor.

Schmitz, Andrew, and Charles Moss. 2015. "Mechanized Agriculture: Machine Adoption, Farm Size, and Labor Displacement." *AgBio Forum* 18, no. 3.

Scruggs, Otey. 1960. "The First Mexican Farm Labor Program. Arizona and the West." https://www.jstor.org/stable/40167678.

Senate Committee on Education and Labor. 1940. "Violations of Free Speech and Rights of Labor." Subcommittee Investigating Violations of Free Speech and the Rights of Labor. Seventy-Fourth Congress, Second Session.

Senate Committee on Education and Labor. 1942. "Part III. The Disadvantaged Status of Unorganized Labor in California's Industrial Agriculture." Seventy-Fourth Congress,. Second Session.

SIAP. 2017. "Atlas Agroalimentario 2017." www.gob.mx/siap/articulos/publicaciones-siap-generando-panoramas-claros-para-la-mejor-toma-de-decisiones?idiom=es.

Strom, Stephanie, and Steven Greenhouse. 2013. "On the Front Lines of Food Safety." *New York Times*, May 25.

Strong, Jennifer, and Daniela Hernandez. 2018. "Robots Head for the Fields." *Wall Street Journal*, October 2.

Stupkova, L. Crespo. 2016. "Global Value Chain in Agro-Export Production and Its Socio-economic Impact in Michoacán, Mexico." *Agris On-line Papers in Economics and Informatics* 8, no. 1: 25–36.

Taylor, Edward, and Diane Charlton. 2019. *The Farm Labor Problem: A Global Perspective.* London: Academic Press.

Thompson, J., and S. Blank. S. 2000. "Harvest Mechanization Helps Agriculture Remain Competitive." *California Agriculture*.

Tofani, Loretta. 1987. "Preferring Foreign Labor, Farmers Spurn Americans." *Washington Post*, May 25.

Truman Commission on Migratory Labor. 1951. *Migratory Labor in American Agriculture.* Washington, DC: GPO.

US Department of Labor. 1959. *Mexican Farm Labor Program.* Washington, DC: GPO.

US House of Representatives. 1963. *Mexican Farm Labor Program: Hearings Before the Subcommittee on Equipment, Supplies, and Manpower of the Committee on Agriculture, House of Representatives.* Washington, DC: GPO.

UNCTAD. 2014. "Mexico's Agriculture Development: Perspectives and Outlook." https://unctad.org/system/files/official-document/ditctncd2012d2_rev1_en.pdf.

Verma, Veena. 2002. "The Mexican and Caribbean SAWP." http://www.nsi-ins.ca/wp-content/uploads/2012/11/2002-The-Mexican-and-Caribbean-Seasonal-Agricultural-Workers-Program-Regulatory-and-Policy-Framework-Executive-Summary.pdf.

Vialet, Joyce, and Barbara McClure. 1980. "Temporary Worker Programs, Background and Issues." Congressional Research Service for Senate Judiciary Committee. https://babel.hathitrust.org/cgi/pt?id=umn.31951d00817043c&view=1up&seq=3.

Vosko, Leah F. 2016. "Blacklisting as a Modality of Deportability: Mexico's Response to Circular Migrant Agricultural Workers' Pursuit of Collective Bargaining Rights in British Columbia, Canada." *Journal of Ethnic and Migration Studies* 42, no. 8: 1371–87.

Vosko, Leah F. 2018. "Legal but Deportable: Institutionalized Deportability and the Limits of Collective Bargaining Among Participants in Canada's Seasonal Agricultural Workers Program." *ILR Review* 71, no. 4: 807–22.

Vosko, Leah F. 2019. *Disrupting Deportability: Transnational Workers Organize.* Ithaca, NY: Cornell University Press.

Weil, David. 2014. *The Fissured Workplace: How Work Became So Bad for So Many and What Can Be Done to Improve It.* Cambridge, MA: Harvard University Press.

Weil, David. 2018. "Creating a Strategic Enforcement Approach to Address Wage Theft: One Academic's Journey in Organizational Change." *Journal of Industrial Relations*.

Weil, David, and Amanda Pyles. 2005. "Why Complain? Complaints, Compliance, and the Problem of Enforcement in the US Workplace." *Comparative Labor Law and Policy* 27, no. 1: 59–92.

Weiler, Anelyse, and Janet McLaughlin. 2019. "Listening to Migrant Workers: Should Canada's Seasonal Agricultural Worker Program Be Abolished?" *Dialectical Anthropology* 43: 381–88. https://link.springer.com/article/10.1007/s10624-019-09563-4.

Zahniser, Steven. 2022. "U.S.-Mexico Agricultural Trade in 2020." US Department of Agriculture, Economic Research Service, AP 97. https://www.ers.usda.gov/publicati ons/pub-details/?pubid=103087.

Zahniser, Steven, Nicolás Fernando López López, Mesbah Motamed, Zully Y Silva Vargas, and Thomas Capehart. 2019. "The Growing Corn Economies of Mexico and the United States." US Department of Agriculture, Economic Research Service, Feed Outlook FDS-19F-01. https://www.ers.usda.gov/publications/pub-details/?pubid=93541.

Zhang, Zhao, Paul H. Heinemann, Jude Liu, Tara A. Baugher, and James R. Schupp. 2016. "The Development of Mechanical Apple Harvesting Technology: A Review." *Transactions of the ASABE* 59, no. 5: 1165–80.

Zlolniski, Christian. 2019. *Made in Baja: The Lives of Farmworkers and Growers Behind Mexico's Transnational Agricultural Boom.* Berkeley: University of California Press.

Index

For the benefit of digital users, indexed terms that span two pages (e.g., 52–53) may, on occasion, appear on only one of those pages.

Tables and figures are indicated by *t* and *f* following the page number